If Not Now, When?

Mathijs Koenraadt

If Now Now, When?

Writings in Defense of Europe

Contents

Preface

This book is an assorted collection of articles and essays I wrote between 2015 and 2018. They cover themes of urbanization, identity, diversity, and the future of Western civilization.

I believe that the supporters of open borders have turned the West, its territories and its nations, into a Ponzi scheme. The scheme requires a continuous flow of goods and people from elsewhere in the world, the sources, to Western nations, the sinks. In so doing, the West has absorbed the brightest minds it could not produce itself. It has employed a foreign-born labor force to fuel its low-cost industries because white women, keen on luxury lifestyles, have failed to produce the babies needed to populate the underclasses. And let's not ignore the vast resources procured through a colonial legacy of theft and oppression, both in the past and in the present. In short, immigration to the West is a scam.

With the use of mass media and its 24-hour cycles of deception, Western civilization has convinced the whole world that "life is better" there. It has awoken a wanderlust, mixed with opportunism, jealousy, and greed, in nearly all of the world's populations. But under this façade of commercial lies, the West is behaving as a cash-strapped technology startup forced to hype untested products in order to lure in new, uninformed investors. Indeed, that's what immigrants coming to the West really are: uninformed investors. They are at risk of being exploited, followed by intense disappointment. At some point, the world will run out of fools stupid enough to buy into the scheme.

It wasn't always like this. Between the late 8th century and the 11th century, Europe nearly completely de-urbanized. Its native peoples left or fled the cities, embracing a traditional rural way of life. The city of Rome, once home to over a million people around the time of Julius Caesar, had shrunk to a village of fewer than 20,000 people. Europeans were willing to forgo having more children over condemning their offspring to a life in the urban prisons. Especially in Northern Europe, where its Germanic peoples never built cities until the Romans forced them to, people felt that living in cities was a humiliating experience. German nobility would shun cities for as long as they could.

Perhaps it is a sign that cities are most unnatural habitats that cannot sustain human life in the long-term. Europe would not see the light of megacities until the Industrial Age and its technological advances made it possible for cities to house and feed millions. The city of Berlin, for example, did not reach a million inhabitants until the late 19th century, almost two millennia after Rome did.

In our time, Western nations are again undergoing such a process of de-urbanization. White families are leaving their nations' major cities in favor of smaller towns in the countryside. The advent of the consumer car has made it possible to work in the big city but still live closer to the land. Fearing economic and social decline, Western ruling elites, always acutely aware of their relative position in the global power play, have decided to open the borders to mass immigration. By enticing the world to come to the West, they hope to restock 'their' cities with immigrants in need of their management.

And so, it has come to be that cities such as London, Paris, Rotterdam, Hamburg, Chicago, New Jersey, or Malmö have seen the rise of majority non-white populations, whereas the British, French, Dutch, U.S., and Swedish countryside still host a significant white majority. The same phenomenon has played out throughout the West. Western societies have meanwhile split into two: a white rural West tolerating many non-white urban enclaves. Is it a recipe for durable social progress or for catastrophic social tension? One needs only one glance at South Africa to know the fate of rural Westerners. Once a non-white majority has taken charge of the nation's political system, illegal land confiscations follow, and thereafter brutal farm killings, together resembling the first stages of genocide.

Can whites really survive as rural minorities in urbanized, multiracial nations run by globalists?

There is a dark reason why, recently, European nations have set their sights on black African immigrants, personified in the office of the French President, Emmanuel Macron, a former Rothschild banker whose public appearances give off the air of a pharaoh who thinks he can unite white Europe with black Nubia. Presumably, that is to be the first step in establishing George Soros's "Open Society". The truth is that black immigration has more to do with robbing Africa of its potent labor force than with building open societies. Black blood is the new oil. By robbing Africa of its economically viable men and by putting their labor to work, Europe's elites hope to stay wealthy, while simultaneously assuring Africa will stay poor.

Since, presently, nobody can work for lower wages than the black people of Central Africa, Western civilization will not—and can not—continue to thrive any longer than Central Africa's women are able to sustain high birth rates. That means the West as we know it will cease to exist, sometime during this century, once black birth canals have exhausted themselves. After that, nobody will be able to undercut Chinese wages. Oswald Spengler, Joseph Tainter, and others were right: the decline of the West is the inevitable outcome of the law of diminishing returns.

Mathijs Koenraadt, Budapest, July 6ᵗʰ, 2018

1

Autonomy and the Collective

"Without stable traditions, no civilization; without the slow elimination of these traditions, no progress..."

—Gustave le Bon

According to French historian Fustel de Coulanges, "The Roman Empire didn't maintain itself by force, but by the religious admiration it inspired." By definition, a people's traditional faith competes with a belief in the State. It's why progressive liberals so often look down on the religious right. God may be the only thing standing between personal autonomy and collective slavery.

The Rural Revolt against Urban Politics: From Trump to Orbán

April 9ᵗʰ, 2018

On Sunday, April 8ᵗʰ, 2018, Viktor Orbán secured his third term as Hungary's President. Unheard of in the United States, his third-term presidency continues an undemocratic wave seen around the world. In The Netherlands, Mark Rutte is serving his fourth term as Prime Minister. In Germany, Chancellor Angela Merkel has started hers. Russian President Vladimir Putin won his fifth term and China's Communist Party awarded President Xi Jinping indefinite rule.

As we see democratically elected emperors spring up around us, rotative democracy's waning prestige points to a conflict, a global conflict. I believe it stems from the growing divide between the countryside and the city, namely between diverging interests of rural and urban voters. No side is right or wrong but in a stagnating economy, each side can only defend its way of life at the expense of the other.

Orbán's Fidesz party won the entire countryside. The Greater Budapest Area, Hungary's only metropolis, is the only place where the opposition won. Out of a handful of parties, Fidesz won 49.5% of the popular vote, with 91 out of 106 electoral districts, and over two-thirds of the seats in the Parliament.

Looking at the 2016 election results by county, the Republican Party, headed by its nominee Donald Trump, took rural "Middle America", whereas the majority of urban "Coastal USA" voted for Hillary Clinton. Although Trump won 46.1% of the popular vote, less than Clinton at 48.2%, his rural backers helped him win 304 electoral votes over Clinton's 227.

The first round of Austria's 2016 election saw Norbert Hofer's FPÖ, the Austrian Freedom Party, win the countryside. Because no party won more than the required 50%, the second round of elections awarded the Presidency to Alexander van der Bellen of the Green Party later that year. His party dominated populous urban and industrial areas, including Vienna.

Following the adagio "privatized profits and socialized costs", modern society—meaning progressive society—tends to generate its profits around urban centers while externalizing the cost to the countryside, both economically and environmentally.

City populations tend to lean left. They are more often progressive voters who favor open borders because the influx of consumers into the city secures economic growth. Rural populations tend to lean right. They are more likely conservative voters who favor the status quo because the influx of immigrants taxes their wealth.

Rural areas do not benefit as much from immigration as urban areas do. First and foremost because immigrants don't migrate to the countryside as much as they do to cities. Policies that benefit megacities such as Chicago and Miami do not benefit the country as a whole. Progressive-liberal reality is a particular urban reality that lacks universal application. Urban wealth doesn't logically trickle down from the city to the countryside.

On their own, places like New York City could never sustain themselves. Like ancient Rome, modern cities are net importers of wealth and net exporters of dung. Yet, despite the fact that disposable incomes are lower in the countryside than in cities, rural folk tend to foot their nation's bills. They pay taxes into a system that unfairly redistributes wealth from the country to the city.

Progressive voters look down on conservative folk. Not only because the agricultural communities of the latter are still relatively homogenous—one luxury the former can never afford—but also because rural folk work as slavers at the bottom of an urban-centric civilization.

Before she lost, Hillary Clinton called half of Trump's voters a "basket of deplorables": homophobes, xenophobes, sexists, racists, and nationalists. Voters right-of-center are often met with such insults coming from urban-centric media. Indeed, Trump's voters, like those of Orbán and Hofer, were more religious and less educated, but the insults hurled at them overlook the key difference: they inhabit the countryside.

Are rural folk really less educated? They may be but they also have better mental health than city folk. Besides, the smartest kids from the country are the ones who move to the city. Are rural folk really more racist? Rural taxpayers are required to pay into a system that prefers foreign immigrants over their own offspring. By pitting natives against newcomers in the competition for a better life, the state has become the primary cause of racism.

Cities lure people by brainwashing them with advertising meant to hide bitter reality. Cities are smog-infested, stress-inducing, hyper-competitive environments that reduce people to gears in a machine stuck in reverse.

My grandparents were farmers. My parents grew up on a farm but moved to a small town later in life. I am the first generation to spend a life in towns and cities. I did not enjoy it. I feel robbed of a more autonomous, more meaningful, and healthier life. I can only accede to what a young woman from Lithuania once told me. After spending a year living in Paris, she and her husband returned to the countryside near Vilnius to settle there. She said,

"Paris is nothing like the romantic image tourists hold of it. If you are rich and you can have whatever you want, a sports car, luxury item, then Paris is good for you. But for the rest of us, where we lived, people were pissing and shitting in the middle of the street. Cities are the end of people."

Today, urban planners are spreading their vision for a concrete world like cancer. Like an elephant cemetery, I fear that urban areas will someday be where our human species goes to rest. If we want to preserve a livable Earth, if we want to rebuild meaningful communities, we must continue to support the rural revolt against urban politics.

Fighting Collectivism:
Marginalization, Assimilation or Eternal Struggle?

March 16th, 2018

"The world conflict of today is the conflict of the individual against the state, ... The names change, but the essence—and the results—remain the same, whether it is the individual against feudalism, or against absolute monarchy, or against communism or fascism or Nazism or socialism or the welfare state." (Ayn Rand)

Liberal ideology and its socialist, social-democratic, Marxist or outright Bolshevik counterparts share a common, religious belief in progress. The names of the religion change, but what exactly do its acolytes think the world is progressing towards?

When the possessed speak of "progress", they mean the progressive industrialization of the entire Earth. They want to urbanize the whole world at the expense of traditional rural society. If living in balance with nature was a hallmark of such rural societies, industrial societies aim to maximize the human population size, namely to maximize the economic output for its owner-class.

Those who push for progress seek to assimilate all free human beings into a single, global collective called the Global Open Society, a prison from which no one can escape. The collective is to be ruled by a self-proclaimed "far-sighted elite", as American billionaire George Soros once put it. If you see yourself as the shepherd of mankind, you also come to regard those who oppose you as wolves: fascists, reactionaries, anti-Semites.

Regardless, progressive liberals don't really give a damn about people. All they care about is how much they can make off others. People are just a means of production, mindless tools to be programmed with new laws, new culture, correct thoughts and compelled speech. If you refuse to play along, your economic value drops to zero.

Autonomous, self-determined peoples can't be exploited and have no value to the collective. They are to be discarded.

To expedite your conversion to the Religion of Progress, liberals will first cast you as a potential victim of unfair treatment. Next, they will promise you salvation through diversity, inclusion, and equality ("die"), coaxing you into complete and total obedience to the collective, your new gender-neutral family.

Contrary to progressive claims of universalism, this brand of economic progress is highly particular, namely in that it serves only the interests of a chosen clique, the owner class of industrial society. Once you realize progressive liberals are paving the way for global empire, everything else starts to make sense.

To achieve humanity's complete assimilation, both the new totalitarians and their Bolshevik predecessors have for centuries deployed their version of "draining the swamp". By deliberately depopulating the countryside, and by luring families into cities with the false promise of "a better life", the urban puppet masters learned to secure power over people's hearts and minds.

Totalitarians, whose aim is to have total control over all people, have historically used war and famine as a conducive. By pitting strong countrymen against each other in suicidal wars, such as the trench wars of the First World War, the totalitarians could then herd the surplus of surviving women into urban areas, where Father State would substitute for a husband.

Repeated over centuries of time, the process of war has thus turned rural areas into ghost towns. Indeed, it has happened that way every time. The Second World War eradicated a large portion of the rural populations from the North Sea to the Ural mountains. After the war, its mentally broken survivors returned to the cities to find shelter.

Now, finally, men's belief in God had been broken to the point of accepting a belief in the State! It takes the horrors of war to make a man lose his faith in God, and the totalitarians know it all too well.

Our urban masters are continuously at war with autonomous peoples who choose to live free from the global collective. The ever-hungry collective justifies the initial depopulation and subsequent urbanization of the countryside by dehumanizing its inhabitants as 'backward rednecks', 'right-wing extremists', 'gun-toting Republicans', 'religious fundamentalists' or 'alt-right fascists'.

These people should have no rights. But whatever the epithet, in the West the collectivists have already won. In Europe, nearly three-quarters of its continental population now live in cities. Mechanized agriculture has all but wiped out Europe's rural populations. All that remains of traditional life survives in suburbia, bastions of white yearning for a long-lost past.

To efface even the suburbs of conservative blood, progressive liberals now justify the biological replacement of any and all individualists with a more docile breed, preferably imported from the collectivist civilizations of the Middle East and North Africa. It's not 'whiteness' or 'privilege' that progressives fear, but the strength and determination to withstand the false god of collectivism, the State.

If mass immigration is sure to wipe out white suburbia, and if there is no possibility of a return to a more meaningful life in rural towns, then what will the future of the West look like?

Alt-right cult leader Richard B. Spencer promotes the idea for a white ethnostate, presumably somewhere within North America. This is the dumbest idea I have recently heard of. The idea is as absurd as Native Americans volunteering to be locked up in Indian reserves upon the arrival of European colonists.

No. Building a white ethnostate, even if to escape multiculturalism, amounts to auto-ghettoization. It is a sign of surrender, weakness, withdrawal, and retreat. Rather than flee into marginalization, the willing and able must choose the flight to the front.

If we want to live free from the manipulations of the upper classes, both our own and those biologically different from us, then we must convince urban families to turn their back on the State. They may seek refuge from collectivism in the countryside, where they may slowly rebuild a more meaningful existence in a community of like-minded people.

To expedite their exodus, the bravest souls among us must wage a guerrilla war against the collectivists' holiest institutions, including the supranational organizations of the United Nations, the World Bank, even the European Commission and the Federal U.S. Government.

To save humanity from all forms of statist slavery, what choice do we have but to burn these temples of statism to the ground? Anything with a flag or anthem deserves our contempt. Yes, this is where I part ways with alt-right nationalists. Hitler, too, was a globalist who dreamed of making Berlin the capital of the world.

Arguably, the only difference between Adolf Hitler and George Soros is that Soros uses soft power to replace the Germans, whereas Hitler marched his own people to their deaths. Reading Hitler's Table Talk paints a picture of a mentally unstable man who thought he could program people to behave the way he wanted them to behave. There's no doubt in my mind Hitler was a collectivist.

Those of us who are not yet prepared to flee in white reserves, as the alt-rightists seem to be, must, therefore, prepare for eternal struggle. We must fight it, and we must keep fighting it. Only through our relentless resistance of urban collectivism may we hope to restore some balance between God and the State.

Fight or Flight? Politically Correct Self-Delusion Helps People Accept Their Demise

November 13th, 2015

Up until the very last seconds before a disaster, people possess the ability to delude themselves into thinking "everything will be alright". While the allied forces were bombing Hitler's Berlin bunker, Eva Braun and her friends were dancing on the tables, singing, drinking champagne, and toasting to the victory they thought would come any moment. Paralyzed by the possibility of an insurmountable setback, they fled into self-delusion.

Decent citizens can delude themselves, too. Psychologists have invented a phrase for it, coping behavior. We cope with a setback by adopting self-destructive behaviors so that we can continue to believe in a false truth, despite negative events engulfing the world around us. Likewise, by pretending we have fallen in love with the newcomers, our collective Stockholm syndrome is expediting our end. We choose to share our freedom and our wealth with the rest of the world, hoping to delay the end long enough for just one more meaningless part. Deep inside, though, most of us already know that the party's over.

Western self-delusion expresses itself best in political correctness. We continue to deceive ourselves into thinking that the relentless flows of immigrants from Arab, African, Asian, Indian and Latin American nations will 'enrich' our future rather than exterminate us. Our love for the multicultural experiment blurs the fact that not even a combined European-American army could effectively protect the borders of our civilization. Rather than admit to our weaknesses and prepare for deserved—and underserved—blows, we continue to say to ourselves, "Everything will be alright."

There are simply too many immigrants to stop them. Our self-delusion has reached the pinnacle of naiveté when so-called welcome committees festively embrace the new Islamic Crusaders into their midst. As we've seen in the wake of the stage Syrian crisis, the majority of refugees is made up of single males of fighting age. Most aren't even Syrian. They have left their hungry women and children behind in war zones but our self-delusion refuses to acknowledge them. Soon, we will have to swap the freedom we inherited from our ancestors for the benefits of Sharia law. To the gallows with us!

It's our privilege to hang ourselves, our politicians say. The few freedom-loving Europeans must find the courage to cut themselves loose from this sinking ship we once called our civilization. Precisely in the light of the insurmountable setback that our pending colonization poses to us, we must rise up to the challenge and change our attitudes towards it. We shall not bend, we shall not budge. Instead, we have an opportunity to show the world that we are, indeed, descendants of the Spartans, the Batavi, and the Cherusci.

For over 2,500 years, our ancestors withstood the threat of collectivism. There is no reason for us to surrender now. We shall fight and we shall win, no matter how long it takes.

Unfree Man: From Managed Child to Civilized Citizen

September 9th, 2016

In Scandinavia's North, the Sami live, the inhabitants of Lapland. Despite modern influences, many grew up as a child in a self-subsistent society. Early on, Sami children learn to bake their own bread, find fresh water, catch fish, or milk reindeer.

Sami parents treat their children as human beings. Their society assumes Sami children possess the ability to take care of themselves.

That way, they grow up to become independent adults that don't need anyone to tell them what to do. Their innate abilities have been brought to light by humane educators.

At the Tjäktja Fjällstuga, a remote mountain cabin in Swedish Lapland, I spoke with a blond-haired Sami woman. She had heard about Britain's 'Brexit' on the radio. She was thunderstruck by the power our politicians wield. Thinking of Britain, she said, "What a strange place that England must be! All those politicians telling people what to do… what use do they have?"

The contrast with modern 'civilization' could not have been greater. Precisely in our highly educated, technological societies we no longer treat children as competent human beings, but as flawed pawns that media and education must 'civilize' into citizens. Citizens are a sort of afflicted people that, despite a higher education, fail to take care of themselves. It's not expected of them to do so. Modern citizens ought to be thankful that the government steps in to decide what's the best for them.

Modern society warns of the angry citizen but forgets to realize that citizens may be angry because they are not being treated as adults. Some citizens haven't been able to become adults, which is what socialism wants: turn people in the sheeple. It is the citizen who is born to serve the government with taxes the way sheep provides wool to the farmer. We are being farmed.

Through taxation, citizens are expected to donate their productivity to the owners of our society. Taxation also serves to punish competence. To stay in power, the leaders of the herd must have a means to beat down successful people. They threaten the status quo.

The Sami show us how life might have been without an overbearing government. All people are born with competence and resilience. In order to become sheep, we have to unlearn the self-reliance we were born with. That's the purpose of education, to make teach you. Your new masters reward obedience with luxury goods—the tell-tale sign of a materialistic conspiracy.

Born into a civilized society, people quickly adjust. Old ways are forgotten, new ways are passed on from parents to their children. Modern parents have taken after Father State. They have begun to treat their children as mini-citizens. Parents have become politician and police-officer, charged with 'managing' their children.

They forget to raise them as competent, self-reliant and responsible human beings. All people who deviate from the societal dogmas are branded willfully disobedient. They deserve punishment and jail.

Modern civilization has bred a generation of know-nothings. Politicians teach people that they cannot take care of themselves. So, they assure themselves and their owners of the people's dependency on their divine redistributive powers. It's what made socialism big. In our society, the less you know how to do yourself, the more you'll come to rely on government hand-outs.

The same modernity that made our lives easy also robbed us of the most basic right to an independent and free life. Despite his wealth, modern man is unfree. The economic progress that politicians promised us has enslaved us.

A World without Owners: Why We Submitted to Financial Slavery and How We Can Be Free Again

November 10ᵗʰ, 2015

We all enjoy modern technological advances, whether it's the internet or our favorite cereal brand. But the way society is organized today has captured our individual productivity in the benefit of financial elites. If we had not surrendered our productivity, we could earn up to four times as much wealth as we do today. The solution is to break away from centralized hierarchies towards smart decentralization. And we still get to keep our modern benefits.

If you haven't heard of Bitcoin yet, it's magical internet money. But Bitcoin's major innovation is not its board-game money, but a way to decentralize ownership of a financial ledger. The Bitcoin ledger, called the blockchain, has no owner, no central bank or other authority. The ledger is distributed across participants' computers who run the Bitcoin software.

Shutting down one participant doesn't harm the Bitcoin network. Anyone can send and receive Bitcoin without restrictions. While some thieves could steal Bitcoins, so far nobody has succeeded to seize control of the Bitcoin network itself. Compare Bitcoin to how your bank works. Banks maintain their customers' accounts, while at the same time owning and controlling the ledger that records these accounts. This gives commercial banks the power to create money from nothing.

In fact, creating money from nothing is precisely how modern economies actually control the money supply. The role of central banks is limited to setting the rent percentage that banks have to pay on loans, thus only influencing money supply indirectly. When European Central Bank director Draghi announced to "print" a few trillion Euros, what he meant was to give commercial banks a license to make up more money—fairy dust.

However, the world banking system is based on legacy security principles developed back in the 1970s and 1980s, and therefore open to global-scale fraud. Two known scenarios recently lead to the theft of billions of dollars worth of currency:

- Bank account balances are just numbers in a database. Those numbers can be altered. Surplus funds can then be wired out of the bank without the bank ever noticing. A top security researcher at Kaspersky Labs Inc., Mr. Golovanov, explains, "We found that many banks only check the accounts every ten hours or so. So in the interim, you could change the numbers and transfer the money."

- Banks can create money from nothing! This means that insiders can plot to rob a bank from within. Forget about Hollywood movies like The Insider. There's no need to haul around bags of cash. Instead, when banks give out business loans or home mortgages, they create the money from nothing. Bank account holders can then withdraw that money. That's exactly how in October 2014 a gang of criminals robbed Bulgaria's KTB bank and stole over $2B USD, "due to what appears to be a Ponzi financing scheme aimed at draining the bank."

You've probably heard of Peak Oil, the point where extracting a barrel of crude oil costs more than its market price. Peak Centralization is the point where world government and world banking converge into a single global organization—the World Government. The question is whether it will ever come to that because the forces of centralization are countered by forces of decentralization. This is the age-old struggle between power elites and free masses.

Going back in history for a moment, most of us believe that prehistoric man came up with money—clams, gems, rocks, salt or anything—to cope with the inefficiency of bartering. For example, if you bartered a bag of potatoes for a chicken, how much chicken could you get for just one potato? You'd have to kill the chicken, which was impractical. But in reality that never happened. Instead, prehistoric man bartered asynchronously, e.g. he would trade a potato on many different days and ultimately receive a whole chicken in return. We can't scratch each others' backs at the same time, there's a delay.

The barter system works well for as long as you can remember who owes whom what. This system is inherently decentralized because every participant stores a personal copy of the financial ledger—the who-owes-whom memory—in their own minds. This memory was not perfect, but it works up to communities of around thirty or forty members. Beyond that point, the human mind could no longer cope with remembering. We were forced to switch to accounting using rocks, ropes, sticks and later coins, gold, paper money, credit and debit cards, and Bitcoin.

(Peak Centralization actually occurred in the West during the past two centuries. In the year 1800, 90% of Western people were self-employed. Self-employment went down to 50% in 1900 and 10% in 2000 .)

Ever since prehistoric bartering, the financial system moved away from a perfectly decentralized system towards a centralized global banking system. This solution helped mankind's population to scale up to almost seven billion members, but there is a downside: we surrendered our lives to financial elites who took control of the who-owes-whom ledger. The reason is that centralized systems only work when we submit our trust to them.

Because we could no longer rely on our own memory, we were forced to accept the authority of bankers, accountants, notaries and others who specialized in this field. But absolute power comes with absolute corruption. For example, in the decades before letting go of the gold standard, banks would run a fractional reserve where they possessed only a small fraction of the gold they were supposed to, on the assumption that the people would not redeem all their gold at once. (For this reason, many governments criminalized publicly calling for a bank run.)

Once financial elites mastered the skill to control local, national and global financial ledgers, they effectively took control of the people's productivity. In one way, the financial elites have the power to declare one business owner bankrupt while extending a loan to another 'promising entrepreneur'. Bank managers can extend billion dollar loans to corporate friends while denying loans to honest middle-class families. Banks benefit themselves from corporate centralization and therefore have an incentive to disrupt middle-class competitors.

Since we can go no further than 100% centralization, the only other way we can go is decentralization. Using emerging technologies such as the Bitcoin blockchain we can reorganize society, governance, and finance. While prehistoric men and women were forced to remember who-owes-whom records themselves, Bitcoin's technology solves this problem in a way that doesn't require centralization: the Bitcoin blockchain is a decentralized ledger without an owner, yet it is much more secure than the current global banking system.

In this sense, the blockchain is a modern solution to a prehistoric problem. The applications of decentralized ledgers are limitless:

- Own your medical history. Imagine you go to a doctor and temporarily give them access to your medical history. They can add information to your record, but when you leave, you can retract access again. Nobody can ever access your medical history without your approval.

- Own your education, diploma's, and certifications. Today, centralized authorities such as universities and schools issue and validate your diploma records. Without a diploma, you may not even get a job. Imagine a social proof of your skills, issued and validated by regular people just like you.

- Own your national identity. The Edward Snowden case shows that governments can retract your passport at will, impairing your ability to travel the world—essentially reducing you to a prisoner of your government. With Bitcoin technology, We The People could issue a global passport, one that cannot be retracted by anyone, a sort of proof of existence.

- Own your productivity. We go to work in an expensive office building apparently erected for someone else's grandiosity (The Rockefeller Building, The Trump Tower). Why can't we decide each day what tasks to work from, from friendly environments, even working for a different company each day while owning our productivity? In the future, companies will compete based on creativity and customer service, but not worker exploitation.

- Own your ideas and inventions. The Creative Commons copyright licenses are an example of how to do things differently. The world's patent system, which now benefits big corporations who have the funds to sue small-business, will be overturned, if not abolished completely. Smart patents, or Creative Patents, will accelerate collaborative innovation in the benefit of all mankind.

What caught my attention about Bitcoin most was the story of Silk Road, a 'black' market where drug dealers could buy and sell anything but without having to meet in person. The anonymity of the internet protected drug dealers from getting stabbed, shot at or robbed. Online user ratings discriminated between 'honest' and 'fraudulent' drug dealers. That's an unexpected benefit—because that means we can also organize 'white' markets to operate in this manner, e.g. without violence and corruption.

A decentralized world, one where people lend their productive lives to causes of their own choosing, one without central governments, banks or militaries, can be a world without crime, corruption and even without war. With the Bitcoin blockchain principles available to us, we now have an obligation to use them. Let's build a world without centralized ownership of our lives.

2

Identity and Diversity

"Social oppression is an inevitable consequence of
the continued rise of population. ... Aggressive war
is caused by the continued growth of population in a
relatively rich society."

—Paul Colinvaux

Immigrants coming to the First World, the West, often feel discriminated. In their own view, they fell discriminated against on the basis of the color of their skin. A complaint often heard goes that Western societies look at what immigrants can't do, rather than what they can do.

The truth, however, may be diametrically different. Most Western societies—whether or not founded upon democratic principles of equality, rule of law and economic freedom—tend to be governed by steep social hierarchies, much steeper than elsewhere in the world. Western economic prosperity comes with a catch: the financial pecking order must be maintained aggressively. Despite the meritocratic promise of upward mobility for those who study and work hard, even in the most meritocratic society of the United States of America a citizen's financial class is mostly determined at birth.

Except for a few unique societies with flat hierarchies, such as Denmark or Iceland, your chances of upward mobility depend on how rich your parents are, i.e. prior wealth. Importantly, this prior wealth trap holds true for indigenous (white) Americans and Europeans too. The lower and lower middle classes of white people are also stuck in first gear, or to some perhaps even in reverse. Consequently, the lower classes, including those of the rest of the world, merely serve as a means of production to generate wealth for the upper classes.

Thus, when non-white immigrants, e.g. from Third World countries, arrive in the so-called "land of the free", the American Dream appears to them just as it is, a dream. Immigrants to the First World often come from much more egalitarian societies, especially when everyone is equally poor. They are not at all accustomed to the steep, aggressive social hierarchies of the rich West. The modern West's power happens to be concentrated in the hands of mostly white Americans and Europeans. Therefore, darker skinned immigrants may feel discriminated because of the color of their skin, but really the steeper social and financial hierarchies of capitalist civilizations are to blame, as they indiscriminately bar newcomers and members of lower classes from reaching the top.

The Right to Identity:
Is the Islamization of Europe a Crime against Humanity?

August 10ᵗʰ, 2016

In a shocking interview, German Minister of Finance Wolfgang Schäuble admitted he believed opening his country's borders could save Germans from "degeneration through inbreeding". He hopes to achieve this goal by mixing German genes with those of Arabs and Northern Africans. Perhaps the mass rapes that took place in Cologne and other cities last New Year's Eve were just what Schäuble had in mind. It may forever remain a mystery how German thinking went from full Nazi to full retard in seventy years' time, but it is certain that no one in Europe has ever voted in a democratic election in favor of mass immigration.

Despite that the European continent's rich history has produced hundreds of different cultures of its own, it wasn't until the sixties and seventies of the previous century that artificial multiculturalism was brought into this world, an afterbirth of unrestrained mass immigration. The millions of migrants that have come to Europe would eventually refuse to assimilate. Considering their high degree of welfare dependency, newcomers have generally failed at their economic assimilation. So, European multiculturalism was born as if the thoughtlessness of its introduction was meant to be.

More than half a century later, the tens of millions of non-Western immigrants, including their offspring, have severely put native Europeans' tolerance to the test. It is no surprise that the multicultural society that was never designed to succeed has indeed failed, although it would take European leaders—including former British Prime Minister David Cameron, German Chancellor Angela Merkel, and former French President Nicolas Sarkozy—half their careers before admitting it.

Having failed to assimilate the newcomers, we've now arrived at a phase called 'acceptance'—we, Europeans, will simply have to accept that we will never be our own people again. How did we end up here? Why hasn't the resistance against the erasure of our identities been fiercer? Whence came the idea to flood our nations with a surplus of Arab and African sons, a sociological and demographic disaster that would irrevocably change the future for all European children?

Contrary to Muslims and other non-Western migrants that came to Europe, Europeans that emigrated to the United States have assimilated into the prevailing American culture. For example, about half of today's white Americans descends from German immigrants. German Americans represent the largest minority in the US, yet as a group one can hardly tell them apart from other whites. They've blended into the dominant Anglo-Saxon culture that American colonists had founded. German Americans never 'Germanized' America but Americanized themselves, trading their mother tongue for English.

In comparison to the millions of Mexican immigrants, as well as equal numbers of illegal immigrants, that came to live in the US while refusing to learn to speak a word of English, the contrast could not have been bigger. By now, the US has absorbed a quarter of the Mexican population, over thirty million lives dependent on the US economy, because Mexico couldn't provide for them. On top of that, two-thirds of the immigrants are illegal aliens. As a group, illegal aliens have contributed little to nothing to America because they remained Mexicans or Indians or Asians. While Anglo-Saxon Americans had anticipated the arrival of German immigrants to the United States, subjecting them to mandatory assimilation, European leaders had never expressed any intention to turn newcomers into people like us.

Possibly, this laissez-faire attitude concerning mass immigration has a historical cause. The multicultural societies that Northern and Western Europeans, in particular, have founded may flow from a colonial passion for collecting things, i.e. their ruling elites' urge to possess the world. After having conquered new lands and foreign countries during the colonial days, after having subjugated entire continents of people, after having looted and amassed the world's natural resources, after having declared archeological treasures their private property—for example, put on display in the Louvre or the British Museum, and after even having practiced slavery and slave trade, there was only one more possibility left to satisfy this all-encompassing urge to possess—by establishing a human zoo, a multicultural society.

I'm not kidding. At the peak of colonial bad taste, indigenous families from all over the world were 'collected' and put on display before audiences in Europe and America. We have erased this dubious phenomenon from our cultural memory but even today we can recognize its remnants, for example in the form of Madame Tussaud's museums. Such expositions may be an expression of Western man's dark side, of he who wants to possess the wax bodies of his idols.

Until 1950, day trippers and their children could visit nomadic families living in human zoos. Few Sami families from Lapland, for example, allowed themselves to be put on display in the Hagenbeck Zoo near Hamburg, Germany. Likewise, Sioux Indians were 'open to the public' in Chicago. These families were not slaves. They received pay and sometimes negotiated good deals including hotel stays. Some were professional actors who seized the opportunity that an education in modern Europe offered them. Above all, it offered participants a rare chance to show their nomadic culture to the world at a time without television and the internet. Aside from cases of unavoidable abuse, the human zoos had, at least to some extent, served to educate the people.

The aforementioned Sami peoples still live in Northern Norway, housing about half the total population, as well as in Sweden, Finland, and on the Russian Kola peninsula. They had lived there long before national borders crossed their habitats. The Sami descend from people who settled in the area sometime ten to six thousand years ago. As a people, they form their own ethnic group, independent from the more southern located Fins, Swedes, and Norwegians. For thousands of years, Scandinavians and Sami have shared an overlapping habitat but in a relatively peaceful manner. Each group relied on different types of food and natural resources. Early on, the southern Scandinavians had begun to trade over the sea with other Europeans. They would build farms while the Sami specialized as hunters and gatherers that lived off fishing and reindeer husbandry.

The Sami are indigenous Europeans, white people with blond hair but they differ genetically from other Europeans. Scientists suspect the Sami are descendants of a smaller genetic branch of Europeans that separated from the rest of us in a distant past. Their faces feature a narrower, flatter nose bridge, perhaps to heat the colder polar air when breathing, as well as varying degrees of epicanthic eyes as some East Asian peoples display (with whom the Sami are not related).

The Sami were first mentioned in Norwegian and Icelandic sagas from the eleventh to the thirteenth century, for example in Egil's Saga which recounts how Iceland's national hero and his Viking buddies spent their summers sailing to Norway, traveling to Lapland looking for Sami, bashing in their skulls and looting their food and wealth. Throughout history, the Sami have commonly been depicted as inferior human beings by their European cousins. They have not been treated well.

As the industrialization of Europe reached the far north, the Sami were forced to surrender the land intended for their reindeer herds. In Sweden, they were put to work in a slave mine near Kiruna. European anthropologists would hold members of various Sami tribes at gunpoint, forcing them to undress and undergo the sort of 'bone measurements' inmates of Nazi Germany would later experience. Naturally, such measurements were intended to 'prove' Sami inferiority and the superiority of other Europeans. Even until 1975, Sami women were forced to undergo sterilization in an attempt to halt their continued population growth.

Still, in 2011, the United Nations committee against racial discrimination reprimanded the Norwegian government with a report to improve the position of the Sami. During the past millennium, the Sami's cultural identity has come under pressure. Until recently, Sami children weren't even allowed an education in their own language. All of the nearly dozen Sami languages are listed on a UN list for threatened and endangered languages. As with the other Europeans before them, the Christening of the Sami largely erased the memory of their earlier tribal faith.

But isn't it hypocrite that precisely these Norwegians and Swedes, who are world-renowned for their tolerance, have opened their own nations' borders to non-Western immigrants while at the same time their treatment of the Sami should be a warning for anyone moving north? Is it possible that with the arrival of Arabs, Turks, Northern Africans, and Eastern Europeans the roles are being reversed and that the Scandinavians, like the Sami, now have to guard themselves against the loss of their identity? We will have to determine to what extent the world's peoples have the right to defend their identity.

If people do have a right to defend their identities then perhaps Europeans may also defend theirs against, for example, the veil for women, the erection of mosques in their lands, recurring aggression during Ramadan's fasting month, colonial Islamic education, and, in short, against any attack on native European culture. The taboo of political correctness doesn't help us in trying to answer such questions because answering these questions also extends protection to the rest of the world. Naturally, the United Nations' directives that protect the Sami against Scandinavian colonialism must also be applicable to all other tribes of Europeans. They hold true for all peoples that seek protection against their cultural drowning in a sea of unassimilated migrants.

It cannot be denied that Europe and the North are the white man's evolutionary birthplace, sacred ground similar to what the desert is to Arabs. Here, Neanderthal men roamed for over three hundred thousand years as well as Cro-Magnon who left some of the oldest cave art. From north to south and east to west, modern Europeans are a naturally diverse people. With hundreds of languages, an even greater number of dialects, dozens of countries, thousands of traditions and customs and an equal number of ethnic identities, owing to its overarching civilization based on individual freedom, the continent is perhaps the most diverse in the world.

The idea to make Europe more diverse through uncontrolled mass migration of uneducated and analphabetic Arabs and Africans holds no credibility whatsoever. Europeans have never had a shortage of diversity that could only be solved by importing millions of ever the same, homogeneous Muslims. On the contrary, it is discriminatory and racist to claim that Europeans would be suffering from a sort of cultural or genetic poverty or that they would only be able to pull themselves out of the doldrums through forceful mingling with unwanted newcomers as Wolfgang Schäuble suggested.

The multicultural societies so beloved by our ruling elites have never received the people's mandate. The large-scale multiculturalization of Europe and the West has yet to be repeated elsewhere unless we count among the successes of open borders the Japanization of China, the Germanization of Poland during World War II or the Islamization of Northern Africa during the 7th century. No, multicultural societies contradict themselves because either its peoples blend into one unrecognizable immigrant master race or they split up in monocultural enclaves, reducing each to the living wallpaper at the end of the other's worlds. In fact, this is what we see happening in the US and in Europe. Individuals mix, but peoples don't.

The true multicultural experience is nowhere to be found. Does this idealized form of cohabitation perhaps exist only for the entertainment of bored Bilderberg elites, the super-rich who climb down from their ivory towers once a year to spend an afternoon dwelling among the peasants, aping at the human apes? Whatever it is, Europeans are about to pay an astronomical price to visit this human zoo: the future of our children. The formation of immigrant enclaves that multiculturalism has infected nearly all major Western cities with has led to a social and economic destabilization at an unprecedented scale.

The clash of value systems between native Europeans and non-Western immigrants continues to demand a one-sided concession from the still dominant culture, who, for now, can afford to do so. But immigrants have an incentive to exploit this naive generosity, at least for as long as native taxpayers feel obliged to cough it up, reducing their own family sizes in order to make room for immigrant boom towns. For that matter, Muslim colonists won't need to sterilize white women because white women already volunteered not to have any in favor of the 'career'.

While the hypocrite Scandinavians now treat their Muslim guests better than they've ever treated the native Sami from their own countries, we must conclude that all people have been reduced to mere numbers in a global accounting ledger. The Muslims in Oslo, Malmö, Stockholm, and Helsinki simply provide the capitalist industry with greater profit margins. Those who do not are dumped in welfare programs which demand natives to pick up the tab. The Sami are not economically viable for the Scandinavian states but increasingly, neither are white Scandinavians. Islam, in the view of the globalist elites, is a fast-growing market for products and services. We have sold the future of our children in exchange for short-term profits, giving the money away to migrants without asking for anything in return.

The multiculturalization of the West appears to have been a magic trick. We've magically replaced white audiences with foreign ones. Still, the multiculturalist ideology will not hold up much longer. *Multiculturalism is a crime against humanity.* As with the Nuremberg trials, its architects will not escape their fate. Europeans will not become the Sami of the world but we will, instead, defend our right to be who we are. Unless Europeans and European Americans wish to live in reserves designated for white people, perhaps the time to begin our resistance is now.

The Trouble with Diversity: Diverse Societies Offer No More Stability Than Monocultural Ones

December 8th, 2015

The historical events that gave rise to multicultural nations and cosmopolitan cities also institutionalized new and upcoming forms of social oppression, notably racism. Since people can never change their 'race'—unlike their religion or nationality—racial discrimination both corners its victims and persecutes their offspring. But in the globalizing West, the public preoccupation with racial inequality obscures an undercurrent of failing multiculturalism. The West is in a deplorable state. To allow for repairs, we must first expose that the concept of universal equality is fraudulent.

Racism is one of many forms of social oppression. Despite so-called enlightenment, social progress, and decades of political correctness (itself a form of oppression), people from all over the world continue to suffer elitism, casteism, bureaucracy, intellectualism, tribalism, nepotism, nationalism, (child) slavery, religious fundamentalism, financial inequality, sexism, political discrimination, feudalism, corporate and military hierarchies, hunger, poverty, bullying, ostracism, playground pecking orders, envy and contempt, shame and guilt, and plain verbal insult. Not only have we not eliminated any of these problems, many of these problems keep rising.

Why hasn't humankind yet successfully rooted out any of these types of social oppression? What makes our politicians and social leaders believe we can end racism? Arguably, the West partially solved slavery by outsourcing slave labor to the Third World, and partially by reinventing modern slaves as low-wage migrant workers. So while richer societies to some extent could afford to dump their social inequality elsewhere, globally speaking nothing has changed.

It appears we can't cure social oppression. The reason is: oppression serves a purpose. Acting as a guiding principle both in the distribution of wealth, and in the allocation of living space for peoples and their offspring, without social oppression, the world of human affairs would implode. Life isn't fair.

The world we live in is one giant tragedy of the commons. For thousands of years, human innovation has pushed the boundaries of its global population size through arduous innovation, capitalist trade, and even world war. But as Indians already double-outsource Chinese jobs to even poorer Africans, the global economy is close to reaching its limits to growth.[1] Therefore, the future holds more social oppression, not less. Individuals will carry the burdens of economic stagnation, as per the principle "privatized profits, socialized costs".

Life's inherent unfairness means the politics of peoples is and has always been right wing. Left-wing politics can never transcend neighborhood activism because it is itself the result of economic abundance.[2] You have to be rich to practice leftism. In fact, 'being left' offers those can afford it to exert public status. Nonetheless, only rich societies can afford to look 'progressive'. Therefore, in times of great geopolitical rifts, the left is by definition unqualified to support a people's need for aggressive self-preservation. Yet today we must shamefully admit that precisely those neighborhood activists are leading the West... into the abyss.

Not all forms of social oppression receive proportional public attention, racism standing out. Is the preoccupation with racism today's fashion? Why do many people feel combating racism is more important than combating the more wide-spread problem of oppressed women, or the morally more disturbing problem of child slavery?

The reason for racism's spotlight attention is that minorities suffering from such oppression may disguise their own racism as anti-racism. Anti-racism as a strategy offers minorities an opportunity to assert themselves in the light of an eternal second place. For this reason, members of the majority group suffer their own social oppression at the hands of minorities. This should be no surprise: the modern concept of equality carefully disguises that by equal treatment we really mean equal oppression.

The debate on race and racism characterizes itself by an abundance of logical fallacies. One fallacy goes, "Blacks (Xs) are equal to whites (Ys), therefore whites should treat blacks equally." It's a fallacy because most whites don't treat most other whites equally either (Ys are not equal to Ys). We tend to call whites discriminating against other whites 'competition', while whites treating blacks the same way, which is equal treatment, is nevertheless called 'racism'. The point being that minorities ought to be able to live equal lives without necessitating equal effort.

The debate on racial discrimination has thus lost all meaning. The doctrines of political correctness have lead to a surrealist state of society. On the one hand, members of a majority group must publicly treat minorities as their equals, which means to give more than to get, or at least pretend to do so. On the other hand, minorities are expected to 'be grateful' for such unwanted help, privately aspiring to replace the majority.

Martin Luther King did not dream of equality, but of the reversal of inequality. We practice equality to keep up appearances, but the very idea of equal treatment refutes we possess equality innately. How much political correctness have we embraced in order to suppress our mutual fear and contempt?

Another logical fallacy, or plain lie, states that diversity offers long-term stability. But diversity also incurs great costs—e.g. integration costs, increased governing complexity, decreased economic efficiency, etc. Generally speaking, the majority group, simply because it is the majority, foots most of that bill, which in turn generates growing resentment. Thus, among other factors, diversity itself causes racism. Therefore, diversity destabilizes society. See Ancient Egypt. See Ancient Rome. See the Ottoman Empire. See the European Union.

Leftists mistakenly believe that some new-found moral high ground, which we supposedly discovered right after World War II, lead to our embracing multiculturalism, i.e. the belief that diversity is inherently 'good' and more diversity always 'better'. As the leftists set off to build a society without hate in which educated people would no longer want to go to war, as if war were ever a choice, they conveniently abandoned the realism necessary to defend their own utopia's.

In truth, the multicultural societies we see in the West today are no more than the result of cold mass immigration serving soulless economic survivalism. To avoid social unrest, Western ruling classes reluctantly glued together their rapidly changing populations with taboos on financial inequality, religious intolerance or racial privilege, but Western leaders did so more out of duty than out of choice, the alternative being civil war.

Diversity may also reach a turning point beyond which minorities prefer to secede from the majority, see for example the Catalans in Spain. And knowing that it took only a few thousand supporters to found the state of Israel, what's to stop thirty million African-Americans from demanding independence as a people? Or American Muslims, for that matter?

Historically, collaborating minorities have ganged up on richer majority cultures, as we know happened to Ancient Rome and other empires. Realizing that somewhere between 11 to 30 million Mexicans (plus offspring) have come to live in the US during the past half-century, what's to stop Mexico from annexing part of US territory? While there's no likely scenario for a Mexican army to march north anytime soon, those already in the US could simply plant their flag, with Wal-Mart supplying their ammunition.

Diverse societies offer no more long-term stability than monocultural ones. Multicultural societies exist merely to postpone a tragedy of the commons. Further progressing down this path, the West will have to face its destiny. The European Union will implode. The American majority will revolt. The question is, will be it enough, or will it be too little, too late?

White Guilt: Do People of European Descent Deserve to Take Pride in Their History?

August 24ᵗʰ, 2016
After World War II, historians scrambled to try to explain what could have caused such a destructive event. What was so different about the Europeans that had steered their actions towards the Holocaust? In attempts to answer such a question, historians and sociologists began pointing fingers at four pillars of European evil: nationalism, xenophobia, racism, and sexism.

The dominant view of European history now centers around blaming white men. White women acquit themselves on the grounds of being victims of male oppression, when in reality, European society, especially Germanic society, had always been matriarchal. Regardless, how can women not be guilty of crimes their men committed in their name, for them or for their children?

From the Spartans to the U.S. Marines, men of European descent are accused of having been warmongering, land-occupying, people-subjugating oppressors of women and minorities. Above all, they are accused of doing so for no other reason but for power and for profit. Accusing white men of doing these things and of doing them just for the fun of it, is as absurdly racist as accusing Jewish men of running a global financial scheme to enslave mankind.

Nonetheless, schools continue to teach white children, especially boys, to feel ashamed of their ancestors and to feel guilty for the actions of their forefathers.

Our children no longer learn that the Spartans showed solidarity by standing shoulder to shoulder against the Persians with their former enemies, the Athenians. Instead, they learn that Spartan men were a bunch of raping, looting murderers. School textbooks decry the Crusades as evidence of institutionalized European Islamophobia and antisemitism. In reality, the Crusades were a response to centuries of Muslim aggression against Christian pilgrims.

We are taught that the white male patriarchy—whatever that may be—has oppressed women since time immemorial until feminists finally won the "war on men" and liberated women. No feminist ever points out that throughout history most European men had lived out their lives as serfs, bondsmen, farmers, soldiers or slaves. They, too, had lived under constant feudal oppression. How could such lowly men possibly have conspired to oppress women? It didn't happen.

The ban on abortion introduced by Christianity saved the lives of many women who would have otherwise succumbed to the primitive procedure. Later, male-led advances in medicine began saving the lives of even more women who would otherwise have died in childbirth. Historically, it has been a male privilege to die in battle in defense of women and children.

Haven't men invented the microwave, the dishwasher, washing machines, and dryers, freeing women from the menial household tasks that used to occupy them for most of their day?

According to progressive leftists, either white men make up for their past oppression by paying for restorations voluntarily or society forcefully dispossess them. Whichever way, the white man must pay for his evil sins. Despite the fact that peoples of European descent are already a global minority, in order to absolve whites of their guilt, they must now allow their countries to be overrun with immigrants. Whites are to become minorities in their own cities in order to experience firsthand what it means to be discriminated against.

That's not even a conspiracy theory. Vice President of the United States Joe Biden publicly called for flooding (formerly) white Christian nations with never-ending streams of immigrants, supposedly "a source of our strength".

To curb their decline, what Europeans need to do is rehabilitate their history and their ancestors. They should teach their children to honor their forefathers. With the help of Wikipedia, I've put together a selection of ten notable European conquerors. No child should have to feel ashamed of them.

Leonidas of Sparta
Lived in modern-day Greece, 540-480 BC (aged 60)
During the Second Persian War, warrior-king Leonidas led the allied Greek forces to the last stand at the Battle of Thermopylae (the Hot Gates), attempting to defend the pass from the invading Persian army. The 300 Spartans were real. In 1939, archaeologist Spyridon Marinatos excavated large numbers of Persian bronze arrowheads on Kolonos Hill where Leonidas and his 300 had died for our freedom.

Vercingetorix the Gaul
Lived in modern-day France, 86-42 BC (aged 44)
Vercingetorix came to power after his formal designation as chieftain of the Arverni tribe in 52 BC. He immediately established an alliance with other Gallic tribes, combined all forces, and led them in Gaul's most significant revolt against Roman power. He won the Battle of Gergovia, in which 46 centurions and 700 legionaries died and more than 6,000 people were injured, whereupon Caesar's Roman legions withdrew. In 42 BC, at the Battle of Alesia, the Romans besieged and defeated his forces and captured him.

Arminius the Germanic
From modern-day Germany, 17 BC-21 AD (aged 39)
As a teenage boy, Arminius, also called Hermann in German, had been kidnapped by Roman forces and raised to become an officer in the Roman military. When he returned, he became chieftain of the Germanic Cherusci tribe. After uniting various Germanic tribes, he defeated the Roman army in the Battle of the Teutoburg Forest in 9 AD, after which his influence waned, and he was assassinated by rival Germanic chiefs. Apparently, his wife Thusnelda was a bitch. In today's German language, her

name abbreviated to Tussi is a derogatory term used to describe superficial, materialistic women.

Attila the Hun
Lived in modern-day Hungary, 406-453 AD (aged 47)

During his reign, "the scourge of God" Attila was the most feared enemy of the Roman Empire. He crossed the Danube twice and plundered the Balkans but was unable to take Constantinople. His campaign in Persia was followed in 441 by an invasion of the Byzantine Empire. He also attempted to conquer what is now France, crossing the Rhine in 451 and marching as far as Orléans. He subsequently invaded Italy, devastating the northern provinces, but was unable to take Rome.

Charles the Great
Lived in modern-day France, Germany, 742-814 (aged 71)

King of the Franks, Charles the Great, or Charlemagne, united a large part of Europe during the early Middle Ages and laid the foundations for modern France and Germany. Charlemagne has been called the "Father of Europe", as from 800 he united most of Western Europe for the first time since the Roman Empire. In a lightning march, Charles and his army defeated the Saracen Muslims between Tours and Poitiers. They would come back twice more, only to suffer defeat at Charles' hands twice more.

Rollo the Norman
From modern-day Denmark or Norway, 846-932 (age 86)

Rollo belonged to a noble Viking warrior family. According to one source, he sailed to Ireland, England, and France, where he seized Rouen in 876 and led the Viking fleet which besieged Paris between 885 and 887. Over time, Rollo and his Vikings converted from Norse paganism to Christianity. His son, William Longsword, and grandchild, Richard the Fearless, forged the Duchy of Normandy. The descendants of Rollo and his men became known as the Normans.

Egill Skallagrímsson
Lived in modern-day Iceland, Norway, 904–995 (aged 91)
At the age of seven, Iceland's national hero Egill was cheated in a game with local boys. Enraged, he went home and procured an ax, and returning to the boys, split the skull to the teeth of the boy who cheated him. He later made frequent round trips from Iceland to Norway and elsewhere to fight against King Harald Fairhair, and later for King Athelston. A violent man, he was also a scholar of runes and a poet. Ultimately, Egill returned to his family farm in Iceland, where he remained a power to be reckoned with in local politics. He died shortly before the Christianisation of Iceland.

Godfrey of Bouillon
Lived in modern-day Belgium, 1060-1100 (aged 40)
In 1095, Pope Urban II called for a Crusade to liberate Jerusalem from Muslim forces, and to aid the Byzantine Empire which was under Muslim attack. The leader of the First Crusade, Godfrey took out loans on most of his lands or sold them. With this money, he gathered thousands of knights to fight in the Holy Land. Godfrey was believed to have possessed immense physical strength. It was said that he wrestled a bear in Cilicia and won. He became a legend among the descendants of the original crusaders.

Vlad the Impaler
From modern-day Romania, 1431-1477 (aged 45)
His father Vlad II was a member of the Order of the Dragon, which was founded to protect Christianity in Eastern Europe. Vlad III is revered as a folk hero in Romania and Bulgaria for

his protection of the Romanians and Bulgarians both north and south of the Danube. In 1459, Pope Pius II called for a new crusade against the Ottomans at the Congress of Mantua. Vlad allied with the King of Hungary in the hope of keeping the Ottomans out. As his nickname suggests, he was known for impaling his enemies.

John Sobieski
Lived in today's Poland, Ukraine, 1629–1696 (aged 66)
Sobieski's military skill, demonstrated in wars against the Ottoman Empire, contributed to his prowess as King of Poland. Popular among his subjects, he was most famous for his victory over the Turks at the 1683 Battle of Vienna. On September 12, upon reaching Vienna, with the Ottoman army close to breaching the walls, Sobieski ordered a full attack. After his victories over them, the Ottomans called him the "Lion of Lechistan", and the Pope hailed him as the "Savior of Christendom", and of Western European civilization.

What all of these men have in common is that their "patriarchal, murderous, raping" lifestyles also provided for the survival of their peoples and their progeny. Feminists overlook that they only exist today because their male forefathers laid down their lives in defense of their peoples. Without such brutal men, indeed there wouldn't have been a United States, an Australia, a South Africa, or even a Europe today but other, more brutal systems would have taken root.

Had these warmongering men converted to a progressive leftism, had they shielded themselves off in safe spaces, had they let shame and guilt guide their decisions, then their children would not have lived to tell about it. Without strong men, democracy as we know it could never have existed.

So, the time has come for European men to honor their ancestors. Let us together reconquer the West and defend European civilization.

Mass Migration's True Motive: A Devil's Pact Between the Low-Wage Industry and a Globalist Cabal

January 3rd, 2016

We say migration is of all times, but for the past two millennia, mass migrations to Europe ended in battles the newcomers lost. "We're all immigrants", they say, most of us do not descent from illegal immigrants nor from immigrants drawn to luxury lifestyles. Europe's early settlers in South Africa, North America, Australia and New Zealand arrived in savage lands and had to build their societies up from the ground.

During the 18th, 19th and 20th century, hundreds of thousands of Europeans boarded the Holland America Line from Amsterdam to New York. They met an economic need. If not, they faced poverty as the New World certainly did not provide them with free healthcare and welfare programs. Upon their arrival at Ellis Island, the newcomers were required to pass a medical exam and take an IQ test. If they failed, they were sent back on the first ship sailing out. It didn't change one bit whether the rejects felt insulted or discriminated, on whatever grounds.

Now, look at how the European Union protects its borders, attempting to integrate millions of utterly unassimilable third world immigrants without demanding compensation in whatsoever form. The American colonists of yore strengthened their new nation economically. Either that or they starved. But the majority of present-day 'refugees' lacking the required education for a job in highly technologized Western nations end up being dumped in welfare programs. They weaken the West.

Mass migration only occurs when a large region finds itself in a state of war or when its population is about to face hunger. Think of the Irish Hunger from 1845 to 1850 that drove many Irish to the Promised Land, the United States of America. Mass migration, however, never happens spontaneously. It is always the consequence of misery. Each refugee is one too many.

The hunger and war that drives people to flee their circumstances flow from long-term processes of social decay. With the United Nations at the forefront, the international community has an obligation to arrange for local support systems. Moreover, it is cheaper and safer to arrange for regional shelter programs than to ship millions of people thousands of miles across land and sea to far-away nations.

It makes no sense, yet that's exactly what is happening. Again and again, the unanimous 'solution' sounds: send everyone to Europe. Since when did Europe turn into some kind of heaven on earth? Fooled by commercial advertising, billions of people are dreaming of coming to Europe for a luxury life that only exists in the movies. People certainly don't come to Europe dreaming of lower-class jobs in rural towns. They come because they feel entitled to stardom.

Failing that, it's easy to accuse their new hosts of being privileged racists. But Europeans aren't gods. Before the Second World War, Norway was considered a Third World nation as its citizens often starved to death, trapped between the fjords in winters with temperatures far below freezing. Well into the 1970s, farmers from the eastern provinces of the Netherlands were living in wooden shacks no more impressive than those described by the Roman historian Tacitus two thousand years ago. Today, in Eastern Europe, many small towns still don't have paved roads.

Cities like Shanghai, Dubai, or even Luanda, Angola, are much wealthier and far more advanced than, say, Germany's rural villages. If you're looking for paradise then why come to Europe, where freezing winters can last up to nine months of the year?

For one, the mass migration of guest workers that started during the postwar 1950s came about because Europe needed slave laborers to rebuilt its economies. The flows of guest workers officially ended in 1973, when both Germany and The Netherlands ended their recruitment programs. Indeed, the workers from Northern Africa and the Middle East didn't migrate out of their own movement—they were actively displaced.

Nonetheless, guest workers turned into refugees, refugees into family reunion applicants, and the latter into economic migrants. A higher birth rate ensured the newcomers would soon dominate lower class neighborhoods. White Europeans are projected to become a minority before the year 2100.[3] The Netherlands, for example, has a dense population of 17 million, which includes nearly 4 million non-indigenous immigrants.

On January 2nd, 2016, the American company Cargill fired 190 employees—Somali refugees who had demanded the right to interrupt work to pray for Allah. The company declined because the interruptions would endanger production processes. More likely, it would endanger profits. But the question remains: had these 'refugees', mostly single men of fighting age, really come to America for a better life or were they recruited by big business as slave laborers? It turns out that globalization is a race to the bottom. Karl Marx would turn around in his grave.

The corporate psychopaths who direct these migrant streams don't care for the quality of the immigrant nor for those drowned souls who didn't make it across. From the perspective of financial self-interest, the globalists dictate to the politicians what they must tell the people to believe. To achieve this goal, corporations have bought their own politicians.

Mass migration is an act of war against indigenous populations. This was true when the Spanish Conquistadores invaded Latin America. It was true when Northern Europeans colonized North America. It still true when Arabs, Africans, Asians, and Indians come to invade Europe. But this crime against European humanity is no ordinary event. It is an act of treason by Europe's own financial elites, a treason against their entire civilization.

This is no minor infringement upon our sovereignty or an insult to our national identities. Even Stalin and Hitler didn't plunge their own peoples into the abyss at the rate Western corporate psychopaths are doing. The resistance, once assembled, shall be merciless. I advise the masters of finance to prepare an escape route and befriend a foreign nation where they may need to apply for asylum when the torched and pitchforked masses come for them.

A Civilization Run by Slaves:
Warning the West of Its Hypocrisy

October 29th, 2016
At the height of the Roman empire, nearly 40% of Italy's population consisted of slaves. Slaves represented almost 15% of the entire empire. But as the increasing cost of warfare against ever more enemies on either side of its borders rapidly depleted its reserves, Rome's slave-run civilization eventually collapsed, because it could no longer afford to feed them.

Today, modern Western civilization takes pride in having abolished slavery, yet it increasingly relies on low-cost laborers imported from elsewhere. We, too, have become a civilization dependent on immigrant slave labor. Despite the fact that we abolished the physical chains that limit a man's movements, the social conditions that make a man a slave have worsened.

In the West, the distinction between citizen and slave is very real, albeit that we have invented a vocabulary of soft-sounding words to hide that bitter reality from both our consciousness and our conscience. For example, both in Europe and in the United States we've reached consensus to call certain people "illegal aliens", "undocumented immigrants", "asylum seekers", "guest workers" or even (economic) "refugees".

All such derogatory labels point to someone's lesser social status. Yet, without them, our failing economies could not survive. In general, we employ immigrants to do the most mind-numbing, low-skilled and poorly paid work we can no longer afford to do ourselves.

In fact, the oft false promise of citizenship and equal rights dangling before their eyes like a carrot on a stick is precisely what persuades immigrants to put up with their condition. All Western power thus rests on a mastery of the art of human exploitation.

To an outsider, though, ours could easily be mistaken for the most slave-run civilization in the history of all mankind. A Roman soldier wandering the busy streets of New York today would easily recognize a legal hierarchy based on race and ethnicity. We only differ from Romans in that we've invented elaborate newspeak to manipulate the plebs into disregarding what their eyes can see.

There's just one problem. Like Rome, our globalized economy will inevitably hit a limit to growth. When that happens, our civilization will no longer be able to award immigrants their "equal rights". The (already inflated) value of citizenship will quickly deflate. Angry immigrant mobs — soon a majority in most Western cities — will have no choice but to take to the streets demanding their rightful due.

If we cannot see our reality, because treacherous words of our own invention have hidden it from view, then we cannot act upon it either. I am convinced that the real reason civilizations fail is that of their inability, or unwillingness, to see the truth. And that truth is: once the immigrant classes have achieved a critical mass, they can and will turn their backs on us.

The Reinvention of Slavery: How Elites Will Solve the Global Energy Crisis

November 12ᵗʰ, 2015

As the world runs out of fossil fuel, sooner or later, formerly cheap energy will inevitably become expensive. The cost to extract one barrel of crude oil has been rising for decades. But rather than causing collapse, the transition from cheap to expensive energy forces energy-hungry civilizations like the West to increasingly rely on human labor. This process of replacing fuel with people is already underway; it is what drives mass migration from poorer to richer nations worldwide, supplying the latter with cheap labor.

Examples of this process are undeniable. The European Union has absorbed tens of millions of migrants from mostly Islamic, African and Eastern European nations. In the past few decades, the share of EU citizens of Islamic origin rose to over 10 percent, now representing nearly 50 million people, but the vast majority continue to occupy lower class jobs. The United States is struggling with immigration reform, namely to award legal status to millions of Mexican and Latin-American workers. They too will mostly populate the US lower class. It is even evident in Saudi-Arabia, whose oil riches now afford large numbers of Indian and Asian migrant workers— under conditions of "near-slavery", according to a Human Rights Watch report.

"All poverty is caused by the continued growth of population."[4]

In 1980, ecologist Paul Colinvaux wrote a little-known book called The Fates of Nations, which argues for a biological view of "why history happens". In it, Colinvaux debunks the myth that poverty is the cause of overpopulation, claiming it to be the opposite way around. He warns of political propaganda that tells us that Third World family sizes will decline once we bring the poor our wealth. The reason we think this might be the case is that we observe correctly that richer families indeed have fewer children, but the families of the rich are smaller because it is more expensive to raise wealthier people than it is to raise poorer people.

According to Colinvaux, the laws of ecology dictate that the continuing growth of population is the cause of poverty (see citation). The reason is that packing more people into the same niche-space dilutes the resources available to each individual, such as food and living space. An increasing number of individuals for a given niche, therefore, causes poverty (ceteris paribus).

"Social oppression is an inevitable consequence of the continued rise of *population*."[5]

Colinvaux explains that Ancient Rome failed to advance technologically as modern Europe did, because Roman elites relied on large numbers of slaves to power the economy, eventually draining Rome financially. He points out that the modern West escaped this fate by first turning to steam engines, that run on coal, and later to oil-powered engines, but doing so only recently, during the past two or three centuries. However, with the rising extraction cost of fossil fuels, we may soon be turning to the Roman solution after all, unless we find new cheap energy sources (e.g. nuclear fission, or fusion).

Meanwhile, the Western off-shoring of economic activities to Asia and India has already exchanged local high-energy factories with apparently cheaper human labor solutions abroad. Companies like Foxconn that produce our beloved iPhones may deliver high-tech technology, but their assembly-line factories are far from innovative. Such companies rely on the supply of the cheap helping hands offered by the crowded Chinese countryside ('crowded' in terms of niche-space, not spatial density).

"Aggressive war is caused by the continued growth of population in a relatively rich society."[6]

The reverse of moving Western industries abroad is, of course, inviting cheap labor to come to live with us. As mentioned earlier, evidence of this process is undeniable as Europe, the United States and even Saudi-Arabia already absorb large masses of mostly cheap labor immigrants to power their industries. While governments seeking to minimize social unrest may want to market these migrations as 'multicultural progress', the true motive for modern mass migration is ecological: the wealthier lifestyles of Western (and other) middle classes have become too expensive to be able to afford large numbers of offspring.

High living cost is what limits the size of new generations of (indigenous) Europeans and Americans. Mass immigration, therefore, is the ecological answer to vacant Western niche-space, by leaving it to peoples with less expensive lifestyles. There is, of course, a potential threat to this development — mutiny. If the immigrant masses successfully cling to their cultural identities, they may someday find themselves in charge of Western industries pursuing their own agendas. While the Mongol hordes of

Genghis Khan had to fight their way into China, the open-border policies of the West may have invited a Trojan Horse after all.

Hyper-Diversity: America's Globalist Class is Leading the Destruction of the West

November 11ᵗʰ, 2016

Until recently, I had never really understood the liberal/progressive narrative demanding the West to become more 'diverse'. But when riots broke out in Los Angeles and New York in protest of Trump's election, the missing insight presented itself. And it's a deeply worrisome one.

Those rioting crowds of anti-Trump protesters namely consist of highly diverse university students. In their classrooms, American whites account for slightly under 25% of the demographic. According to UC Berkely 2015 enrollment statistics, East Asians — e.g. Chinese, Korean, Vietnamese, etc. — together represent over 40% of all students.

But the United States as a whole only has Asian Americans at around 6% of the total population. Why do Asians overrepresent student demographics nearly eightfold at universities such as Berkeley? Conversely, African Americans make up about 14% of the total US population but still don't manage to fill 3% of classrooms at Berkeley — over four times fewer than expected.

Isn't that odd. How come Berkeley, arguably the most diverse university in the world, manages to attract that many East Asians, while apparently still discriminating against blacks? More importantly, despite that American whites populate about 70% of the United States, whites are being underrepresented at Berkeley by a factor of three. Isn't that racism?

One instantly notices that Berkeley's population is a highly artificial one. It is in no way connected to the reality Americans live in. But what the Berkeley population does align with more closely is that of the world as a whole. In other words, Berkeley university has ceased to be American and has become a truly globalist institution.

That also means Berkeley no longer serves the American people. At Berkeley's campuses, young minds are trained to think, act, behave and live in their mock global demographic. Students graduating from such institutions have become globalists by training. As a consequence, America's future governing classes will no longer be able to relate to average Americans.

We should expect that in the near future American industry, politics, media, military, science and other branches of society will be led by a caste of trained globalists, consisting of a non-white majority, dominated and led by East Asians, supplemented with Hispanics/Latinos and others.

American whites will themselves only occupy about a quarter of the nation's top tiers, despite still being a demographic majority. That's why the educated classes who have come to populate the editorial offices of major news organizations could not see Trump coming. They cannot relate to white Christian voters—because they don't know any.

American leadership has actively denounced white Christian America. Instead, it has congratulated itself for being part of a fantasy Ivy League world, drowned in artificial, sophist hyper-diversity. But those who surrender or outsource their own leadership to others who cannot relate to them also surrender their continued existence.

If white Christian Americans want to survive, they will have to get organized. They will have to take back leading positions in the nation their European ancestors built. They will have to take charge of their destiny.

When it comes down to securing a future for Americans of European descent, it's either victory or death. And it has come to that.

Racism Doesn't Exist: Economic Arguments against Immigration

April 19ᵗʰ, 2018

Children of Western parents cannot compete with African wages. Chinese incomes do not suffice to pay off Western mortgages. Even though the newcomers to the West may have different skin tones, white people's economic self-preservation has nothing to do with racism. The inequality is found in the cost, not in the benefits. The arguments against mass immigration to the West are economic.

In tandem with unpredictable winters, Northern landscapes make life more expensive for the people living there. We sometimes say people living in Africa have to survive on a dollar per day but raising children in Europe and American costs well over a *million* dollars. Who is going to pay for that?

If you want to survive and procreate in North America or Europe, you will need a higher income than someone living closer to the equator who can survive off a bowl of rice a day. Therefore, Westerns may not allow themselves to be outcompeted by cheaper types of people. It would bankrupt Western societies. In such an event, even recent refugees who came to live with us will have to flee elsewhere again.

Despite the fact that feudal serfdom was abolished hardly two centuries ago, a progressive mafia maintains that we, whites, have a white privilege. They mean to say we were born racist like an original sin. The accusation comes in hand to disown whites now and later.

Do the motivations to accuse whites of racism perhaps have something to do with racism?

A large part of the conflict between black and white comes down to warped imaging. People living in Africa or Asia who have only heard about the West from commercial advertising, mistakenly believe the West is a Valhalla. But if they'd open their eyes to the reality outside of our gated communities, they would see that life in the West is a struggle.

Migrants don't come to the West to become a poor farmer or a factory worker They dream of becoming successful soccer players, singers, and movie stars. While they dream of a better life, migrants prefer to outsource their new society's daily maintenance to dumb white folks who still believe in taking responsibility for one's actions.

In Christian terms, one might call the mass migration to the West a flood. Of course, half a century of peace and prosperity had to be punished with the arrival of hundreds of millions of migrants. They, too, want to have their fair share of the wealth we generated.

If predictions come true, the tsunami of immigrants will collapse Western economies. The baby boom generation is retiring, will then demand high medical costs, and will ultimately go extinct. The surviving generations will inherit a plundered continent. They will live as minorities among the immigrant tyrant.

Europeans are fifteen times as productive as Chinese people. Americans are twenty times as productive. For this productivity disparity, Westerners ought to receive back a little bit more wealth, but leftist media nonetheless point out how 'unfair' this 'unequal distribution' supposedly is.

Productive whites ought to give away a larger share of their wealth, without compensation, in order to make less productive people wealthier.

Westerners have more because they produce more. By only regarding the benefits, it seems as if Westerners are unfairly advantaged. But if we take the costs into account, too, then the so-called poorer people are actually better off. They don't have to work so hard. They don't have to facilitate a global civilization that feeds the rest of the world.

The anti-racists are the real racists. Behind their mask of hatred, they hide their own incompetence. By wrapping their jealousy in progressive vocabulary, the migrant losers, who, upon their arrival at age twenty-five, still need to learn to read and write, try to hide their inflated ego's.

Most immigrants coming to the West do not contribute anything to our economies and they never will. At home, they have grown used to the eternal easy life. They only came here to reap the benefits of Western labor, like a locust plague pillaging the future of white children.

If Westerners want to defend something of a future for their offspring, they must revolt. When they do, they better follow the principle of *first the traitors, then the enemy.*

Collective Blindness: Are Victims of Racism and Discrimination the Victims of a Universalist Worldview?

April 3rd, 2018

During my many travels, I have found that especially travelers from strongly collectivist backgrounds sometimes fail to adjust to new environments. Whether they are Indians from India or Indians from the United States, whether they are Asians from China or Asians from Britain, the collectivist nature of their mother civilization has still left an indelible impression on their thinking.

This inability to adjust, I believe, rests on the false assumption that one's own life experiences must be universal and that, therefore, the *other* must change *his* ways to be assimilated into *our* collective. If the other refuses to do so, and if he happens to be white, he is being 'racist', i.e. rebellious. Since a collectivist has been conditioned to believe that his own culture is the Right One, he cannot adopt new ways that either differ or even contradict his own.

What migrants to the West experience as 'discrimination' and 'racism' may, therefore, be the consequence of having a false, universal worldview, namely their own. Migrants from collectivist backgrounds—e.g. from Asia, India, the Middle East, Northern Africa and Latin America—fail to compete with Westerners because the former believe opportunity is something to be allocated to them (by some authority), whereas the latter believe opportunity is something to be seized (by oneself).

A historical example of this passive attitude can be found in the book *The Open Veins of Latin America*, a Marxist favorite. Its author, Eduardo Galeano, laments page after page how the European conquerors robbed, sacked, raped, pillaged and enslaved his continent. His analysis is correct. Not a word of his treatise is a deliberate lie. Galeano even admits to the technological flaws of Incan and Mayan civilization, which, for example, had never invented the wheel.

But in his own blindness, the author failed to reveal the reason why Europeans were able to take over so easily: Incan and Mayan societies were themselves strictly authoritarian, centrist, and collectivist, and had been so for thousands of years. They were ruled by families who claimed a divine ancestry, organized like a social pyramid with a pharaoh on top, in this case, Emperor Atahualpa. All that the colonial Europeans had to do was replace the presiding ruling family with either a European administrator or a local vassal. And so, no more than a few thousand Conquistadores subjugated an entire continent.

To the common people of Latin America, though, not much changed. They submitted to European rulers willingly because they had been conditioned into obedience by their own divine masters. Today, such inbred obedience still governs most of the world, including the oldest surviving civilization on Earth, namely China and its satellite states. Reading Confucius's *Analects*, one cannot escape the repetitive calls to obey a higher authority. For at least two thousand years, Chinese people have been coaxed into obedience by its emperors and prime ministers.

People raised in collectivist households also raise their children to be collectivists. The many migrants from collectivist backgrounds who have moved to Europe or to the United States have failed to become free-thinking individuals. Instead, they and their offspring have remained collectivist and centrist, waiting for opportunity to be allocated to them by some socialist authority. A belief in personal competence is wholly absent. In my view, the majority of our human species has long been domesticated by 'divine' ruling families. Their people's slavish condition only became apparent once white colonials took over, such as the British in India.

Collectivist blindness may also explain the socialist worldview, which has sided with the 'oppressed victims' against the 'oppressive West'. Socialists, too, describe the world in terms of authority and power, with the exception that socialist leaders known they want to crown themselves humanity's divine allocators. Left-wing and right-wing politics fight each other for the right to exploit the people. Neither wing gives a damn about you.

Regardless, the colonial success of the Europeans relied on this distinction between individualists and collectivists. While

the more collectivist parts of the world were slaving in purgato-
ry, eternally waiting for opportunity to come to them, the more
individualistic Europeans broke free and seized it.

3

Reviving the West

"Nietzsche predicted that in the 20th-century hundreds of millions of people would die because of the replacement of these underlying dreamlike structures with this rational, but deeply incorrect representation of the world."

—Jordan B. Peterson

Jordan Peterson, Savior of the West? How Canada's Martin Luther Is Preparing Christians for the Battle between Good and Evil

February 14th, 2018
Exactly 500 years after the Great Schism of 1517 that split Western European Christianity into a southern Catholicism and a northern Protestantism, Jordan Peterson published a series of lectures on Christianity on his YouTube channel. The timing is no coincidence. In his lectures, Peterson presents an 'alt-right' revaluation of Biblical scripture, justifying society's need for God, hierarchy, and inequality. Intermittently, he teaches confused post-modern men how to become real men again.

Peterson, a Canadian clinical psychologist in his mid-fifties, believes "we're at the end of post-modern despair", and that it is time for a "discussion of first principles". He preaches to his online followers they must "transcend the catastrophe of being and prevail". Peterson is literally telling Western men — meaning *white* men — to transcend the catastrophe of the 20th century and its world wars and prevail in the 21st.

No, Peterson is certainly no supremacist. But his energetic insights, heavily drawing on the philosophies of Carl Jung, Friedrich Nietzsche, and Martin Heidegger, have an unmistakably Germanic signature. If beliefs evolved to serve their peoples, Peterson's insights may effectively reinvigorate Christianity with pre-Christian values, perhaps even completing the Reformation that Martin Luther (not King) had once begun five centuries ago.

Indeed, we've grown so accustomed to 24/7 news cycles that we've imprisoned our minds in the Now. We've forgotten how grander social movements play out over centuries rather than in Tweets. If Martin Luther once helped Germans break away from Catholicism (literally meaning: universalism), Peterson has laid the foundation for the West's spiritual revival.

In order to fight globalism, cultural relativism and Soros-funded mass migration meant to eradicate European civilization altogether, we were going to need a manlier Christianity. Whether he meant to do so or not, Jordan Peterson has given us precisely that.

Before Christianity, the peoples of Northern Europe who would later colonize North America, Canada, South Africa, Australia and New Zealand had never had their own religion, aside from a loose collection of stories and superstitions involving Thor, Freya, Odin and other deities, especially female ones. But before the Germanic Northerners had a chance to organize themselves, Catholic missionaries got to them first. From the

7th to the 13th century, they converted — and submitted — the North to Roman Catholic rule.

It didn't last very long. Barely two centuries after their conversion to Catholicism, German thinker Martin Luther set off the Protestant Reformation. Catholicism and its more collectivist worldview simply never sat well with people of Northern European descent.

Historical events leave their marks. Ancestors of Southern Europeans were once subjects of the Roman Empire, whereas Northerners resisted their subjugation, halting further Roman expansion northward, first under Arminius of the Cheruscii in 9 AD, and later in 69–70 AD under the joint command of Batavii leader Julius Civilis and the Frisian chieftain Bruno. For nearly 2,000 years, Northern Europeans would continue to fight Roman conceptions of *one-worldism.*

Perhaps ecology provides a better explanation for Northern stubbornness than a room full of sociologists could. Studying the bottlenecks for human life in ancient Europe, access to potable water was what restricted life in the warmer, drier South. The Romans solved their water problems with grand works of aquatic architecture. But aqueducts also diverted already sparse water away from the dry countryside, forcing people to huddle together in cramped urban areas from where water was distributed.

The Roman Empire relied on controlling the life-giving water resource in order to control the population. It went along well with totalitarian conceptions of "One State, One Church, One People". But in the North, the conditions for life were very different. Indeed, the Germanic barbarians couldn't build waterways, but they didn't need to either. Rainy summers and snowy winters provided the Northerners with an abundance of water. Even today, one can easily notice that German agricultural lands look considerably greener and more fertile than France's or Spain's.

Climate matters and forces people to adapt. As a consequence of the climatic differences between North and South, the easier access to water allowed Northern peoples to settle wherever they liked, giving way to a more individualist and dispersed society. Around the time of Christ, the Roman historian Tacitus noted that the Germanic tribes didn't even have any cities. There was simply no need to huddle people together in dense urban areas. Instead, each family could settle on a patch of earth of its own.

What was the ecological bottleneck for life in the North, then? Most certainly it was the availability of *fuel*—in the form of firewood and food—that needed to be stored up before the arrival of long, harsh winters. Temperatures often drop below freezing point for months in a row. The short summers put a lot of pressure on the inhabitants of the North since they had little time to amass what resources they could get their hands on in order to prepare for the coming frost.

In short, even within Europe, individualist Northerners have historically evolved their societies very differently from people living in the South. Different environments produce different peoples with different cultures and different attitudes towards their survival. But there's an even more profound truth: people who adapted to different landscapes and climates *also evolved different collective psyches.*

That means people don't just look different, they think differently too. The Mediterranean and Middle Eastern principles of collectivism, rationalism or universalism may suit them well but may have a detrimental effect on more individualist peoples. No wonder, then, that Martin Luther sought to reform Catholicism, it didn't work for the Germans. Similarly, North American notions of democracy may suit them perfectly, but may not be of any help to the collectivist peoples of East Asia, let alone those of the whole world.

Coincidentally, this insight predicts that if Catholicism couldn't subdue the Northern Europeans, then neither will Islam; even if the process takes several centuries to sort itself out.

Yet, today, precisely the more collectivist Catholic ideologies appear to be governing the United States, and by extension the West, even though most Americans are Protestant. It doesn't surprise me. At around 43 degrees latitude, New York, and Washington lie closer to Madrid and Rome than to Northern European cities. (By comparison, Jordan Peterson grew up in Edmonton, Alberta, which at 53 degrees latitude lies on par with Hamburg and Berlin.)

In addition, mainstream media have shut themselves off from reality by incessantly promoting the principles of equality, one-worldism, the global open society, and scientific rationalism, because these are the principles that govern the inhabitants of cramped urban areas. Since the world's most powerful media companies, as well as their employees, generally live and work in big cities, all they know is to promote their subjective, urban view of the world, ignoring the fact that the world isn't New York City. Ultimately, that may prove to be an unsustainable worldview.

As urban governments in both Western Europe and North America have taken the Christian love of strangers to the point of committing demographic suicide, it turns out that a slave's religion doesn't quite transform men into the wolves they need to be to fight off the barbarians at the gates. That is, until now. Jordan Peterson has de facto established a new Christian religion. More specifically, he has reinvigorated Christianity with manlier, Germanic ideals of individualism, authority, hierarchy, and inequality.

It isn't the first time Northern peoples have tried to 'upgrade' Christianity. As I mentioned, it was Martin Luther who started the Reformation. Later, in those dreaded 1930s, it was ideologue Alfred Rosenberg who called upon the German people to do away with Christianity altogether. He urged them to replace this middle-eastern "superstition" (*Zauberglaube*) with something of their own. Swiss psychoanalyst Carl Jung had noted a similar trend, writing,

"As the Christian view of the world loses its authority, the more menacingly will the 'blond beast' be heard prowling about in its underground prison, ready at any moment to burst out with devastating consequences."

Rosenberg's best-selling book *The Myth of the Twentieth Century*—outselling Hitler's *Mein Kampf*—shocked Catholics so much the Catholic Church added the book to the index of forbidden books. But unlike *Mein Kampf,* Germans actually read *The Myth*. It electrified them. Priests and pastors began openly questioning the truth of Christianity with churchgoers. Many more, though, found Rosenberg's calls way too radical. Moderates suggested an intermediate solution, i.e. a *Deutsches Christentum* or Germany Christianity that would gradually return Protestant Christians to the values of their ancestors over the course of several centuries.

Jewish psychoanalyst Erich Fromm later aptly remarked that Northern Europe's conversion to Christianity had never been completed, to begin with. According to Fromm, European Christianity was really just heathendom with Christian symbols. Perhaps he was right. Catholicism civilized the rational side of Northern Europeans but failed to convince their emotional, barbaric soul. Christianity was always the religion of the Catholic victors who subdued Northern minds. What the

Romans couldn't achieve by the sword, Catholic missionaries achieved with words.

Rosenberg's plans were soon forgotten. Out of fear of international ridicule, Hitler vetoed against a religious revolution. Rosenberg would be hanged at the Nuremberg trials for his antisemitism.

Nevertheless, the fact that Rosenberg's ideas had resonated so strongly with the German people indicated a crisis underneath the surface. Jordan Peterson has rather put the focus on *reinterpretations* and *revaluations* of Biblical scripture. By applying the teachings of Jung, Nietzsche, Heidegger and other Germanic and Nordic thinkers, Peterson offers his YouTube followers a version of Christianity that suits his followers and our time better.

On a recent episode of *Rubin Report*, Peterson discussed some of his ideas with orthodox Jew Ben Shapiro. At some point halfway through, Peterson said of religious experiences that "the downside of transcendence is something that's *not to be trifled with*". Those words rang a bell. Carl Jung, in opposition to Freud's reductionist view of human beings as biological machines, had written them too,

> "I can understand very well that Freud's reduction of everything psychic to primitive sexual wishes and power-drives has something about it that is beneficial and satisfying to the Jew ... [but] these specifically Jewish doctrines are thoroughly unsatisfying to the Germanic mentality; we still have a genuine barbarian in us who is not to be trifled with ..."

According to Peterson, "Jews put a tremendous amount of emphasis on the State as a mechanism for salvation," and that "the [Protestant] Christians come down more strongly on the side of the individual, and the Jews come down more strongly on the side of the [collective] State." Although Jews are certainly not sending missionaries around the world to convert everyone to Judaism, the ideal of an overarching, abstract State certainly affects the non-believers.

In recent years, Europeans' greatest fear has been that the European Union would turn out to be a transnational superstate, and indeed it has. Such abstract organizations, copied after the United Nations and the Federal U.S. Government — themselves undoubtedly inspired by ancient Rome and the Roman Catholic Church — as well as their invented anthems, flags and postmodern moralities merely serve to submit European peoples to even more convoluted systems oppression they cannot oppose.

Soon, we may expect the United States and the European Union to be absorbed by an even more abstract entity — the World State and the Global Open Society. It's just that the global open society that includes everyone is also a prison no one can escape from.

That is where we are today. There is a war going on. But it is not a war between Jews and Germans, not one between Christians and Muslims, not between natives and immigrants, nor between men and women, *but between free individuals and the collectives that aim to assimilate them.* If the rulers of U.S. Empire, their EU vassals and their propaganda arms at the United Nations thought they could stay the radar forever by hiding themselves behind puppet elections, they are wrong. The world has long taken notice.

If anyone is going to halt the advance of yet another attempt at Global Empire and save humanity from collective slavery, I predict it will be the Western peoples of Northern European, Germanic descent. If Protestant Christians accept Peterson's reinvigorated religion, they might pull it off. They are the descendants of the men and women who resisted globalism for nearly 2,000 years. There's no reason to surrender now.

Storm and Frenzy:
A Call for European Unity in Defense of Our Continent

October 8th, 2016

After a council with his bishops, on November 27th, 1095, Pope Urban II held a speech on a field near the French town of Clermont. He called on all Europeans to stop fighting their brother wars and ushered them to take up arms against the Eastern heathens—the threatful Turks and Saracens that had invaded Europe. According to the Pope, the crimes these barbarians committed against the Eastern European population justified a new kind of war. He called it an armed pilgrimage, a Crusade. Led by Godfrey of Bouillon, a man in his early forties from present-day Northern France or Belgium, the first crusaders would defeat everything in their path and liberate Jerusalem from Islamic occupation.

Today, all major Western European cities are Jerusalem. Our cities are being occupied by the migrant foot soldiers that appeared from the Trojan Horse's pregnant belly, the Meccan Camel of uncontrolled mass migration. The war in Syria became an excuse to flood Europe with millions if not hundreds of millions of Arab and African migrants. Allegations of gas attacks by the Assad regime have altered European public opinion to welcome the 'refugees'—along with the extinction of their own civilization.

If we still want to defend a European Europe, we, too, will have to call upon our European brothers to stop their brother wars and unite in defense of our continent. As opposed to U.S. citizens, Europeans with their many languages are like the family that never speaks to each other, until the time is come to divide our shared inheritance. That inheritance of Germanic-Celtic culture mixed with modern Christian civilization is at stake. The legacy that our forefathers spent the last 2,500 years fighting, for now, threatens to fall into the hands of a barbarian occupier that seeks to erase our speech, our lifestyles, our future, and even our past.

Like the Latin American continent under Spanish rule, Europe is to be subjugated to Islam, its people to be effaced and usurped. Above all, Europeans must accept their forced miscegenation—the rape of Europa.

The Crusaders once fought in the name of Christ and for the freedom of all European peoples. They served God's battalions out of piety. Isn't it time for us, European brothers, to gather as one behind such a higher ideal? If we want to defend the cultural diversity that our continent boasts against migrant homogenization, then we, too, must be prepared to fight a new kind of war, a spiritual Crusade, a prolonged guerrilla war whose decisive battles are going to be waged on the streets of Paris, Amsterdam, Vienna, London, and Berlin.

Our cities have fallen to migrant populations who deem their cultures superior to ours. The mass immigration that was set in motion far outside of the European has, in some places, already replaced over 30% to 50% of the native city population. It is not uncommon for a city in Western Europe to boast a 75% non-indigenous kindergarten population; replacement immigration is real. That means, in only twenty years' time Western Europeans will have become the absolute minority in their own countries. Are we going to let it happen?

Make no mistake. Europe's open borders were a crime planned by our own governing elites. After the guest worker migrations of the sixties and seventies, and after half a century of family reunification, and explosive minority population growth, in 2008, the European Commission decided that Europe must further import over 60 million more "guest workers" (whether as migrants or as 'refugees') between now and the year 2050,

"[The European Parliament] recalls that projections present-ed by the Commission estimate the need for 60 million mi-grant workers by 2050 and this requires the opening-up of channels for legal migration."[1]

By that time, native Germans, Swedes, Dutchmen, Belgians, French and British will be a minority in their own countries. Western Europeans may face the risk of genocide at the hands of an aggressive invader. If Europe supposedly needs so many guest workers to solve the problem of aging demographics, then why don't European governments fund indigenous women to bring more children into this world? Instead, Western Europe-an governing officials have chosen to pursue the politics of our replacement.

If we do not revolt against our planned genocide now, our civilization will make way for the poison that is digesting our cultural inheritance. The mass migration that ought to have brought us economic prosperity instead brought us welfare-de-pendent illiterates. But the fact that Europe's Islamization poses a threat was clearly understood by a twenty-five-year-old Win-ston Churchill, in 1899, when he expressed harsh criticism of Islam in his book *The River War*,

"How dreadful are the curses which [Islam] lays on its vota-ries! Besides the fanatical frenzy, which is as dangerous in a man as hydrophobia in a dog, there is this fearful fatalistic apathy. The effects are apparent in many countries. Improv-ident habits, slovenly systems of agriculture, sluggish meth-ods of commerce, and insecurity of property exist wherever the followers of the Prophet rule or live."

Churchill warned that when Europeans would welcome Is-lam, "the most retrograde force in the world", and allow the ideology to take root in Europe, "the civilization of modern Europe might fall, as fell the civilization of ancient Rome." Hungarian writer Imre Kertész, a Nobel prize winner, also understood the pending catastrophe,

> "I should recall how the Muslims are flooding Europe to later conquer, or, in other terms, destroy it; … on suicidal liberalism and brainless democracy; democracy and suffrage for chimpanzees. This is always what it concludes to: the civilization arrives at an overbred condition in which it is not only unable but also unwilling to protect itself; when, seemingly mindlessly, it worships its own enemies."

We must cease to worship our enemies. A storm is coming in Europe, the sleeping giants are awakening. It is time for a new kind of war, a war for survival, pilgrimage past every major city in Western Europe, a war we must fight to secure a future for our children.

After the Fall, a European Empire? Recap of the Book 'The Decline' by Professor David Engels

February 7ᵗʰ, 2017

Within twenty to thirty years, civil wars are going to break out throughout Europe, comparable to the wars Spartacus waged against Rome before the collapse of its republic. That's what professor David Engels of Brussels's Free University predicts in an (as usual) underexposed book *Le Déclin* (*The Decline*) that was also translated into German as *Auf dem Weg ins Imperium* (*On the Road to Empire*) in 2014.

According to this Belgian historian, the similarities between the decline of the present-day European Union and the fall of the Roman republic are so big that civil war in Europe has become inevitable. Countries such as Germany and France will then cease to exist. In their places, armed paramilitary groups will found their own states.

Professor Engels expects that this period of civil wars won't end until an emperor stands up who will once again promise the European peoples social security, just as the first Roman emperor Augustus did. (But by that time, twenty- and thirty-somethings saving for a pension today will probably be left standing empty-handed.)

The professor draws his conclusion from detailed, fact-based comparisons between Rome and the present-day European Union. In his book, he analyzes several 'politically incorrect' topics such as the multicultural society, mass migration, aging demographics and replacement immigration, but also the decay of the family as the cornerstone of society, as well as the overall shift from traditional values towards abstract ideas such as equality, tolerance and personal development.

In the following paragraphs, I summarize the first three of the professor's twelve main arguments.

Tolerance on Steroids (§2.1) Despite the fact that white skin color has determined European identity for a long time, inhabitants of the European Union now regard tolerance of the 'other' a sign of civilization. The racism of the twentieth century has traumatized them. Exclusion, they believe, only leads to hostility. But they have idealized their tolerance to such an extent that they have effaced their own ethnic identity.

Europeans now believe in universal values and welcome anyone from any place on Earth. But rather than selecting quality, they've opened their borders to everyone on mere humanitarian grounds. Nearly 20% of the German population now consists of people (and their progeny) who immigrated there since 1950. Almost 25% of French people have a migrant parent or grand-parent. This has had consequences: in 2006, 9% of the German population was found to have committed nearly a quarter of all crime—criminal immigrants.

Similar developments had taken place in old Rome. Professor Engels writes that, because of this, native inhabitants had begun to feel disenfranchised from the societies their forefathers had built. Because of replacement immigration, the original population slowly began to lose its loyalty to a country increasingly less their own.

New Births and Aging Demographics (§2.2) "With the massive integration of women into the workforce, Europeans have little time to spend on their families," writes professor Engels. As a consequence, the native population has begun to age in a catastrophic way: European families hardly produce any children anymore.

By contrast, people of African or Arab descent do keep their families large. In Switzerland, native women give birth to 1.7 children on average, but migrants give birth to 2,8; Turkish and Moroccan migrants even to 3.4. By the time the native *baby-boom* generation has gone extinct, one in three Germans will be a migrant, predominantly Muslim. The fear of *Eurabia*, a Europe populated by Arabs, will then have become reality.

A comparable demographic catastrophe had taken place in Rome. Over time, Roman slaves had become the majority and 'free' citizens a minority. On top of that, the critical difference between a larger generation of older citizens versus a smaller, younger generation led to mutual distrust between them. In any case, Roman elites were more interested in satisfying their hedonistic needs than in the continued existence of Rome's free *populus*.

Family and Individualism (§2.3) As a result of low births, Europeans have begun to rearrange their families. For example, nearly a quarter of French children no longer grow up with both biological parents. On top of that, Europeans have collectively begun to normalize gay marriage and adoption from abroad, even by gay couples. The rights of children are no longer put front and center in European societies, but rather second to their parents' personal needs.

Professor Engels calls it worrisome that the family as a cornerstone of society is disintegrating, among others because of the growing number of divorces. How can a human being stay loyal to his society when the stability and the security of his own family are continuously being undermined by 'progressive' changes?

Strikingly: even in the final days of the Roman republic, women had begun to become financially independent. Not their own husband, but State and employer from then on maintained a woman's life. A Roman author complained that the city only kept slaves in order to artificially boost its numbers, whereas the original Romans preferred to see "their race and their name" perish.

According to professor Engels, Europe's decline is part of a global phenomenon also visible in its former colonies of North America, South America, Australia and South Africa. They, too, struggle with aging demographics. The signs are identical everywhere, namely that the collapse comes from within:

> "In fact, cosmopolitanism and the decay of family and marriage complicate and hinder cultural identification. Because the urban insulation and the unbridled materialism it creates, apparently justified by the right to personal development, careerism dismantles the social cohesion between citizens, the most important element of identity."

In short, we keep working more for more money, but keep receiving less life and fewer children for it in return. That breeds feelings of jealousy, distrust, and anger towards others. As a consequence, citizens eventually stop trusting the judicial system, whose universalist attitudes render it both incapable and unwilling to protect its own citizens.

With that, Engels concludes his book, at least in his role as a historian. In an epilogue, however, he goes one step further: can we draw any lessons from the comparisons between Rome and the European Union, and if so, what do those lessons tell us? First and foremost, Engels emphasizes that the Roman Empire superseded a decaying democratic republic. In Rome, it was Emperor Augustus who then rose to power and who would rule from 27 BC to 14 AD.

The people supported Augustus because he promised them a quick restoration of societal order, as well as an efficient social security system. In case Europe disintegrates indeed, it is likely that modern Europeans will also support a strong leader, just as they had once chosen a Napoleon or a Hitler. In order to survive, Europeans will grow willing to accept the risk of voting for a radical party that centralizes power.

Professor Engels expects that the Europe of the future will no longer be progressive and cosmopolitan. A future European emperor or president will, once again, embrace family values and tradition in order to revive its native population: a Europe of *law and order*.

Erasmus's War against the Turks: A Warning from the Past

August 7ʰ, 2016

To enslave a people, one must first erase the memory it has of its own history. That's how European colonials had succeeded in converting entire African peoples to Christianity. In doing so, the subjugated had not only lost their older pagan faith but had in many cases even forgotten their mother tongue. Even now, for example, hundreds of millions of Africans speak French, English, Dutch, a blend or a derivative of a European language. As a result, many have lost their oral traditions as well as the memory of their collective pre-colonial identity.

From this practice of identity-laundering perhaps flows the progressive belief in socially engineered man: the person programmed by his conquerors with new language and culture in order to be someone who he really is not. With one difference: today's social activists are applying these tactics on their own people. Europe and the United States are to be 'multicultural'— in order to make room for tens of millions of non-Western foreigners that reject our way of life. Westerners must learn to be more 'tolerant'—in order to submit to the intolerant ideologies that will forever change who we are, but without our consent.

For that matter, the Islamization of the West did not start with the erection of mosques, nor with public acceptance of veiled women in the streets. The Islamization that intends to erase the memory of our identity already began in the late sixties, early seventies of the last century. It began with historical revisionism, with reinterpretations of our greatest writers and thinkers. For example, new readings of the works of famed Dutch philosophers Desiderius Erasmus, Baruch Spinoza and poet laureate Joost van den Vondel have changed them into so-called early supporters of multiculturalism, into global citizens that naturally rejected nationalism even before it becomes popular.

Today, many high schools in the Netherlands willingly teach students the aforementioned in their multiculturalist propaganda. The originally Flemish-Belgian Van den Vondel had fled to the Republic of the Netherlands to find "a better life", as it is called. In the Amsterdam Vondelpark named after him, occasionally groups of asylum seekers, mostly from majority

Moslem nations, leave behind flowers or wreaths at the base of his statue, as if it were a homage to a man who surely would have personally welcomed millions of Moslem immigrants.

Children gobble it up, but who will dare tell these Moslems that the very same Van den Vondel had had in mind a strong, masculine Christendom to violently defend Europe against Islam? Even our Spinoza was never tolerant at all. He called Islam the most deceitful religion on Earth. In turn, Erasmus outright supported new crusades against the Turks, who in his time were knocking on Vienna's gates. He edited his long letter to Johann Rinck on this subject into a whole book, De Belli Turcico, or On the War against the Turks (1530).

"The world is your fatherland," it is written, dedicated to Erasmus, in neon letters on the side of the Central Library of Rotterdam, his birthplace. Desiderius Erasmus, writer, philosopher, humanist and above all, Christian, had himself written 'my fatherland', but the man of a thousand letters had borrowed the phrase in his turn from a Greek saying, "The whole earth is the fatherland."[2] When offered to become a citizen of Zurich, Switzerland, he did write in an irritated manner, "I want to be a citizen of the world, not of one city."[3]

The city of Rotterdam, just as the left-leaning Dutch intellectual circuit, enjoys flaunting Erasmus as a sort of early anti-nationalist idol, a multicultural global citizen who supposedly had advocated open borders, e.g. a pacifist who had opposed war, and a tolerant human being who would have warmly welcome visitors from afar and all their many cultures and beliefs. He had to have been someone who, if we suppose he was a US citizen today, would have voted for the Democratic Party, or even the Green Party. Oh, that cheeky little Erasmus! What a decent man he was.

That image of him is, put straightforwardly, a load of bullshit. According to Jan Papy, a researcher who has actually read

Erasmus's works, "[his] worldview never reaches beyond that of Christendom; an interest in or appreciation for foreign cultures and religions is alien to him." At all times, Erasmus had been a part of the Christian world of medieval Western Europe. If he had ever called himself a global citizen, a cosmopolitan, it would only have served to emphasize his intellectual independence.[4]

But nowhere in his writings has Erasmus argued that Europe ought to open wide its borders in order to let in masses of foreign immigrants. While Erasmus supported the free movement of studied individuals, he definitely did not support endless migration of entire peoples. Nowhere in his writings does Erasmus set forth his views on nationalism or world citizenship. The subject didn't occur to him.[5] And as a pacifist, it is true that he vigorously argued for Christian Europeans to cease waging wars among themselves, but he was "no naive advocate of surrendering Europe to the Turks."[6]

In a time when Europeans understood the word 'Turks' to mean all Moslems, Erasmus had been worried about the danger they posed. In the letter to Johann Rinck dated May 30, 1530, i.e. written in the year after the Siege of Vienna, he first elaborated on the objections to wage war, but then continued:

"Someone will perhaps deduce from all this that I have undertaken the task of arguing against a Turkish war. Not at all; on the contrary, my purpose is to ensure that we make war against them successfully and win truly splendid victories for Christ. ... I have more than once been astonished by the nonchalance of other Christian lands, and especially of Germany herself as if these things in no way affected the rest of us. We become tight-fisted, and spend on pleasures and trivialities what we do not wish to spend on rescuing Christians."[7]

According to Erasmus, Europeans first had to become better Christians before they could defeat the Turks, "a race softened by debauchery".[8] Holding a low opinion of the opponent, he resorts to hate speech:

"It is easy to see how profitable their false religion has been to [Moslems], as long as we have neglected the duties of true piety. While we have been endlessly fighting among ourselves over some useless plot of ground in what is worse than civil wars, the Turks have vastly extended their empire or, rather, their reign of terror."[9]

Erasmus goes one step further and compares the Turks to the ten plagues God had sent the Egyptians:

"How many defeats have the Christian peoples suffered at the hands of this race of barbarians, whose very origin is obscure? What atrocities have they not committed against us? ... [There] can be no doubt that the Turks have won an immense empire less by their own merits than because of our sins ... We have frequently taken the field against the Turks, but so far with little success; either because we have still clung to all the things which have angered God and caused him to send the Turks against us, just as he sent frogs, lice, and locusts upon the Egyptians long ago ... [We] conducted ourselves like Turks against the Turks."[10]

Admittedly, Erasmus wanted nothing to do with violence-loving warmongers. He would remind his addressees of their duty to commit themselves to introspection. But despite the acts of horror that Christians had done onto other Christians, this had not given him reason to support dogmatic pacifism, "for there are those who claim that the right to make war is totally denied Christians. I find this idea too absurd to need refutation, ... My message is that war must never be undertaken unless, as a last resort, it cannot be avoided..."[11]

Regarding the Turks, Erasmus had been more worried about the corruption that drove destitute Christian soldiers to loot than about Moslems' feelings, "What is there to say about people who prefer the damnable and criminal man Mohammad before Christ?"

Thus. we have to establish as fact that Erasmus had neither been a multiculturalist nor tolerant of foreign faiths. Those are the pleasant labels social justice warriors have given him only since the late 20th century. In reality, Erasmus had limited his tolerance to differences between European peoples. He had wished for peace for all Christians in Europe but had seen no problem with warring against the Turks. He had been a global citizen of the Christian world, not of the world beyond it.

At the start of our present century, we may have arrived at the point that we, as a last resort to save the free West, will have to engage in war. Erasmus would not have disapproved of a war against the Islamic occupier of his lands. In fact, in his book on marriage he advised what to do against the Turks:

"The same individuals who are so pleased with virginity are not displeased with warring against the Turks, who outnumber us by so many; if their judgment is correct, it will follow that it should be considered especially right and honorable to strive with all one's might to produce children, and thus provide enough young men to serve in war. Unless perhaps they think artillery, missiles, and ships should be provided for this war, but that men are not needed."[12]

For such hate speech against the Turks and Moslems, today we would be convicted of racism and Islamophobia. Luckily, Erasmus had lived in freer times when European economies operated independently from Arab oil. Despite his nuance and self-critique, Erasmus had warned his audience about the threat of an enemy occupation. It is time to once again hear his unfiltered warnings.

Why We Fight for the West

November 10th, 2015

"A people that yield to tyranny will lose more than life and property, then darkness falls." (H.M. van Randwijk)

After the 9/11 attacks, President Bush assured the world that America was not at war with Islam. But terrorist attacks throughout Europe showed that Islamists are war with the West. Rooted in traditionalism, Islam despises freedom, stifles progress, and buries critical thought. Islamic doctrine rejects everything that Europe and the West have built up over the past three thousand years. Islam is not a religion, but an oppressive ideology posing as one. We owe it to history to defend the future of the West.

Islamic terrorism is but another wave of the collectivist threat that European peoples so bravely fought throughout history. Leonidas and the Spartans stalled the Persian hordes at the Battle of the Hot Gates in 480 BCE. The ensuing events gave birth to Greek democracy and its recognition of the individual. In 9 CE, Arminius united the Germanic tribes that slew the Roman dragon in the Black Forest, thwarting further Roman conquest. Alaric and the Visigoths first sacked Rome in 410.

In the eleventh century, European knights waged the Crusades against Islam in their attempt to restore the holy lands. In the thirteenth century, we held our ground against the Mongol invaders led by Genghis Khan and his successors. Vastly outnumbered, fearless European soldiers decimated the Islamic Ottoman armies at the Siege of Vienna in 1529, and again at the 1683 Battle of Vienna. We emerged from the Dark Ages to conquer the world, promote modern medicine, introduce the rule of law and spread education everywhere we established a civilization. Facing the worst in ourselves, we defeated twentieth-century fascism and communism.

Who are we to forsake freedom now? While attacking foreign nations may not be in our best interest, we have no excuse but to defend civilization at home. In the name of liberty, our forefathers demand that we fight tyranny wherever it shows its face.

Islam's terrorists don't hate the West for its perceived wrongdoings, but because the West's technological advancement and economic success make Islamic civilization look bad. According to the World Values Survey, Islamic nations value traditionalism over rational thought, and survivalist attitudes over self-expression. Thus Islam diagonally opposes everything that Europe and the West stand for. While many Westerners mistakenly believe that "the desire for free choice and autonomy is a universal human aspiration", the collectivist peoples of Islam, in fact, reject freedom. Muslims renounce their own equality for they consider equality to non-Muslims an insult to their prophet, the perfect Muslim whose life they wish to imitate.

Unsurprisingly, all of over fifty nations that suffer a majority Islamic population have failed to produce a single democracy. Turkey, at one time being the only exception under the secular rule of Atatürk, has fallen victim to Islamists who swiftly reversed progress. Traditionalist Islam effectively hates modernity. For example, the name of the Nigerian terrorist group Boko Haram literally means 'to forbid Western education'. But then how do Islamists, who reject Western knowledge, acquire Western levels of wealth? Conquest.

Who are we to submit our lives to barbarism? We have no alternative but to defend a culture of rational thought and self-expression. In the name of life, we must fight traditionalism wherever it robs children of their future.

In the past half-century, Europe in particular absorbed mass immigration of mostly poorly educated people from the Islamic world. Contrary to a persistent belief held by the progressive left, immigrants do not assimilate their social, cultural and religious values. The values of any given civilization are neither superior nor universal, but they are Spenglerian, i.e. specific to a people. While many immigrants integrate well in terms of jobs and paying taxes, most retreat into ethnic enclaves that remain visible for centuries. Mass immigration's Trojan horse not only brought cheap labor and educable talent, but also hostile attitudes towards recipient populations.

When we extend the idea of equality not just to people, but also to their beliefs, then the naive welfare states of the West end up serving as Lebensraum, or birth ground, for anti-Western ideologies to take root. Ideologies that hate individual freedom. Ideologies that hate you. The solution is to recalibrate and solidify our values. Firstly, freedom is not what you hold hostage for yourself, but what you grant others. Secondly, tolerance and equal treatment are two-way streets. Thirdly, those who seek the democratic vote in order to undermine democracy disqualify themselves from the electorate.

Who are we not to defend our values? We must offer future generations the foundations that they need in order to thrive and succeed. In the name of love for our culture, we must defend Western values wherever uncontrolled immigration threatens to eat away at them.

For the first time in history, the common enemy that is Islamic terrorism unites the peoples of the world. Together we can make a stand for the progress of all mankind. We fight Islam because we prefer light to darkness. We fight because we must.

Progressive Dehumanization: The Belief in Political Progress Substitutes for Genuine Religious Belonging

February 20th, 2017

Reminding people of death strengthens their belief in social and moral progress, especially when those people are not very religious.[13] Hence, in our deconfessionalized time, a growing number of people has substituted genuine religion for a belief in progressive politics.

But history warns us. Decades after Karl Marx called religion "the opiate of the people",[14] Soviet Premier Vladimir Lenin declared war. Although the majority of 20th-century Russians were believers, Lenin and his successor Stalin waged two decades of anti-religious campaigns against their own people.

According to historians, anti-religious regimes such as communist Russia "turned mass crime into a full-blown system of government",[15] leading to the death of over 94 million people worldwide.[16] But neither Stalin, Lenin nor Marx had invented this political disdain for religion. Anti-religious sentiment had been aroused by profound social changes during the Industrial Revolution.

The industrialization of the world uprooted millions of people from their traditional country lifestyles and brought them into dense cities to work in factories. Industrialists enslaved them with the false promise of a "better life"—the same lie we tell immigrants coming to the West today. But life never got better. Except for the bourgeoisie, mass poverty made life a lot worse.

The industrial age reduced human beings to mechanical gears fueling a giant soulless machine. By replacing a rural faith in God with an urban belief in the State, state bureaucrats now crowned themselves the high priests of progress. Herein lay the birth of communism, the anti-human ideology that would quickly spread its disgusting tentacles all over the world.

Today, communist indoctrination has been so successful that after graduating from high school most young people now say they would rather be "gears in a big machine" than free individuals. Such convictions are taught. Technology has disconnected people from what it once meant to be a human being, namely *to be in charge of one's reality by thinking for oneself.*

German philosopher Martin Heidegger recognized this danger, warning of its consequences in a speech given in 1955. Heidegger foresaw the power of nuclear technology, even warned of Third World War. But man, he believed, would overcome war. The real danger lay not in a potential nuclear holocaust, but in what would come after:

> "Modern man's down-to-*earthiness* is deeply threatened. ... This is because a change of all leading ideas has been taking place for several centuries. ... Nature will become a single gigantic gas station, an energy source for modern technology and industry. ... And then what? Then, mankind would have denied and discarded his own self, namely that he is a thinking being."[17]

Modern technology, Heidegger believed, is in the process of transforming human beings into calculators who spend little thought on meaningful activity. Radio, television, and the internet have since standardized the human experience. We all watch the same shows, see the same movies, listen to the same commercialized music and share the same news.

This standardization has made it a lot easier for globalists to shepherd mankind. By effacing religious, ethnic, national and racial differences, progressive politics has molded people into a dull gray mass primed for consumption. When Facebook's Zuckerberg promotes a future where people upload themselves to the internet after their bodies die, we know that our progressive dehumanization is nearing completion.

Globalists believe all nation-states should one day be replaced by a single global open society. But how can a global society be 'open' if all people are born into it and no one can ever escape from it? What about the freedom to be different? The open society is a totalitarian state no different from the Soviet Union, the Islamic Ummah, or Star Trek's *The Borg*.

That's not progress. That's collective slavery. If we want to break free, we will have to fight the machine and hold its engineers accountable.

In Praise of Patriarchy: Patriarchy as a Response to Natural Disaster and Sudden Population Decline

February 14th, 2017

In 1900, about 1.6 billion human beings lived on Earth. One hundred years later, the human species nearly quadrupled to 6.1 billion.[18] Before the end of 2020, we may pass 8 billion, adding in a single generation's time what had once taken us thousands of years to achieve. But human populations aren't evenly distributed across the globe. Different geographies, climates, and cultures have allowed for different growth rates and different population densities.

For millennia, Asia has been humanity's center of gravity, currently housing nearly 60% of the world's population, despite China's one-child policy. At the peak of its industrial age, Europeans had once fathered a quarter of all living people, while many more had spilled over to its colonies. But today, aging European and Northern American demographics have long begun their decline, despite immigration.

Europe and Northern America combined now make up no more than 12% of the world's population, whereas African, Arab and Asian numbers continue to rise explosively. This brings me to several questions. What is causing Western nations to throttle back despite their wealth? What is enabling Third World populations to continue to grow despite a lack of wealth? And what had set off the human population bomb in the first place?

I'd like to try and answer that last question first. One might think advances in technology are what has been driving human population growth, perhaps through increased agricultural productivity and greater economic efficiency. I agree, except for the fact that the earliest and most effective growth technology was not scientific, but Biblical. Two works of early human literature shed some light on this matter: the story of Enkidu from the *Epic of Gilgamesh* and the Biblical story of *Adam and Eve*.

The Gilgamesh epic is a Sumerian tale preserved from oral tradition, written down on cuneiform clay tablets about 3800 years ago. The epic tells of a wild man named Enkidu who is brought to the city of Uruk (a city whose archaeological remnants were heavily damaged during the Gulf Wars in the 1990s)[19]. A promiscuous woman introduces Enkidu to urban civilization, which involved "the wearing of clothes and the eating of food that is cultivated (bread and wine)".[20]

In Enkidu's time, women were still considered equal to men.[21] Patriarchy had not been invented yet. Thus, in contrast to the Biblical Eve, "woman is viewed as the medium of raising man to a higher level".[22]

The story of Enkidu, a tale popular among citizens of ancient Mesopotamia and Babylonia, must have influenced the Biblical story of Adam and Eve, but with a moral twist. Two historians explain, "The [newer] Biblical point of view is that he who drinks wine becomes drunk; the [older] Babylonian says, if you drink wine you become happy."[23] Unsurprisingly, in the story of Adam and Eve, woman is no longer an educator, but "the tempter who brings misfortune to man".[24]

By rewriting women's role from educator to tempter—a crime punishable with children—the Biblical Genesis contains the greatest social innovation in human history: patriarchy. Moses (or the author, or authors, known as Moses) subordinated woman's child-giving ability to man's sexual desires, setting in motion a chain of events that have led to today's overpopulated world. This instruction from Genesis to "be fruitful, and multiply"[25] could not have been any clearer.

In a sense, Christianity has become Judaism's more potent younger brother, namely a social and cultural technology that would secure its followers' global presence, at least in the West. In return, though, the invention of patriarchy condemned men to carry the burdens of labor and war in order to feed their offspring.

But where did Moses, and others like him, get the idea for patriarchy? From handling livestock. Since the lives of early nomadic tribes depended on maintaining a healthy animal stock, people were naturally educated in dealing with animal disease, famine, natural disaster, or the occasional rain season that flushed away their herds.

There is plenty of first-hand evidence proving that primitive people understood how to multiply animal herds. Inanna, the world's earliest known female author, wrote almost 5,500 years ago, "As the farmer, let him make the fields fertile, As the shepherd, let him make the sheepfolds multiply".[26] The Egyptian *Tale of Two Brothers* mentions, "And the cattle which were before him became exceedingly excellent, and they multiplied greatly."[27]

Such literary evidence points out that whoever wrote Genesis knew exactly what he was doing: the author was applying lessons learned from animal husbandry to 'herds' of humans. Why would he do this? Because, on occasion, natural disasters also hit human populations. It was in the interest of mankind's survival to convince tribes of people to be "fruitful", especially after a catastrophe (see the story of Noah's Ark). Biblical propaganda did the job.

Hence, the invention of patriarchy must be understood in terms of a people's evolutionary struggle. We may not dismiss patriarchy as merely a way of discriminating against women for the fun of it, but rather as an important *social technology* that helped prevent human extinction.

By submitting female sexuality to male sex drive, patriarchal societies gained an evolutionary advantage helping them to survive natural catastrophe. Moreover, as a result of at least 5,000 years of cultural selection, we should expect most of today's societies to be patriarchal. In fact, most are.

Now I can answer the two remaining questions. Why do poor Third World populations continue to multiply despite a lack of wealth? Because they have patriarchal societies that seize every opportunity to reproduce, like Adam and Eve. And why do rich Western nations fail to do the same? Because they have ceased to be patriarchal. Like Enkidu and the whore, Westerners rather spend their money on luxury goods they don't really need.

If the West chooses not to reverse its course, future historians will say that primitive Islamic, African and Asian societies defeated a technologically superior West by simply populating Europe and Northern America with their own children. In other words, *by promoting feminism, liberal leaders have brought Western civilization to the verge of suicide.*

A Comment on the Invention of Christianity: Caesar's Messiah

May 21ˢᵗ, 2018
Joe Atwill's 2006 book *Caesar's Messiah* makes the case that Christianity's New Testament was written by a scholar named Flavius Josephus and/or a group of people surrounding him. Josephus was an adoptive son of the ruling Flavian dynasty, which provided three Roman Caesars: Vespasian, Titus, and Domitian. It turns out that the New Testament contains clever references to Josephus's book *The War of the Jews*, in which prophecies made by Jesus Christ later seem to be confirmed as historical events. Atwill argues that the author of *The War of the Jews* must have invented the Christ from the New Testament.

There is, of course, circumstantial evidence that corroborates such a hypothesis. The many authors who wrote during the time Jesus Christ was supposed to have lived never mention him. The Christ we know from the New Testament appears to be a character only ever mentioned in literature, decades after his supposed life and death. For example, Philo Judaeus, a contemporary scholar living in Alexandria, does not mention the existence of Christ nor does he mention his miracles. If his Jewish Messiah had indeed appeared, one might have expected him and other Jewish authors to have mentioned Christ as a historical figure. Yet, none did. Jesus Christ was a literary invention.

However, Joe Atwill then suggests that the Flavian dynasty invented the New Testament in order to trick the Jews of Judea, a colony once at war with Rome, to worship Titus Caesar as their Messiah. Passages from the NT refer to historic events from Titus Caesar's life, mapping things Titus said or did onto things Christ supposedly said or did. Still, this idea seems far-fetched and simply wrong, since the suggested author of the NT, Flavius Josephus, was born as Yosef ben Matityahu, a Jew. Why would a Jew trick his own people into submission to Rome?

It is much more likely that Josephus invented Christianity in order to sell Rome a progressive, open border, and multiculturalist doctrine. How did he do it? He played rich people's egos. By tricking the Roman emperors, especially Titus, into believing the NT had the Jews worshiping them as gods, the Caesars would be willing to adopt and spread Christian religion across the Roman Empire—unaware of the literary Trojan Horse they would welcome into Europe. This hypothesis seems more plausible. Converting kings and emperors first is exactly how Catholics would later spread Christianity northwards. For example, in 995 AD, Norway's King Olaf Trygvasson had himself baptized. Only thereafter did the conversions of his people begin.

Everywhere in Europe, the Christianization follows the pattern that presumably began with the conversion of the Flavian Caesars: first, you convert the power elites and then the people will follow. Power elites can be swayed to adopt any belief system they think will help increase their wealth and their power over people. Perhaps Christianity offered Europe's rulers an ideology to make their subjects more docile and easier to tax. A conversion to Christianity also invited ruling elites into a Roman collective of Christian allies to fight non-Christian enemies. In other words, Christianity benefited the power play of the upper classes at the expense of the common folk, who were now submitted to a slave's religion.

Notably, the New Testament altered the nature of God. The God of the Old Testament was a Patriarch, whereas the God of the New Testament begot a Mother, the Virgin Mary, placing the Matriarch before God in the logical hierarchy. Does one have to wonder what the purpose of this gender transformation was? Judaism and Islam, by contrast, both retained their patriarchal God. Islam does not recognize Christ as the son of God and Judaism does not recognize Christ as the true Messiah. Jewish scholar Maimonides would later declare that Christ wasn't the real Messiah since he died prematurely and did not complete his task.

In conclusion, I must reject Atwill's thesis that Roman Caesars invented Christianity. I support the opposite thesis that Flavius Josephus tricked the Flavian dynasty into adopting Christianity by making Titus Caesar believe the Jews, and others would come to worship him as their Messiah, thereby spreading a multiculturalist, pro-immigrant, progressive open border ideology across the Roman Empire.

Revolt of the Oppressed:
Patriots Will Defeat Progressive Appeasement Politics

February 17th, 2016

"Faith in a holy cause is to a considerable extent a substitute for the lost faith in ourselves," wrote American longshoreman Eric Hoffer.[28] Still today, people spoiled by wealth prefer to escape reality, rather than having to admit migrants threaten their civilization. The faith in progressive appeasement politics has become a substitute for the lost faith in ourselves.

Hoffer, a simple and poor worker, gained fame with his insights among intellectual circles. President Dwight Eisenhower quoted him during a televised speech.

In the nineteen sixties, a black man confronted Hoffer. The man was full of rage over the unequal America that had supposedly made him a victim of discrimination, but Hoffer torpe-doed him: "Mister, it is easy to be full of rage. It is not easy to go to work and build something."

Because of this remark, Hoffer was publicly accused of being racist. But Hoffer was right. It's easy to surrender to rage and setback. It's hard to do something about it. Conversely, it's easy to give demanding others everything they want. But it's hard to say "no" and stand up for oneself.

As a consequence of progressive appeasement, the whole world watched how Europe couldn't defend its borders against the Trojan horse of the refugee crisis. Already, African and Syrian migrants battle it out in asylum centers—because they hate each other's race. Women and children who came looking for a safe haven have become victims of sexual violence by the very men they tried to escape from. And Europeans haven't lifted a finger.

The whole world now knows that when in Europe, it pays to behave as aggressively as possible. Migrants have observed that white suckers neither have the guts to stand up for their history nor fight for their future. In Cologne, thousands of young women became victims of robberies, intimidation, sexual assault, and rape. But German men didn't act.

Western peace politics has turned into the politics of capitulation. From 9/11, through Madrid, London, Charlie Hebdo and the Bataclan massacre, Islamic migrants have successfully intimidated the West with sadistic violence. To avoid confrontation, our leaders give the terrorists and their 'moderate' supporters everything they demand. The attacked civilians, however, haven't done anything in their self-defense.

It's very easy to act 'progressive'. Then, you don't have to defend anything, and along with your Stockholm syndrome, you can be best friends with the people who hate us. It's very to step aside in order to house migrants at the expense of one's own population. It's very easy to lay down the sarcastic pen out of fear of insulting others. It's very easy to surrender oneself to the enemy.

But Islam, mass migration, and multiculturalism didn't invite themselves. Self-hating politicians did that, those who sold the future of their grandchildren to barbarians and who spent the money on people illegally occupying their own lands.

When will we, the oppressed, finally revolt?

We defend civilization when, in any confrontation between ourselves and others, we choose to defend our own values, precisely when it is hard to do so. Westerners—Europeans, Americans, Canadians, Australians, South Africans and others—have no right to evade the conflict with the world.

In order to save the West, we will have to overcome ourselves first. Fate leaves us no other choice.

Before PC, Everyone was Alt-Right: The Fight for European Identity

June 8ᵗʰ, 2017

In 1953, Albanian film director Yutkevich decided to portray the life of his nation's greatest hero, George Scanderbeg, a true story. Named after Macedonia's Alexander the Great, Scanderbeg was taken hostage by the Ottoman Turks as a child. He was to be raised a Muslim and a slave.

For twenty years, he became the most feared warrior, even fighting the Albanians. He secured many victories for the Ottoman Empire as leader of the Janissaries, an elite infantry made up of captured foreigners. But Scanderbeg grew homesick and eventually returned to his people. Embracing his native customs, he converted back to Christianity. For the next thirty years until his death, he would unite the Albanians and keep the Ottomans from invading.

Islam could neither erase Scanderbeg's European soul nor that of the Albanian people. His campaigns against the powerful Turks helped to keep all of Europe free. In the film, a supporting actor explains why:

> "What are the Turks even doing in Albania? It is the bridge
> for them. The jump from here will take them to Europe."

Today, the film about Scanderbeg's life could never get past the censors. It is a most politically incorrect film, perfectly lacking Hollywood's self-loathing. Upon his return to Albania, Scanderbeg speaks to his people, reflecting on his time with the Turks:

> "I would like to tell you something. Today is the happiest day
> of my life. For twenty years I have lived among dogs as if I was
> a dog myself. Now, finally, am I allowed to be a man again."

Can you imagine a European leader saying this about growing up with diversity? For fifty years, open borders have forced both Europeans and Americans to live as immigrants among immigrants in the countries their ancestors built. When did this begin, this belief that we are all equal? Our progressive leaders have tried so hard to make African and Asian immigrants our equals but ended up doing the opposite. They made us equal to *them*.

Yutkevich depicted Muslims as mouth-foaming barbarians defacing Greek statues. But it wasn't just his prejudice. In our time, we've seen ISIS destroy the historic city of Palmyra. We've seen Muslims waste their energy destroying Western art. If you've ever wondered why so many ancient Greek and Roman artworks have lost their faces, it's because Islamic invaders really did destroy many of them. Where does this hatred of humanity come from?

Raised by faceless mothers hiding behind the veil, perhaps nothing enrages a Muslim man more than the sight of a European woman's face. Unlike women in Islam, women in Albania were not slaves to their husbands. Having given Scanderbeg a son, the free woman Mamitsa plays the role of a Wagnerian Valkyrie. Armed to the teeth, she joins the men in battle to fight the Ottomans.

She dies, but the Albanians live on. European history is littered with such sacrifice.

Like Scanderbeg, a German boy named Arminius was presumably taken hostage by the Romans around the time of Christ. He received Roman citizenship and rose to the rank of equestrian. But as one historian explains, he probably never felt like one of them.

Arminius, too, returned home a man. He, too, united his people. Having tricked general Varus to take a shortcut through the Teutoburg forest, the Germanic allies annihilated his legions, ending further Roman expansion to the north. Mass migration may have made the West multicultural, but it is only a matter of time before people of European descent will reassert themselves.

We will never be Africans and Asians. We are Europeans. With patience, we will liberate our cities from multiculturalism and diversity. And when we do, future historians will know the greatest story ever told.

Uproar! Europeans of All Tribes Must Unite to Resurrect
Their Civilization

March 18th, 2018

In a poem from the Icelandic *Edda*, the Norse god Thor wakes
up without his hammer. He has lost his phallus. A giant named
Thrym, whose name means uproar, has taken it. He won't bring
the hammer back unless the fair-haired Freya, Odin's wife, mar-
ries him. But the otherwise promiscuous goddess refuses the
ugly troll; her anger sends an earthquake through Asgard.

Instead, Thor and Loki decide to dress up as Freya and her
bridesmaid. They fool the giant, but barely. Once Thrym re-
trieves the hammer to hallow the bride—with the blessings of
Vár—a fiery-eyed Thor smashes him to death, kills the giant's
sister, and then exterminates the entire race of giants, saving
Asgard.

This 14th-century Icelandic poem, *Thrym's Lay*, can be
traced back to a 10th-century Norwegian origin, perhaps it was
authored by Þjóðólfr ór Hvini in a time of heathen insurgence
against the Catholic conqueror. It is around this time that archaeological evidence shows Nordic peoples began wearing the
phallic hammer amulet.

The Icelandic Thor's hammer looks like a Christian cross
turned upside down. The heathens were giving Catholics the
finger, quite literally. We know what happened next. The Catholics won, the heathens lost. It would take another five centuries
before Martin Luther instigated the Protestant Reformation
that ended Catholic universalism in Europe.

But the poem's contents may be based on a much older, oral
tradition spread around North-Western Europe via the North
Sea. One or two lines from the poem appear to have a 7th-centu-
ry origin. Could the chronology of events described in *Thrym's*

Lay refer to a historical event, perhaps the events leading up to the Battle of the Teutoburg forest?

In the poem, Thor loses his masculinity and leaves Asgard defenseless. The same thing happened between 50 B.C. and 20 AD when the Germanic tribes were forced to pay young men as tributes to the Roman oppressor to serve as mercenaries. The loss of men left their Asgard, the gardens of the Æsir or the agricultural lands of the Germanic peoples, unguarded.

The poem describes a council of such importance that the female deities were allowed to attend it. Perhaps the threat of a foreign conquest?

According to Roman sources, around the year 15 AD, a young 16-year-old girl known as Thousnelda was to be married off by her father, Segestes. A true progressive, Segestes praised peace with the Romans, because the slavery of his people would profit him personally. When Thousnelda was 25 and pregnant, Segestes would sell her into slavery in exchange for a home in Gaul.

It seems plausible, then, that young Thousnelda, a fair-haired Germanic girl of noble birth, was to be married off to a Roman officer in exchange for peace. It was customary among Germanic peoples to forge peace by marrying the noble daughter of one tribe to the prince of another. The most important Roman around the time of the Battle was general Varus.

Was Thousnelda given to Roman general Varus, a fifty-four-year-old, fat, lazy man, according to a contemporary historian? The girl's anger must have sent an earthquake through Asgard indeed.

At either Varus's summer or his winter encampment, somewhere along the Rhine and the Weser rivers in North-Western Germany, Thousnelda would have met her future savior and husband, a young man known as Arminius. He was twenty-three years old at the time. For at least two more years, Arminius would serve the Romans well and rise through their ranks to become a lesser Roman nobleman, one of only a handful living in the North.

Like Thor in the poem, Arminius dressed up as a "woman" to get close to the ugly general, namely in Roman battledress. In fact, a recurrent theme in Nordic literature of Odin (e.g, in Adam van Bremen's chronicles) or of Thor dressing up as a woman may have nothing to do with transgenderism, but rather with the historical reality of "joining the Romans", namely dressing up as a Roman soldier.

From the Germanic perspective, Roman soldiers must have appeared feminine. Roman battledress, tunic or toga must have looked ridiculous to the traditionally pants-wearing Germans. Roman soldiers were also several inches shorter than average Germanic men, let alone the Northern fighting males who could be over six feet tall, even then. Romans were clean-shaven; Germanic men grew beards.

(If the poem's Thor has lost his masculinity and dresses up as a bride, perhaps he has joined the Romans?)

Despite Arminius' stellar career among Varus's legions, he would ultimately choose Thousnelda over Rome. He led general Varus and his army into a trap at the Battle of the Teutoburg Forest. Like Arminius, he retrieved his hammer—his Germanic manliness—and killed Varus. A union of Germanic tribes, among others the Marsi and the Cherusker, then slaughtered the three legions, effectively exterminating every single last one of them.

It is unlikely, though, that the battle took place in an actual forest; you can't throw a spear very far and you can't see the enemy. We don't know the historical truth, in large part because the Germanic peoples didn't leave a written history. The stories they told their children and the songs soldier sang were lost.

Perhaps Catholic book burners have been too effective. Perhaps there was and is no connection between the historic *uproar* of the Battle and Thrym's Lay, even though the chronology of events in both stories seems to match. What is certain, though, is that Northern Europeans are the descendants of a subjugated people whose pre-Christian history has been forgotten and effectively erased.

Today, not only Northern Europeans but all Europeans face a new potential onslaught. Europe is under threat from being flooded by a billion immigrants from Africa, the Middle East, India and Asia. I'm not exaggerating. The United Nations projects Africa's population alone to rise from 1 billion to 4 billion people, whereas white Europeans will decline from 500 million to below 200 million before the end of this century.

Black men will outnumber white women 10 to 1. Europe is about to be gang-raped. Our wealth will be plundered, our lands desecrated. In times like these, we must look to the past in order to bridge a path towards a more desirable future.

The Germanic ancestors of Northern Europeans defeated a numerically and technologically superior Roman army. They applied the tactics of a surprise attack, lured the Romans into a trap and slaughtered them. How can modern Europeans thwart the threat of our biological extinction through mass rape and murder? What can white Europeans do to prevent their genocide?

4

Demography is Destiny

"The pursuit of material wealth contributed to un-sustainable levels of debt, with suddenly higher pric-es for food and oil contributing to defaults—and the [Global Financial Crisis]."

—The Club of Rome

The UN projects that the African population will grow to 4.4 billion individuals by the end of this century, over a third of the entire global population. Despite its ethnically diverse peoples, Africa will not only become the world's largest consumer market but potentially also the biggest supply of cheap labor to the developed world. An overlooked question, however, is whether African peoples will submit to such a secondary role willingly, or perhaps choose to conquer the world on foot instead.

Western capitalists have long understood that, after having saturated their home markets, the only way to further increase demand was to breed new consumers. They have done so first and foremost by irresponsibly turning the African continent into a human factory, producing the surplus births needed to grow Western economies.

As a consequence, since the second half of the twentieth century, Africans have suffered an involuntary population boom, brought about by money-hungry Western agriculturalists and capitalists that forced their surplus production onto Africa, under the manipulative guise of "development aid". Posing as humanitarians, Westerners deliberately created Third World hunger as an excuse to westernize the region.

Like China briefly had become a playground for the madness of Western architects, Africa has now become a breeding ground for Western consumerism. Modern-day capitalists thus succeeded in doing what European colonials could not: the submission of all of Africa.

Once Africans realize what has been done to them, they will already vastly outnumber the populations of the West four-to-one; Europe nearly ten-to-one. Much like the angered Germanic tribes that had once gathered at the gates of Rome, Africa's rising numbers will give them an incentive to try to conquer its former masters. Future historians will tell us whether they succeeded.

Population Overshoot: Limits to Growth

December 22ⁿᵈ, 2014

Assuming the world can feed five billion Asians, four billion Africans, and 2 billion 'other', the United Nations predicts all but white populations will grow. However, a different set of predictions was published in 1972 in a book titled Limits to Growth, which takes into account declining birth rates, pollution, and depletion of resources leading to a premature collapse of the global economy.

What is driving population growth? I believe that the developing world's demand for consumer products and services drives demand for human capital, namely large numbers of (low wage) laborers and the required managerial talent to lead them. But by incorrectly projecting a linear growth of demand beyond sustainable levels the global economy incentives an unprecedented overshoot of 'labor production' i.e. new births of people destined to become future workers.

According to the supply chain theory complex chains suffer greatly from inefficiency when intermediaries hoard supplies in anticipation of future demand. This causes an overshoot in production by producers upstream of the chain. In the case that demand is not met, unsaleable supplies and products may put companies out of business and hurt the economy as a whole. In some cases, the entire chain may collapse.

Historically, and even today, we have seen large numbers of people from rural areas migrating to nearby cities in hopes of better lives. The upper middle and upper classes will not be very willing to give birth to large families of children merely to send them off to work in crowded factories.

This means that not all people are born equal. The majority of people from undeveloped rural areas are considered human livestock born to populate factories or perform other menial jobs. The mechanism is that wealthy people are not willing to send their children off to poor, unrewarding jobs.

As Europe started rebuilding itself after World War II soon economic growth outpaced population growth. I call it the great detachment because local economies no longer served local communities. AS the demand for mostly low wage labor skyrocketed several European countries such as France, United Kingdom, Belgium, The Netherlands, Germany, and others invented a scheme we now know as the guest worker mass immigration.

Dutch researcher Paul Scheffer wrote a book about the guest worker phenomenon, a political policy that officially ended in The Netherlands and Germany around 1973. Businesses in demand for labor were allowed to recruit workers from Morocco and Turkey. Scheffer describes how Dutch companies selected workers based on their level of education, namely: a high school diploma was considered over-educated.

Although the mass guest worker immigration policy officially ended, it was essentially extended through legal family reunion, including brothers, sisters, and their families. Even today many descendants of the former guest workers marry a partner from their home countries. Whereas indigenous native Dutch continue to have low birth rates, the first and second generations of guest worker immigrants provided ample offspring.

But while guest workers are employed in the western world, a much larger hidden class of workers is employed overseas. How many people in China are employed in factories that refine or produce parts that end up in Apple's iPhone, sold to mostly western consumers? They range in the hundreds of thousands. Western demand for consumer products employs hundreds of millions if not billions of people worldwide.

The point is that human population growth -mothers deciding to have children- is based on exaggerated estimates. In reality, a stagnating or even dropping demand for consumer products in the western world will have a ripple effect across the global economic supply chain. Ultimately the least productive people, manual laborers in Third World countries, will be hit with hunger and extreme poverty.

It requires dedicated global leadership to slow down economic growth and prepare for a world without growth for growth's sake, towards a world of quality over quantity, and happiness over money.

The World Population Bubble:
We Can Still Cancel the Apocalypse

June 3rd, 2016

"We, at the height, are ready to decline." *(Shakespeare)*

Civilizations come and go. History recorded the rise and fall of dozens of peoples and their societies, among others Ancient Egypt, Old Greece, the Roman Empire, and more recently, the Third Reich and the Soviet Union. So, we, at the height, have to wonder: Is the modern world immune to collapse? The possibility that it might not be spells worry. In his book The Collapse of Complex Societies (1988), among dozens of examples, professor Joseph Tainter describes the decline of a Mesoamerican civilization centered around the city of Teotihuacan:

> "The city leaders had the ability to mobilize labor at an unprecedented level. For 600 years or more, 85 to 90 percent of the population of the eastern and northern Valley of Mexico lived in or near the city. About 700 A.D. Teotihuacan abruptly collapsed. The population dropped within 50 years to no more than a fourth of its peak level. A period of political fragmentation followed."[1]

This sounds eerily similar to modern times. Today, globalization mobilizes a historically unprecedented level of labor. In developed nations, over 50 to 70% of their populations now live in cities. As hundreds of millions of people struggle each day to find housing in densely crowded cities, futurist dreams of space colonization signal a desperate need to expand mankind's living space. But if we fail to accommodate this fast-growing world population — whether on Mars or at the bottom of the ocean —

I predict nothing will stand in the way of bursting the human bubble.

We have reached Peak Humanity—but are we ready to decline?

It has taken mankind since the beginning of history to arrive at a population of over 7 billion individuals. An unfathomable number, but as with Teotihuacan, within only the next 50 years, a concurrence of economic breakdown, resulting in poverty and famine, failing antibiotics and the subsequent outbreak of global epidemics, and—ultimately—global war will accelerate the descent of man towards near-complete collapse. As we risk losing billions, we carry a responsibility even Atlas's shoulders cannot.

But if fortune favors the bold, the survivors entering the 22nd century will have descended from those able and willing to act now. The price for apathy is death. We who still dream of a better future must abandon the naive policy of freedom without a struggle. Freeing ourselves from the politics of appeasement, and from a culture centered around sheepish consumerism, the future calls on the heroic to guide humanity through the apocalypse.

For decades, even the best government forecasters have repeatedly overestimated our chances of economic recovery. This naive optimism has fooled the world into adopting a wait-and-see attitude, forestalling the psychological preparation to combat a recession spiraling out of control. As one German historian put it, "Optimism is cowardice." Given that the bureaucrats who mean to reassure us have been so wrong for so long, we urgently have to open our eyes and face reality as it is.

Is the threat of a human population collapse real? In this section, I argue that our expanding population, like Ponzi schemes and stock market bubbles, has formed a human bubble ready to burst. But first, in order to familiarize the reader with a basic concept, please imagine a classical S-curve graph. Going from left to right, we see a typical S-shaped curve. We see such graphs in almost every college textbook. This particular graph may, for example, represent the number of skyscraper stories construction workers have built over time. Once the workers have painstakingly laid out the foundations, developments accelerate as the tower stacks more identical stories. Then, developments slow down again in order to finalize the peak.

But such graphs fool us into thinking that growth processes always end in success, i.e. in the upper right corner of the graph. This survivorship bias, people's preoccupation with explaining success rather than with looking at causes of failure, blinds us from seeing a bigger picture. Skyscrapers collapse or are demolished. Stock markets crash. We have to ask ourselves, "What comes after success?"

What happens next, we can learn by studying nature. Studying social insects such as ants, bees or termites, we can track the size of a colony's population over time. The various species of social insects, with biomass as a measure of the total number of individuals, generally follow an identical series of growth cycles. They start with zero and end with zero. Having established a new colony during the founding stage (F), its total biomass is described by successive stages of exponential growth (E). Near the end of each cycle, the population reaches its natural limits to growth, limited by both external and internal factors. Then, a new reproductive cycle (R) begins, during which the colony regroups resources necessary to revitalize the colony, affording itself another growth cycle.

For their survival, social insects find themselves under a constant pressure. A colony runs the risk of being overrun by invading armies. Environmental disaster may cut off a colony's food and water supply. Some social insect colonies even deploy the practice of slavery. But of equal threat is the risk of internal collapse. During the reproductive stage (R) the insect population experiences a sudden drop in numbers, losing up to 40–60% of its members. Individuals either pass away of old age, starve, succumb to disease, abandon the colony, or die defending it.

Whatever the causes, deaths now exceed new births at an alarming rate. In the end, the colony collapses with the death of its queen. We can now apply these lessons to human populations.

If we say the study of apes tells us something about the human animal—the naked ape—then social insects can tell us a great deal about how we behave collectively. Not just insect colonies face the possibility of extinction. Famously, the dodo bird went extinct around 1662. Short of a century ago, about 5 million elephants still roamed the African planes. Today, no more than 12% of that remain. Given the growing number of mammalian species faced with extinction, what about that brainy one, Homo Sapiens?

We know the Neanderthal went extinct about 40,000 years ago, after having roamed Europe for several hundreds of thousands of years. Surely, by now modern man must have developed the required intellect to control his own evolution, right? If only we had the time, we would cure all disease, end all war, save the whales, lock the climate in a fixed state–preferably at 80 degrees Fahrenheit—and stop the universe from expanding. But these are the delusions of politicians whose only currency is the false promise. In reality, more than having outwitted nature, man has escaped fate by chance.

No human settlement, city, nation or empire either has endured or will endure forever. Societal collapse is a historical certainty. In the past, even entire continents of people were faced with the possibility of collapse. In medieval Europe, the bubonic plague, also known as the Black Death, killed nearly 30% of all Europeans, amounting to 25 million individuals out of a population of 85 million. It took Europeans three centuries to recover.

Because cities have denser populations, they allow for disease to spread more quickly. In some medieval towns and villages, the plague had killed up to 85% of their inhabitants. A recent article in The Guardian states that "people who lived through the epidemic saw their world collapse around them." In some neighborhoods, "'ruinous' houses were still being reported two centuries later." With the majority of human beings living in cities today, professor Carenza Lewis points out:

> "This disease is still endemic in parts of today's world, and could once again become a major killer, should resistance to the antibiotics now used to treat it spread amongst tomorrow's bacteriological descendants of the fourteenth-century Yersinia pestis. We have been warned."

The plague, however, does not tell us a story of a human bubble bursting, but one of resilience to disaster. In order for populations to deal with nature's blows, they must be able to withstand and recover from all sorts of setbacks, including epidemics, foreign invasion and changing habitats. Evolution favors these more resilient systems over less flexible ones.

Another well-known example of such resilience is the impact the arrival of the Europeans, and the diseases they brought with them, had on Native Americans. In North America, between 1490 and 1890, their numbers dropped from around five million individuals to below several hundred thousand. However, recently, the Native American population appears to have recovered to pre-Columbian levels. Again, in this example we do not observe a sudden collapse — there is no flash crash — but instead, we see a rather steady rate of decline over a period of several centuries. It evidences Native Americans' extraordinary resilience to a complete takeover of their habitat.

In the previous two examples, disease and invasion disrupted populations of people, but they did not collapse. When it comes to collapse, what we're looking for lies in internal factors. In an article titled Time Is Running out for Japan's Dwindling Population, professor Kohei Wada of Chuo University mapped 2,000 years of Japanese population growth, including a catastrophic projection of what happens next:

The professor predicts that during the next 50 years the Japanese population will fall from over 125 million people today to below 45 million. This sudden drop equals a population loss of over 60%, most likely the result of an aging baby-boom generation phasing out, while new births have dropped to all-time lows. To grasp the scope of such a decline, picture Tokyo, but with six out of every ten homes abandoned. At this rate, megacities will become mega ghost towns.

However, if such a collapse occurred in isolation from the rest of the world, Japan would no longer be able to participate in the global economy. Also, its dwindling population—and therefore its diminishing military might—would open the door to foreign conquest, possibly forever erasing ethnic Japanese people. Population decline is a dangerous thing.

Early in November 2013, I emailed a researcher of stock market crashes if he could assess whether internet money Bitcoin had formed a price bubble. It had happened before, when in April 2013 the price of one Bitcoin rose to about $265 before crashing back down to $80. Later that year, from October onward, Bitcoin's price began to surge again, rising to well over $1,000. Using a mathematical method called a log-period power law (LPPL), the researcher I had contacted examined Bitcoin's price movements, publishing his results on November 16th:

"In this post, I will respond to a request to publish an analysis of the Bitcoin/USD index (Mt. Gox). Based on these graphs, there is quantitative evidence to suggest that the recent increase in the Bitcoin/USD has been the start of a bubble. While The Bubble Index: Bitcoin has not reached its highest levels seen earlier this year, investors in the currency should be cautious."

Then, just a few weeks later, in early December 2013, the Bitcoin bubble indeed burst as he had predicted. The price of a single Bitcoin plunged from its $1200 high to well below $600, losing over 50% of its value on a single day. Today, investors are still waiting for recovery.

What exactly had made Bitcoin a bubble in the first place? To answer that question, I refer to research by professor Didier Sornette of the Financial Crisis Observatory based in Zurich, Switzerland. Sornette explains why bubbles form in his book Why Stock Markets Crash. To cut a long story short, bubbles form as the result of positive feedback loops. People bought more Bitcoins because they saw other people buying more and making great profits—i.e. "monkey see, monkey do". Most financial bubbles thus form in and out of themselves, regardless of external factors.

We can apply this insight —positive feedback loops create bubbles in and out of themselves—to the historic growth of the entire human population, from 10,000 BC to today. During only the past two or three centuries, exponential innovations in agriculture, accelerated by fossil fuels, first coal then oil, allowed for a dramatic expansion of the human population size. We went from 1 billion to 7 billion members within a timespan of 10 generations.

That exponential growth also paints a picture of a highly risky bubble formation.

We like to think our numbers either continue to grow or stabilize. We like to believe our technological skills will solve whatever problems stand in our way. We think we are going to build floating cities or off-world colonies. But the reality is, that a declining marginal return on investment that governs human societies will force stop further growth. Not external factors, but the declining rate of human efficiency is what will most likely kill the species.

Alarmingly, compared to 50 years ago, the speed at which the human population is growing has more than halved. At this rate, within the next few decades, human population growth will cease. For the first time since the birth of modern man, we begin our decline. But it won't be the first time a species of man collapses. Homo Neanderthalensis, too, was erased, as were Homo Habilis, Homo Erectus, and Homo Denisova. Is there anything we can do to cancel our demise?

Right before the possible collapse of humankind, we would expect to see a societal breakdown. We can indeed see evidence of such a breakdown. Yet not all of our leaders want to be made aware of that fact and flee in self-delusion. A few weeks after dropping out of the race for the Republican nomination, former US presidential candidate Jeb Bush held a speech in Amsterdam, The Netherlands. Without shame, he claimed, "Babies born today will easily become 120, 130 years old."

Bush said this while accusing his former competitor Donald Trump of being a populist, but this typical false promise of old age is the oldest form of political demagoguery. Children born today will most certainly not grow older than their parents. Firstly, genes still cap our average longevity at more reasonable levels. Secondly, since people spend nearly 50% of their medical budgets in the final years of their lives, economic stagnation will force governments to divert the cost of old age away from the elderly.

Next, in order to provide for younger generations so desperately needed for a culture's survival, governments will also be forced to divert pension funds. Ultimately, with governments running in panic mode, the unproductive elderly that no longer contribute to society may be actively 'discarded', freeing up resources for the young. In fact, Nazi Germany's euthanasia programs targeted not only minorities and Jewish people but also the sick, the elderly and those deemed unfit for work. (Fascism may very well be the politics of collapse.)

In his book on collapsing societies, professor Tainter writes a great deal about why societies collapse. In some cases, the decision is perfectly rational as "under a situation of declining marginal returns collapse may be the most appropriate response." People choose to cut themselves loose from a failing system, rationally accepting a lower standard of living, but thereby saving their lives. In case of the Mesoamerican Casas Grandes civilization, Tainter paints a grim image of what might be the future of the modern world:

> "Sometime about 1340 A.D. Casas *Grandes* political supremacy came to an end. The site fell into disrepair. Goods were still produced in large volumes, but civil construction and public maintenance ceased. Public and ceremonial areas were altered for living quarters. The dead were buried in city water canals and plaza drains. As walls crumbled, ramps were built to reach still usable upper rooms. Casas Grandes finally burned, at which time corpses were left unburied in public places, and altars were systematically destroyed."[2]

The collapse of complex societies follows a general schedule. "There is, first and foremost, a breakdown of authority and central control. Prior to collapse, revolts and provincial breakaways signal the weakening of the center," writes Tainter. Indeed, in recent years, the collapse of authority and control in the Middle East has led to the so-called Arab Spring revolutions that plunged many regional governments into chaos. The European Union, too, is showing signs of weakness as the Dutch have voted against Ukraine joining, and the British are set to hold a referendum on leaving it.

Next, "revenues to the government often decline." In Europe and America, both an aging demographic and mass migration of low-wage laborers have lowered national and federal tax incomes. As a consequence, "foreign challengers become increasingly successful, because, with lower revenues, the military may become ineffective." Europe doesn't even have an army to defend itself. The US pulling funds out of NATO, Germany's Angela Merkel was forced to strike a very bad deal with Turkey to protect European borders against floods of migrants. Likewise, the US army would not be able to afford another Iraq invasion — and its enemies know it.

Eventually, "the populace becomes more and more disaffected as the hierarchy seeks to mobilize resources to meet the challenge." But failing to do so, "the umbrella of law and protection erected over the populace is eliminated. ... Monumental construction and publicly-supported art largely cease to exist. Literacy may be lost entirely, and otherwise declines so dramatically that a dark age follows."

A declining marginal return on investment in human population growth, alongside a shortage of cheap fossil fuels (Peak Oil), will irreparably disrupt the global supply of food and water. Peak Oil will usher in a global famine because even genetically unmodified crops have been selected for greater yield at the expense of normal plant functions. In other words, most fruits and vegetables we eat today come from crops that cannot survive in the wild, due to weak root systems. Without cheap fuels, farmers will abandon energy-intensive agriculture in favor of lower-yielding crops, which can survive in the wild, but which feed a much smaller number of people.

That agricultural disaster, coinciding with failing antibiotics, spells global catastrophe, as even the bubonic plague may resurface. For their survival, panic-stricken men and women may ultimately surrender themselves to a strongman calling for war against Enemy Others, competing for diminishing food supplies and living space. Professor Sornette calls it the Mad Max scenario. I believe that, within the next 50 years, we may lose up to 60–80% of all mankind, our numbers dropping below 2 billion individuals. The decline will then continue for several centuries as people struggle to hold on to what is left of civilization. In the end, we may never recover.

Perhaps a new species of man will evolve to replace us. No matter how wrong the world's religions may have been about the creation of the universe, perhaps they were always right about the threat of the apocalypse. If we don't act now, children born today will not live to be "120, 130 years old", as phony politicians want us to believe, but instead, our children will witness the world collapse around them as the human race implodes.

I wrote this admittedly depressing article as a necessary warning. Human beings can show remarkable resilience to natural disaster, foreign invasion or war, but we are equally oblivious to our own weaknesses. With this article, I meant to argue that we must prepare ourselves for the inevitable. We must prepare for the one catastrophe we may never recover from: population collapse. It is comparably easy for us to see a rain of meteorites coming towards Earth, but when it comes to human arrogance... it's our heel of Achilles.

In my view, the Western world should take the lead. Abandoning the oppressive politics of political correctness, we must make it our duty to leverage both our wealth (Europe) and our military power (US) in order to guide humanity through the collapse. We must do so with the help of allies, while defending the weak who deserve protection, but without any hesitation to obliterate old and new enemies.

With the spiritual support of a toughened-up, manlier version of Christianity, the West should restore its dominance in the world, and by doing so, save mankind from itself. Because if we don't, no one else will. I conclude by citing rule #16 from the Manual for a Christian Soldier, written by medieval intellectual Desiderius Erasmus, in 1501:

> "If you ever receive a mortal wound, never cast your shield aside, never give your weapons away, and never surrender to the enemy. I have seen this happen to a lot of people whose minds are naturally weaker and more effeminate. Once they have fallen to the ground and ceased to offer resistance, they surrender entirely to their emotions and no longer think of winning back freedom. This pusillanimity is very dangerous, and even if it does not happen to the worst of people, it often does lead to the worst of things, namely despair. Against this, the mind must be strengthened through this rule of conduct that when we fall into sin we may not despair. Instead, we must imitate courageous soldiers who often not only refuse to flee out of shame, or out of pain inflicted by a wound, but who, because of that, are encouraged and awoken anew to fight more fiercely than before."

We can still win back freedom and cancel the apocalypse. Let us follow the courageous and let us fight more fiercely than ever before.

White Decline: Benefit or Danger?

February 5ᵗʰ, 2017

"By 2050, only 5 percent of the world will be European."
(Russel Shorto)

When mass immigration makes a society more ethnically diverse, the narratives that maintain social order shift from traditional ones to abstract ones. Blood and soil make place for equality and diversity. But when a people becomes too diverse, e.g. when the dominant culture becomes a minority culture, the inevitable realization takes root that one is no longer one people, but many.

We can observe the collapse of social order in real-time in the present-day United States. Demographics play a leading role. In 1965, non-Hispanic whites represented over 80% of the total population. Down to about 65%, Pew Research projects white Americans will become a minority by 2040.[3] By that time, newborn children of white parents will represent less than 25% of all births. Since 2015, non-white births already outnumbered white births.[4]

The decline of whites in the United States has two key causes. First of all, a rapidly aging white demographic is failing to reproduce its replacement generation. Unwilling to let go of wealthy lifestyles and invest money into having more children, American whites have been forced to cut family sizes down to an average of one to two children per woman.

Secondly, a mostly Hispanic and Asian low-wage immigrant population is having a baby-boom. Concerning the African American population, researchers project it will remain relatively constant at around 13% of the population, though still growing in absolute numbers.[5] Researchers believe the immigration made possible since the 1965 Kennedy Immigration Act will bring in nearly 60 million mostly non-white immigrants (excluding offspring) by 2065.

These demographic changes have divided the United States into two distinct peoples, namely a rural Middle America populated by whites who helped vote Republican President Donald Trump into office—dismissively known as "flyover country"—and a hyper-diverse urban rabble that houses much of the U.S. industry's slave labor force—known as "coastal America" and home to Democrat voter bases.

Although much of the United States is still white-owned, rapid white decline implies that this former British colony, too, must one day follow in the footsteps of other former colonies such as Suriname, Rhodesia (Zimbabwe),[6] and South Africa. These former colonies were once ruled by whites, but their falling numbers toppled the balance of power in favor of (indigenous) non-white majorities. However, Australia, Canada, the United States, and even Europa herself may be facing a similar fate if whites fail to respond to the 'black wave' with more babies.

For example, in South Africa, according to the 1904 census, whites represented about 22% of the total population, namely 1.1 million individuals.[7] In 1960, whites had grown to 3 million individuals but constituted a relative 19% of the total population as the non-white population began to explode.[8] By 2011, whites had grown to around 4.6 million, but now represented less than 9% of the total.[9] In 2016, the non-white population hit a staggering 50 million individuals, with whites further declining to 8% of the total population.

Reduced to 4.5 million, South African whites have begun to decline in absolute numbers for the first time in history.[10] The above figures exclude about 3 million illegal immigrants left unaccounted for.

Foreseeing white decline, it is feasible that a future majority of non-white Americans may overthrow white dominance in a civil war. Mimicking the abolition of South Africa's Apartheid regime, non-white Americans may demand their own non-white government. America's revolutionaries may argue that, since institutionalized racism had historically disadvantaged them, they have the right to disown whites of their lands and properties.

Once non-whites have established themselves as the dominant political power in America, they may aggressively pursue white dispossession. This has happened in Suriname,[11] it has happened in Zimbabwe, it is presently happening in South Africa,[12] and it is eventually going to happen to Australia, New Zealand, Canada, the United States and even to the mother continent Europe. The economically successful whites are failing to win the reproductive game.

Indeed, white decline is a global phenomenon. For decades, Europe's aging white demographic has been dropping in absolute numbers. By 2050, Pew Research expects Christian Europeans to decline from 550 million down to 450 million.[13] At the same time, the European Union believes it should actively import tens of millions of non-European immigrants to replace its aging workforce,

"The cumulative effect of net migration assumed under the EUROPOP2008 convergence scenario is to increase the EU's population by 56 million by 2061."[14]

People of European descent are set to become a fringe minority. In the case of Europe alone, Russel Shorto reasoned,

"Around the time that President Kennedy went to Germany and gave his Ich bin *ein* Berliner speech, Europe represented

12.5 percent of the world's population. Today it is 7.2 percent, and if current trends continue, by 2050 only 5 percent of the world will be European."[15]

By 2050, only 5 percent of the world will be European. By that time, white Americans will only be 2% of the world. Indeed, being white will be a privilege. In such a scenario, white *people* are unlikely to maintain their wealth and power. Instead, whites shall play the role of an economically successful though a politically powerless rural minority.

White dispossession is real. Once dictator Robert Mugabe had usurped Zimbabwe's rule, his all-black government began brutally torturing and killing whites and their families in order to seize their property and scare them out of the country.[16] Faced with such violence by an overwhelming anti-white mob, Western civilization may be flushed out and replaced by the triple-A doctrines of African superstition, Arab traditionalism, and Asian collectivism.

Notably, as an unintended side-effect of Mugabe's "well-planned" policy to drive out white farmers, a quarter of the Zimbabwean population, and counting, now faces mass starvation.[17] Millions of Zimbabweans have already migrated to South Africa illegally, happily consuming the food South Africa's white farmers still produce there... What happened to Zimbabwe is also happening in South Africa. Since the fall of Apartheid in 1994, South Africa has become a net importer of food in order to feed its ballooning black population.[18]

Disowning white farmers has led to a collapse in the local food production chain. The resulting hunger sets off a mass migration from places with low to places with high agricultural activity. With Europe being a most productive agricultural region, Europeans risk being overrun by hundreds of millions of hungry Africans, Arabs, Indians, and Asians, once their failing home-societies force them to make a run for the European continent.

It is time people of European descent face these facts. We are economically successful but only because we keep our family sizes small and subsequent inheritances large. Our numbers are in decline everywhere in the world, both relatively speaking and in absolute numbers. Before the end of this century, we risk becoming a global fringe minority. Replacement immigration is real and eating away at the societies we have built.

But world overpopulation and its environmental footprint are not our faults. They are rather the fault of non-white masses whose numbers keep rising exponentially. The hungry Third World hordes may soon choose to invade our lands in search of food, wealth, and living space—at our expense.

Before the end of this century, people of European descent face the real possibility of their near extinction, namely through a combination of aging demographics and mass immigration, followed by potential mass rape and genocide at the hands of our new masters.

The most worrying observation? Western upper classes seem only interested in their own survival and are perfectly willing to sacrifice the plebs as a human shield. That means us commoners are on our own. We have no choice but to prepare for total war, both against our enemies and against the traitors among us.

Gulag or Hunger Games? The Tragedy of the Commons

February 8th, 2017
Writing on the problem of human overpopulation in a 1968 essay titled *The Tragedy of the Commons*, American ecologist and philosopher Garrett Hardin asked,

"In a welfare state, how shall we deal with the family, the religion, the race, or the class (or indeed any distinguishable
and cohesive group) that adopts overbreeding as a policy to
secure its own aggrandizement?"[19]

Indeed, *overbreeding as a policy* is the strategy immigrants
to the West have been pursuing in order to conquer Europe and
America from within. A Western welfare state drunk on cheap
immigrant labor that willfully opens its borders to an unrestricted influx certainly risks the possibility of self-induced extinction, namely *suicide by immigration*. Hardin further notes that
there is "no technical solution to the problem" of overbreeding
in an enclosed setting, whether local, national or global. Regardless of technological advances, overall human reproductive
rates eventually catch up with the latest developments.

Those dreaming of building underwater cities will not escape the Tragedy either,

"It is fair to say that most people who anguish over the population problem are trying to find a way to avoid the evils of
overpopulation without relinquishing any of the privileges
they now enjoy. They think that farming the seas or developing new strains of wheat will solve the problem—technologically. I try to show here that the solution they seek cannot
be found."[20]

The finite world we live in is what Hardin calls the *Commons*. A term taken from political economics, the commons
refers to all natural and cultural resources people or societies
hold in common such as air, water, and the habitable earth, as
opposed to privately-owned property. The phrase *Tragedy of
the Commons* refers to mankind's inability to escape the consequences of its own continued population growth, namely over-

population, resources shortage, war, famine, disease outbreak, and the subsequent reality of (partial) population collapse. Hardin explains the Tragedy of the Commons as follows:

"Picture a pasture open to all. It is to be expected that each herdsman will try to keep as many cattle as possible on the commons. Such an arrangement may work reasonably satisfactorily for centuries because tribal wars, poaching, and disease keep the numbers of both man and beast well below the carrying capacity of the land. Finally, however, comes the day of reckoning, that is, the day when the long-desired goal of social stability becomes a reality. At this point, the inherent logic of the commons remorselessly generates tragedy."[21]

The impossibility of a peaceful solution led Hardin to the conclusion that an individual's freedom to reproduce lies at the heart of the problem:

"Each man is locked into a system that compels him to increase his herd without limit—in a world that is limited. Ruin is the destination toward which all men rush, each pursuing his own best interest in a society that believes in the freedom of the commons. Freedom in a commons brings ruin to all."[22]

Hardin proposed a political solution to the unsolvable technical problem, stating, "The only way we can preserve and nurture other and more precious freedoms is by relinquishing the freedom to breed, and that very soon."[23]

In his view, individuals should no longer be allowed to reproduce at will. Hardin's suggestion is surprising because it is precisely the sort of 'solution' Nazi Germany employed by enacting racial purity laws that barred 'impure' people from having children. Still, the idea of licensing parents to have children is gaining popularity among the progressive left.[24] But there's a problem. If we would go full leftist and choose to license only economically successful people, whites would remain a substantial part of the licensees—the whole world would cry racism.

(There's a risk that progressives may decide to down-breed the human species in order to create more obedient specimen.)

Hardin's solution to overbreeding was an argument for *communism,* namely the belief that individual people may not be left to decide for themselves what is best for them. Under communism, it is the State that decides who may (or must) start a family, how many children each woman may have, and who should be barred from having children—like a shepherd in charge of his flock.

What, then, is the solution to the Tragedy? There is none. At some point in time, the human species must either face the Gulag or the Hunger Games. Those who prepare for it today have a better chance at winning tomorrow.

Make Boys Men Again

January 27th, 2017

President Trump's election confronted mainstream journalists with something they had never seen before: a male role model. But the damage eight years of Obama's feminism has done to male minds may take decades to unwind. Unlike our European forefathers who struck fear in primitive people's hearts, today's frightened white twenty-somethings call themselves 'gender-fluid hipsters' or 'third-wave feminists'. What they really lack is a pair of full-grown testicles. If Western civilization does not aggressively reinstate a *rite of passage* that teaches teenage boys how to be a man, future historians will point to their feminization as the reason why the millennial generation so easily surrendered to the enemy.

One man with the courage to act on foresight is South Africa's Colonel Franz Jooste. Having served in the South African Defence Force, Colonel Jooste now leads the *Kommandokorps*. Several times a year, the corps organizes paramilitary camps for teenage boys and young men. They are the *Afrikaners* or in the colonel's own words, "the white tribe of Africa". Once a majority, many members of today's South African white minority of about 4.5 million are lost in a sea of over fifty million non-whites. Colonel's Jooste's boot camps prepare Afrikaner boys to become members of their tribe.

In 2011, photographer Ilvy Njiokiktjien and journalist Elles van Gelder produced a short documentary film about the Kommandokorps titled *Afrikaner Blood*. The documentary portrays a dozen boys aged thirteen to nineteen who feel a need to "become a real man, no longer a sissy". During nine days of physical hardship and verbal abuse, the boys undergo a visible psychological transformation. Short interviews with the filmmakers show that the boys, at first, appear unsure of their place in multicultural South Africa. A few days later, after having shed tears struggling to obey Colonel Jooste's orders, the boys appear to have found their true identity. They now confidently reject Nelson Mandela's doctrine of the *rainbow nation*.

Colonel Jooste understands why so many of today's whites feel lost,

> "When I love my own nation, my own language, my own culture, and my own race, and someone says I'm racist, yes, then I am a racist. I am not ashamed to say I'm a racist."

Themes of Afrikaner manhood and identity returned in a feature-length 2015 documentary by Tarryn Lee Crossman, titled *Fatherland*. The female director chooses to focus on the extremist nature of the camps. She shows how a batch of insecure boys win confidence. After nine days, the boys know who they are, where they are from, and what they stand for, both as members of the Afrikaner tribe and as men. Fifteen-year-old 'Sparky' says, "Now I know I can be like my dad one day."

The camps provide the boys with a rite of passage that questions modern Western taboos on manhood and white identity. The Colonel's rite resembles that of traditional passage rites found elsewhere in the world. First, the boys depart from their families. Then, they travel to an unknown location where they arrive in a men's only setting. Given nicknames and new clothing, they complete the separation from their family's protective environment. At this point, they cease to be their parent's children. Colonel Jooste and his crew teach the boys discipline, how to execute an order, and, most importantly, what responsibilities their Afrikaner society expects of its adult members. Deprived of sleep and food, the boys must complete several trials. A ceremonial celebration signals their successful transition to manhood. They've earned the right to call themselves men—*Afrikaner* men.

The rite of passage helped to separate the boys from the feminine family. They were absorbed into the masculine Afrikaner tribe. In today's world, media and politics teach us to believe that manhood and tribal identity are the cause of racism and sexism. We are taught that men threaten the socio-political position of minorities and women. We are taught that war and conflict are men's fault.

At the same time, though, minorities living in the West continue practicing their passage rites. The Amish *Rumspringa*, literally "jumping around", allows Amish boys and girls aged fourteen to sixteen to leave their strict fundamentalist communities and explore the modern outside world on their own. In Ancient

Rome, during the *Liberalia* festival, a father would take his adolescent sons to the Forum where they received new clothes and were presented to the public as adult citizens with voting rights.

Although no written evidence of Nordic passage rites has been preserved, one can still observe certain ancient rites of passage in remote areas of rural Europe. Dutch filmmaker Arnold-Jan Scheer spent three decades of his life traveling to small towns and villages in rural Austria, Switzerland, France, and Germany. There, he recorded traditional Saint-Nicholas festivals held in early December. In some of these places, teenage boys would dress up as wild beasts. For several nights, the frenzied boys run around chasing and harassing young women—deliberately. An elderly father figure—sometimes in the form of Saint Nicholas and sometimes as Wotan, the Germanic god of storm and frenzy—fires them up. The boys, in a trance, keep roving until they collapse from exhaustion.

The taboo on manliness explains where gender disorders come from. They come from the feminist oppression of boys who are denied their right to become men. In the interest of the psychological health of young Western males, our societies must immediately restore teenage boys' access to publicly acknowledged rites of passage.

5

The United States and Europe

"But what is more than curious—indeed, piquant to
a degree—is that an ancient god of storm and frenzy,
the long quiescent Wotan, should awake like an extinct volcano to a new activity..."

—Carl Jung

America, A Prophecy:
Can the United States Avoid World War III?

November 7th, 2016
No civilization lasts forever. The Etruscan civilization vanished.
The Roman Empire collapsed. The Ancient Egyptians disappeared. But if no civilization lasts forever, in the global struggle for natural resources fueling our economies and feeding our
peoples, which civilization might be first to fall? And which one
shall outlive all others? The world we live in isn't the Garden of
Eden where all people can coexist in peaceful harmony for all
eternity. That's just a fantasy. The globalization of our struggle
means human history has entered its endgame.

We all take for granted that we can use money to buy something we need. Money is a promise that sometime in the future

I will be able to purchase something of value. But, knowing that the United States owes the rest of the world nearly 16 trillion dollars worth of debt, what might the United States be offering its creditors of value in exchange for that much money? There are a few ways to answer that question. Inflating the dollar handily lowers the value of US debt, but when economists run out of such peaceful options, aggressive war may become inevitable.

Currently, the United States holds about 30% of the entire world's government debt, making it the most indebted government on the planet. That debt now burdens each US citizen with at least $50,000 from the day they are born. If today all foreign creditors at once demanded the United States repay its debt, they could bankrupt the American people. Therefore, the United States government holds an obligation to its citizens to find ever new ways to convince foreign creditors to hold onto large reserves of USD currency—i.e. reserves they keep but do not spend.

So far, the US government has succeeded. Since World War II, the US dollar has been a so-called world reserve currency, which is a preferred currency other governments use to store their national wealth, like a personal savings account. Throughout recent history, there have been several world reserve currencies, which supersede each other in terms of importance about once every century. Today, there are several currencies competing for the dollar's alpha status. In order of importance, they are the Euro, the British pound sterling, the Japanese yen, and, as of November 30, 2015, the Chinese yuan.

But why is the US dollar so popular internationally? It would be foolish to think people just really love the great American example, or that American democracy makes people drool as if the world fell in love with America. No, since even its worst enemies keep large reserves of USD, meaning they are forced to, we must accept that American power rests on some threat of physical violence.

After Europe's decolonization of the Middle East, and after the US army emerging from World War II victoriously, the global balance of power shifted in favor of the United States. It was American military muscle power that finally ended the age of European dominance. With their superior army, the United States could control many of the world's energy supply routes. As a result, the dollar replaced the British pound as world reserve currency.

To persuade foreign parties to hold large USD reserves, the United States can either offer them access or protection. Foreign creditors may receive access to US controlled trade routes or US military protection. Conversely, those who refuse to accept this 'generous' offer risk being cut off from global trade, or risk a US military 'intervention'. Given the power of the US military, the logic of economics dictates that most nations simply choose to submit to American demands. For example, with the US providing NATO's biggest army, Europeans wouldn't dare dump their USD reserves. Their relatively weak and underfunded armies simply could not defend their own peoples.

Next, during the Cold War, Americans successfully stared down the old Soviet Union. Even Russian President Putin today admits that the United States is the only real superpower left in the world. But after seizing power comes the struggle to maintain it. To stay on top, the United States needs to control humanity's most important sources of energy — e.g. oil, gas and uranium — but this has forced the US army to stay involved in increasingly complex and costly wars, notably in the Middle East, a region holding one of the world's largest known oil reserves.

It should be understood that undiscovered fossil fuel reserves might dramatically disrupt the balance of power in the world. In fact, it did. With the discovery of massive oil fields in Russia, for example, the Vankor oil and gas field, Russian has recently overtaken Saudi Arabia and the United States as the number one oil-producing country. The United States remains a superpower because it can use (the threat of) its military force to bully other parties into paying for oil in USD currency — commonly known as the petrodollar.

The power to rule the world, then, does not come from any perceived moral, cultural or technological strength, but from the brute ability to physically control the trade in natural resources, notably energy. The downside is that superpowers have to relentlessly maintain and continuously upgrade a massive army with military bases spread all around the world — outposts of the American empire. Without such a powerful military, an inheritance of winning World War II, there would not have been an America today.

In conclusion, the ability to price oil in dollars, and only in petrodollars, backed up by US military threat, is what effectively forces foreign parties to hold large reserves of USD currency. Without such dollar reserves, foreign nations would only cut themselves off from the oil trade that fuels their economies and feeds their peoples. To them, USD currency acts as a granary, an insurance that helps them survive through future drought. And that's why in turn the United States can run massive trade deficits and survive a multi-trillion dollar debt.

But the story isn't as straightforward. American dominance is under constant attack by foreign parties trying to escape or circumvent America's stranglehold. All attempts to price oil currently traded in USD in any other currency will necessarily weaken the US economy. For example, if China could force the world to price oil — or whichever energy source becomes more important in the future — in Chinese yuan, all foreign nations would instantly want to dump their USD reserves, forcing Americans to either pay off their debt or file for bankruptcy.

In such a scenario, a debilitated US economy would no longer be able to enter new loans, and it would no longer be able to maintain its massive army. To cut expenses, Americans would have to shut down foreign military bases. They would have to give up their luxury lifestyles. With much of American industry already shipped to China and Mexico, America itself would risk becoming a Third World backwater.

On top of that, US debt is spiraling out of control. In 2000, US national debt counted around 5.6 trillion dollars. By 2016, that debt has more than tripled in only fifteen years time. That hyper-exponential debt growth makes it less attractive for foreign investors to hold US dollar reserves, for several reasons. Firstly, any sane person knows debt cannot keep on growing. At some point in time, debt has to be repaid. The faster US debt continues to grow, the less likely that debt will be repaid. Secondly, investors know that with growing debt USD interest rates will have to come down, making other currencies more attractive.

At this point, it seems that the most powerful nation, the leader of the free world, has caught itself in a web of debt and an almost exponentially increasing dependency on the petrodollar. It is becoming a historical certainty that the US dollar eventually will be superseded by some other world reserve currency, perhaps the Chinese yuan, or some other currency, thereby bringing down the West as we know it.

Talk of an Amero—a North American currency tying together its hemisphere—may offer a temporary solution. Another might prefer the 'Atlanto', a currency bridging the more homogeneous regions of Europe and America, but such preference is irrelevant. In the years leading up to third world war, we expect to see more of such economic centralization. The European Union's aggressive eastward expansion, likely to usurp Ukraine and Turkey, provides another example of a people's attempt to survive economically. The move would bring in millions of new guest workers, sacrificing fresh blood to fuel Europe's aging economies.

But while such expansionist and centralizing developments may postpone global war, they do not suspend it. In fact, they make global war more likely. That's because there are physical limits to centralization. We will undoubtedly stop short of one world and accept the great divide between East and West, both struggling for global dominance. The most unlikely of allies may join in this all-or-nothing tournament. The United States' dependence on oil likely forces them to align with the Arab World, perhaps even sacrificing Europe to Islam in exchange for Saudi oil.

On the other hand, Orthodox Russia, its former Soviet satellite states, and China will together form the second axis. Other civilizations—India, Africa, etc.—will choose a side depending on their interests. Such a third world war will be truly global. While WWII saw mostly European nations fighting each other to the death, WWIII will see entire civilizations fighting each other to extinction. But there is a reason to suggest that the United States will strike first.

In 1980, ecologist Paul Colinvaux spent a year of his life researching the Fates of Nations. Based on historical evidence, he concluded his research with three social laws that relate to aggressive war:

1. All poverty is caused by the continued growth of population.
2. Social oppression is an inevitable consequence of the continued rise in population.
3. Aggressive war is caused by the continued growth of population in a relatively rich society.

When we apply Colinvaux's three social laws to the current state of the world, we learn the following. Firstly, the poverty we see in the world, from the Third World to the lower classes of the West, is not a consequence of failing economies or politics, but of continued population growth. In fact, globalization itself was merely another attempt to cope with the world's explosive population growth. The golden years when economies grew faster than populations lie behind us. Today, the demands of growing global populations have been greater than our economies could possibly meet. In other words, mankind's untamable fertility has put us all on a path towards self-destruction.

Secondly, as richer Western societies with historically lower birth rates try to cope with an influx of poorer peoples migrating to their countries, Western nations have been forced to develop all sorts of social oppression to secure a future for its own people. The wealth that feeds a people quickly dilutes when populations explode. For example, since the Kennedy Immigration Act, the United States has added over 60 million new residents through immigration. Racism and discrimination are just two of many ways to oppress immigrants and their unwanted reproductive rates.

Thirdly, the West happens to be a relatively rich civilization. In case of global economic collapse, we have most fat to burn. Through our colonial heritage, Western nations together still control more natural resources than the rest of the world combined. The United States has the most powerful military force and seems more than willing to use it in order to protect its interests. And because of mass migration to the West, America, and Europe are now suffering an artificial population growth that will force them toward aggressive war.

It is not the case that Western nations are necessarily lead by "bad" people who "love" war. Apart from collective suicide — the leftist option— the West will likely see compelled to go to war with the world. Although they will blame the Russian, America will lead the first charge. The question, therefore, is not if there will be a global war, but when. It will come sooner than we think. In his essay on Wotan (Odin), German psychologist Carl Jung described the events leading up to World War II like a wind that began blowing throughout Europe:

> "Armed with rucksack and lute, blond youths, and sometimes girls as well, were to be seen as restless wanderers on every road, ... faithful votaries of the roving god [Odin]. Later, ... the wandering role was taken over by thousands of unemployed, who were to be met with everywhere on their aimless journeys. By 1933, they wandered no longer, but marched in their hundreds of thousands."

Have not youthful Americans and Europeans long been flocking to open air summer festivals? Have not hundreds of thousands of unemployed, homeless wanderers been looking for a purpose throughout the West? Have not nearly a million Americans attended Donald Trump's rallies? Trump is the archetypal Wotan. Whether or not he wins the 2016 election (tomorrow), he has already unleashed a storm. Americans are ready to march.

By this I do not mean to compare present-day America to Nazi Germany, nor am I comparing Trump to Hitler. Rather, I mean to compare the conditions that predict aggressive war. In my view, Americans have an extraordinary opportunity. Under American leadership, the West has the potential to jump over its own shadow, to be the first civilization that avoided its own demise.

High Treason: How 15 Years of U.S. Military Intervention in the Middle East Surrendered Europe to Islam

August 16th, 2016

Recently, Russia launched another attack to "bomb the shit out of ISIS", as Donald Trump would say. The question is, why hasn't the Obama administration done the same? If the US wanted to take out the Islamic State, they could have done so easily. Is there perhaps truth to Trump's claim that President Obama and then-Secretary of State Hillary Clinton through their actions helped create ISIS?

The answer to that question lies in the US response to the September 11 attacks. On that day, 19 hijackers, most of them were foot soldiers in their early twenties, murdered thousands of innocent American civilians. Of the terrorists, 15 held the Saudi-Arabian nationality. According to 28 now declassified pages from the 9/11 Commission, US intelligence had known early on that high-ranking Saudi Arabian officials had provided the terrorists with support, even from within the United States. The United States, therefore, had been attacked by Saudi Arabia, yet the Bush administration decided to cover up any links to the Saudis and blame the Taliban instead.

Almost immediately after 9/11, the US military shifted its War on Terror to Afghanistan, but the Taliban people, however backward, hadn't played any role in 9/11 whatsoever. The US army moved in any way, on the weak assumption that Afghani supporters were hiding Osama Bin Laden in the Kandahar mountains. Since then, for almost a decade, the US military began framing its operations in the Middle East as a national quest to find the ever-elusive Bin Laden.

Obviously, it made no economic or military sense to spend trillions of dollars of taxpayers' money, sacrificing tens of thousands of US lives, on a hunt that would take a decade before capturing and killing one bearded bogeyman. When they found Bin Laden, he had supposedly been hiding in plain sight in a Pakistani compound, living there with his wives and children.

Never mind that Bin Laden initially denied any involvement, until from December 13 onward US army personnel began "finding" audio and video tapes with belated admissions. Never mind that Bin Laden's medical records showed he suffered organ failure—he traveled around with a mobile kidney dialysis machine. Never mind the bogeyman's own obituary published in an Egyptian newspaper dated December 26, 2001.

Bin Laden's alleged body then thrown from a plane into the sea, the very Navy Seals team that had presumably killed Bin Laden later died in a helicopter accident. The crash conveniently killed the only witnesses of what had really happened in the Bin Laden compound. Today, the only evidence of Bin Laden's death is a series of photographs the US Courts ruled may never be shown to the public.

Sure, I believe all of that. Of course, anyone still left in doubt over 9/11 is a conspiracy theorist, a modern-day heretic. But whether or not 9/11 was a conspiracy, an inside job, or plain opportunism, the United States eagerly adopted the Bin Laden narrative in order to justify a decade of regime change in the Middle East—without ever attacking Saudi Arabia.

It's quite simple. You can't fight the enemy who has you by the balls. Saudi Arabia controls so much of the oil that fuels both the US economy and the US military that post-9/11 Washington had no choice but to slip into vassalage to the House of Saud. Since 2001, the US army has effectively been fighting Saudi Arabia's regional wars. All the Saudis need to do is provide the fuel for US weapons and troops, while conveniently hiding behind "American imperialism" and blaming any social unrest on Western actions.

Nonetheless, it is undeniable that the United States has actively supported Saudi Arabia in exporting its fascist, Wahabbist brand of Islam throughout the Muslim world. In doing so, US leadership supported "regime change" that replaced secular, democratic or otherwise pro-Western leaders with Islamist puppets. Indeed, seen in this light, George W. Bush, Barack H. Obama, and Hillary R. Clinton have together created ISIS—because ISIS is Saudi Arabia.

As with every civilizational fault line, in this case between Europe and the Arab world, there is a grey zone where both civilizations meet, trade and live relatively peacefully. Specifically, this grey zone once consisted of Turkey, Syria, Egypt, and Libya. But not anymore.

First, coming out of the war in Afghanistan, the US military began targeting Iraq. Supposedly, Iraqi dictator Saddam Hussein had hidden yet-to-be-found weapons of mass destruction that posed a threat to the West. In the end, even George W. Bush had to admit Saddam had nothing to do with 9/11. Hussein, however, no matter how evil a man he was, was also a Ba'athist and the leader of a secular movement that strove for an Arab enlightenment. As a result of the US-led regime change that disrupted Iraq's social order, various warring Muslim factions today control the region. Above all, these factions are Islamist, anti-enlightenment and tied to Saudi Arabia's fascist brand of Islam.

Next, the so-called Arab Spring which led to major unrest in the entire Arab world culminated in the toppling of democratically elected, secular Egyptian President Hosni Mubarak. He was a vassal of the West and a dictator to his people, but his reign defended Egypt against the fascist, Saudi-backed Muslim Brotherhood. After Mubarak's fall, that's exactly who took over when the Muslim Brotherhood's own Mohamed Morsi briefly seized power. When the Egyptian people took to Tahrir Square in 2011, they weren't celebrating freedom. They were celebrating the Islamic reconquest of Cairo. Soon afterward, Arab Egyptians began ethnically cleansing Coptic Christians—the true heirs of Ancient Egypt.

The same thing again happened in 2011 when the United States violently ended Muammar Gadaffi's regime. Like Hussein and Mubarak, Gadaffi was a vassal and a delusional despot, but he also defended his people's Northern-African Shi'ite roots, a Persian brand of Islam, against that of fascist Saudis. In doing so, Libya too acted as a sort of buffer zone, the grey zone between liberal Europe and a more fundamentalist Islam. Yet Hillary Clinton and President Obama decided to throw Gadaffi out with the trash when they bombed Libya in favor of a Muslim Brotherhood takeover. Unsurprisingly, Libya has now become a popular passageway to Europe for millions of African 'refugees'.

Around the same time, Syria imploded. Once again a secular, democratic, pro-Western leader Bashar al-Assad was dumped in favor of a Saudi-backed ISIS and the Muslim Brotherhood. Today, Syria is a source of refugees pouring into Europe.

Finally, Turkey. The United States' support of Turkey's Islamist President Erdoğan tops it off by letting him erode the Turkish secular democracy once founded by Kemal Atatürk—the last and only democracy in a majority Muslim nation. While Erdoğan blames the Gülenist movement for staging the recent coup, it is much more likely Erdoğan staged it himself in order to cleanse Turkey of its remaining secular, democratic elements. A self-admitted admirer of Hitler's Third Reich, Erdoğan appears to be following Hitler's footsteps in his ascent to power.

In short, all US-led efforts in the Middle East have ultimately surrendered Europe's regional security, leaving it highly vulnerable to a Turkish-led, Saudi-backed Islamic invasion. Europe either prepares to go to war or prepares to submit to "regime change". Coincidentally, Saudi Arabia has been trying out $130 billion dollars' worth of US military equipment, sold to them by Hillary Clinton and President Barack Obama. The Saudi's ongoing war in Yemen appears to be nothing but an exercise to train its soldiers and test its equipment.

Likewise, Turkey, after having fooled the international community it was NATO's most trustworthy ally, happens to boast NATO's second-largest army after the US. No wonder, then, that there has been the talk of assembling a European Union army. But Europe's leaders are either too late, too naive or too incompetent to do anything about what's coming. If Europe survives this century, it will not be because of its politicians, but because of its people's will to fight.

Perhaps Americans will soon have a change of regime of their own. If the American people elect Donald J. Trump for President, perhaps his reign can start by arresting the most prominent political architect and military strategist, Henry Kissinger, and have him hanged for high treason.

"Anyone who cannot name our enemy is not fit to lead our country. Anyone who cannot condemn the hatred, *oppression,* and violence of radical Islam lacks the moral clarity to serve as our President."—Donald Trump, Youngstown (OH), August 15, 2016.

Europe First: Trans-Atlantic Civilization and the Law of Diminishing Returns

March 10ᵗʰ, 2017

Atlanticism is the belief in a single European-American worldview, as expressed in NATO and many trans-Atlantic trade agreements. But the relationship between Europe and America is far from equal. Since the American armies emerged victoriously from the Second World War, Europeans have been living as vassals, serving the interests of American capitalism.

In exchange for NATO protection, a militarily weakened Europe was left with little choice to accept the relationship. But while Americans reap the benefits of globalization, Europeans have been footing the bill, forced to see their continent flooded with African and Arab immigrants. Why? To satisfy American market expansionism.

Is it time for Europeans to break away from NATO in favor of European independence? Taking a look at ancient history, a break-up between America and Europe may indeed be inevitable.

When Julius Caesar and subsequent Roman generals Drusus, Varus, and Germanicus invaded the territories northeast of the river Rhine between 52 BC and 16 AD, the poor Germanic tribes who lived there often abandoned their mud huts, hiding in the woods for safety. Faced with an invincible enemy, the barbarians saw no honor in meaningless death.

According to historian Christoph Pantle, it is plausible that Caesar's armies slaughtered well over a million Northern Europeans—men, women, and children—in horrific massacres along the Rhine. Not even pregnant women were spared. Such bloodshed certainly united the Germanic tribes against Rome for centuries to come.

Unlike the Gauls, a wealthier people who had mastered the art of goldsmithing, Germania offered Roman conquerors little wealth to take home. In order to pay for bloody invasions into Germanic territory, Roman armies had to take male prisoners to work as slave laborers. Countless blonde girls were likely sold into prostitution.

Rome ultimately abandoned the conquest of Northern Europe. It didn't pay. In economic terms, the Romans faced what we now call the law of diminishing returns.

According to Wikipedia,

"The law of diminishing returns states that in all productive processes, adding more of one factor of production, while holding all others constant, will at some point yield lower incremental per-unit returns."

Roman elites' hunger for wealth forced Rome to continuously expand its territories in search of more wealth, but the incremental expansions offered the empire increasingly lower returns. The growing cost of defending Rome's stretching borders forced it to allocate an ever larger portion of its wealth to military defenses.

Once the cost of Rome's defenses outgrew the benefit of its conquests, the Roman Empire became a losing proposition, a losing stock. As economic decline set in, Rome's defenses crumbled and its armies retreated. Over the course of the next few centuries, the very Germanic tribes Rome had sought to submit would overthrow their previously invincible enemy.

The descendants of these West Germanic tribes would go on to establish their own empires, fight the Crusades, battle with the Mongols, usher in the Industrial Age, establish modern civilization and lead the many conquests of colonial Europe.

Today, they are the Germans, Swedes, Dutch, Belgians, Austrians, Swiss, Norwegians, Danes, Faroese, Icelanders, and many English and Scottish people too. Their colonial offspring includes South Africa's Boers, as well as a large portion of white Australians, New Zealanders, Canadians, and Americans.

Together, these peoples have amassed the largest sums of wealth in human history. But like Rome, the West cannot escape the law of diminishing returns either. At some point in time, global trade and technological innovation will cease to yield desired returns.

Then, the West's defenses will crumble (Europe's borders, for example), its economies will shrink, its populations will age—and the new barbarian hordes may succeed at conquering its lands on foot. The West Germanic peoples have become the new Romans.

It would be foolish to think that some measure or action could somehow magically prevent the decline of the West. Such delusions lie at the heart of both the progressive left and New World Order conspirators. Instead, Westerners will have to make tough choices. To Europeans, the question becomes: *What are we willing to sacrifice in exchange for long-term survival?*

Cutting loose from their American owners, Western Europeans would be free to share their wealth with neighboring peoples in Eastern Europe, the Middle East, and Northern Africa, rather than with Starbucks and McDonald's. Ending Atlanticism in favor of European independence could help secure Europe's borders and end economic immigration.

No longer a vassal to American interests, Europe could guard itself against Saudi, Turkish and Russian aggressors more effectively. If Europeans don't embrace their independence, the alternative would mean to join in America's endless wars for profit, undoubtedly sacrificing millions of Europe's strongest men and women.

I see no honor in such meaningless death. It is time for Europe to become a truly independent continent once again. It is time for Europe to cut its ties with America. Indeed, the loss of its European consumer market would most certainly bring about America's downfall, as well as the demise of its Middle

Eastern outpost, Israel. Then again, the age of colonialism ended a long time ago.

Swedish Pride: Moral Superpower or Jealous Neighbor?

August 4ᵗʰ, 2016
The Kungsleden is an over 250-mile long hiking trail through Europe's last wilderness. The trail beings north of the polar circle in the Swedish town of Abisko. There, the trail snakes southward across Swedish Lapland, where herds of reindeer, moose, lynxes, and bears get in each others' way. The hike rewards the wanderer with breathtaking views, desolate valleys, and wild streams of melting snow water that debouch into lakes and rivers. These are the veins that provided for the indigenous Laplanders, the Sami, and their reindeer herds, for thousands of years.

Arriving at Teusajaure, a mountain hut along the trail, positioned at the base of a waterfall pouring into a massive lake, I spoke to a woman who revealed a national taboo. To outsiders, Sweden is known as the open-border country that has welcomed a great number of guest workers, asylum seekers, and refugees. But, as the result of years of economic depression, since the year 2000, large numbers of native Swedes have themselves left for neighboring Norway to find work as economic migrants. Every summer, tens of thousands of Swedish youths cross the border looking for jobs they think will make them "rich like a troll". Many have emigrated permanently. The Norwegian capital of Oslo alone counts over 50,000 Swedish guest workers, over 10% of the city's population.

What happened? In the past fifteen years, an age-old hierarchy suddenly turned around. For centuries, a formerly richer Sweden had been exploiting its Norwegian neighbor as a sort of colony for natural resources. It had been the Norwegians who would come to Sweden looking for jobs. But from 1969 onward, things changed when Norwegians discovered large reserves of oil just off the coast of their country. Today, Norway has become the eighth largest oil exporter in the world. It has brought the population of barely five million inhabitants unprecedented prosperity.

In the pre-oil boom era, Norway was considered to be the poorest country in Europe, essentially a Third World country whose long winters would hold people captive between frozen fjords, cut off from the outside world. In winter, many Norwegians would experience hunger, fearing the real danger of starvation. But thanks to the oil, they now manage a national pension fund worth over $750 billion USD, the largest investment fund on the globe. In cash, every Norwegian citizen can claim a pension bonus worth $150,000 USD.

The Norwegians now wield so much money they don't know what to do with it. And that hurts their neighbors' feelings because, for the past few centuries, Swedes had felt assured of their dominant economic and cultural role in Scandinavia. The regional power Swedes had amassed had become so self-evident that the country didn't even need to wage any more wars to defend its status quo. As a consequence, like Switzerland, Sweden stayed neutral during World War II, allowing for German troops to march to Norway without offering resistance. If the enemy doesn't want us, the Swedes figured, we'll let them take our neighbor.

In absence of undiscovered natural riches of their own, the Swedish economy has fallen behind that of Norway. In only the past fifteen years, Norway's gross national product rose to twice that of Sweden. Because of its strong economic growth, Norway is currently experiencing a labor force shortage that forced them to call upon Swedish replacement workers to supplement it. After all, Swedes are a highly educated people, and their language is very similar.

Conversely, because of their newly discovered wealth, many Norwegians no longer feel like slaving away at jobs they can hire a Swede to do for them instead. The *norvégien riche* prefer to spend time letting off a long-suppressed national pride. They enjoy rubbing it in, too, now that Norway is Scandinavia's richest country. For a change, Swedes must come and do their dirty work. A popular Norwegian clothing brand was called *Anti Sweden*. Popular musicians depict Swedish guest workers as 'effete drunks'. In response, other Norwegian artists produced a documentary explaining that "Swedes are people" too.

(It is interesting that white people of different denominations can freely discriminate against each other without having to fear legal action.)

For their historic arrogance, the now 'second-rate' Swedes have been dealt quite a kick in the crotch. The loss of status hurts but precisely this loss offers an explanation for the excessively 'progressive' politics the country has chosen to pursue. What Swedes could not acquire with black gold, they solved with black people. While Norway was busy drilling for oil riches, Sweden tapped into an endless stream of cheap economic migrants, mostly poor and socially dependent people from Islamic countries. Sweden has found in mass immigration a means to turn its receding economic tide.

That point of view shines a different light on the land of IKEA and meatballs. To the outside world, Swedes have traditionally marketed themselves as a moral superpower. Driven by nothing but Christian altruism, supposedly, Swedes have transformed their country into a global refugee camp, only to accommodate floods of strangers in need of a so-called better life—a life young Swedes can't even find in their own country anymore and are trying to find in Norway. Sweden is bullshit-ting immigrants into doing their slave labor.

Migrants coming to Sweden are being exploited, just as was once the case with the Norwegians. Asylum seekers who fall for the promise of a house, a car, and perhaps a natural blonde wife, will soon find themselves chiseling iron ore in the northern city of Kiruna. At one time, the Swedes enslaved the native Lapland-ers there. Today's slaves are African, Asian, and Middle-Eastern 'refugees'. They provide cheap labor to Sweden's upper castes while the Swedish taxpayer picks up the social tab. Sweden has adopted the American way with privatized profits and social-ized costs.

This Scandinavian microcosm mimics what we can see is happening at a larger scale between Eastern and Western Eu-rope. Like Norway, Western-European countries have enriched themselves by tapping into global markets, cranking up global-ism while Eastern-European, Middle-Eastern, and African mi-grants have been invited to donate their labor to Western indus-tries. For over half a century, the West has been able to enrich itself at the expense of migrant workers who, much like modern slaves, came to do its dirty work. Al over the world the geopo-litical shifts such mass migrations have set in motion appear to join in the same dead end: a stagnating global economy.

Just like Sweden, the US-led West haughtily considers itself the natural cultural, economic and moral center of the world, much to the annoyance of other world civilizations. In reali-ty, Europe and America have long given up on a vision for the world. The Idea of Europe has burnt out and underneath its glossy lipstick, the US doesn't look much better than a failed British colony. When the ancient Greeks invented direct de-mocracy 2,400 years ago, they couldn't have suspected West-ern man would fritter his freedom away in the manner we have done.

Westerners are living in denial, refusing to accept they have passed their cultural peak.

For our survival, we will have to get back to work. Let us be inspired anew by the Spartans' preparedness to fight, by the architects of the Roman Empire, by the Germanic women who cheered for their men behind the lines of battle, by the brave Crusaders, Columbus' travels, NASA's engineers who safely returned dozens of men from their trip to the moon. Let us tear down the present. Let us rethink our values, decide on a new Idea for Europe and come together to build a bridge between our glorious past and a glorious future. In any case, what is self-evident is that we will build that bridge ourselves.

Will the West Wage War on Russia—Again?
Wars for Living Space

March 27th, 2018

> "Largely unknown in the West, the war against communism already began after the Russian Revolution, when Great Britain and the United States sent secret armies against the newly founded Soviet Union, a state in 'baby age'. Between 1918 and 1920, London and Washington chose to support the Russian right and financed ten military interventions against the USSR on Soviet soil."[1]

When Napoleon and Hitler attempted to take Russia, their empires crumbled. Will the United States of America risk all to win nothing?

When French dictator Napoleon Bonaparte began his Russian Campaign, on June 24th, 1812, the Russian army chose to avoid conflict. It retreated and applied a scorched-earth tactic, burning everything behind it. This put a strain on the French army's supplies. For three months, the Russians kept ceding territory until the bloody Battle of Borodino. The French won, barely, and Napoleon marched into a smoldering Moscow, set ablaze by the fleeing Russians.

Then the tables turned. Napoleon waited a whole month for peace, but Russian Tsar Alexander I never offered it. Instead, the Tsar waited patiently for the French *Grande Armée* to run out of steam. His strategy worked. Hunger and cold forced Napoleon to retreat back to Europe. The man who had marched into Russia with over half a million soldiers now returned home with no more than 27,000 men left.

Russia prevailed and France was no longer a superpower.

On June 22nd, 1941, German dictator Adolf Hitler began Operation Barbarossa, the invasion of Russia. It was part of a plan called the *Generalplan Ost* or the "Hunger Plan". Nazi leadership had decided to colonize Poland, Ukraine, and Western Russia. They wanted to starve local Slavs and repopulate their lands with Germanic offspring. A 1985 film by Belorussian director Elem Klimov, *Come and See* (Иди и смотри), captures the atrocities committed to achieving this goal.

The German Wehrmacht army was operationally and technologically superior to the Red Army, but the Russians once again chose to resist their invader in a war of attrition, steadily draining the Germans of supplies and personnel. The German army retaliated by capturing a total of five million Russian POW's, then starving the majority to death. It wasn't 'enough'; when the war finally ended, the Russians had taken Berlin.

Russia prevailed and Germany was no longer a superpower.

After the Second World War, we said *never again,* yet the West's conflict with Russia flared up immediately. A long-dormant Atlantic Empire—the United States and it new Western European vassals—now emerged as a world power to rival the

Soviet Union. From 1947, the Cold War ensued. This time, Western forces had learned from history. They patiently pursued their own war of attrition in order to bring the Soviets to their knees.

Nuclear technology's mutually assured destruction (MAD) prevented the Cold War from heating up. Nevertheless, the Soviet Union, with its vast geography and its control over Eastern European and Central Asian peoples, never managed to win the economic power to defeat the United States. Western Europe's former colonies now fueled American capitalism, notably with oil. So, a consumerist West successfully impoverished the Soviet Union. Unable to compete, communism fell with the Berlin wall in 1989, followed by the collapse of the Society Union in 1991.

However, it was not the end of Russia. Thanks to *glasnost* and *perestroika*, and a modernized nuclear arsenal, Russia prevailed.

Why has the West been so fixated on conquering Russia for at least the last two centuries? If you want to rule the world, if it is your aim to build a global empire that may last for thousands of years, then you must seize control of the Eurasian continent. In other words, you must conquer Russia. In his classic work *The Grand Chessboard*, geopolitical expert Zbigniew Brzezinski argued as much. Former U.S. Secretary of State, Henry Kissinger, spent a lifetime implementing the strategy.

There are other reasons why the West has set its sights on Russia. Over the next twenty years or so, hundreds of millions of Arab and African immigrants are projected to flood Europe. Aging demographics dictate that by the year 2100, there will be fewer than 10 million white Germans left in Germany, a loss of 80% of today's population. By then, Germany will no longer be a democracy, but an Islamic state.

Similarly, by the year 2050, white Americans will have become a minority in the country their European ancestors built.

Here is my prediction: the Russian people will rather nuke its own cities than allow Westerners to take over. Once the fog of war has cleared, Russia will have prevailed and the United States of America will no longer be a superpower.

Endgame: Europe against the World

November 17th, 2015
Europe and the Arab World meet each other in the final phase of two processes that will come together as in a deadly accident. The first process emerges from the economically failed Arab World that produces little to nothing the rest of the world wants to have and that knows little meaningful trade among itself.

Despite that, Islamic populations have grown explosively. For example, while the Dutch population doubled to slightly over 17 million inhabitants (which includes 2 million non-Western immigrants) between 1935 and 2015, the Turkish population quintupled in that same period of time from 15 to 75 million inhabitants. The same explosive growth can be observed in other majority-Islamic nations. Just like everyone else, these people want a meaningful future, one the failed Arab economies cannot possibly offer them.

The other process emerges from the economically successful though rapidly aging Europe. For several decades, European peoples have experienced a stagnating if not declining population. A likely explanation may be that by reducing the number of children per woman, Europeans could increase the amount of inherited wealth per child and, so, stay on top of the global economy. In effect, white families have paid for their alleged economic privilege by lowering their birthrates to below the required replacement rates.

On the other hand, Arabs, other Muslims, and Third Worlders, a population of which two-thirds are younger than thirty years old, know that the wealth they will need to build up a life lies in Europe. If they do not conquer Western wealth, they will not be able to have families of their own, for the very reason that their (irresponsible) parents have had too many children—coaxed into having large families by an Islamic leadership that has been eying Europe's lands for over 1,400 years. Besides, the Syrian 'refugee' crisis showed them and the world that Europe's wealthy Valhalla can be reached on foot.

Meanwhile, European economies have also begun to stagnate as European nations fail to compete with the billions of slave laborers in India, China, and Africa. Dutch politician Rinnooy Kan (of the *Democrats '66 party*), justly spoke of a 'Japanization' of Europe, namely the shrinking of both economy and population but with the difference that Japan is successfully protecting its borders, so far. The globalization that has long driven on Western profits has no reached its natural limits to growth, as the Club of Rome predicted.

We are at the start of an inevitable economic endgame—or perhaps a *Ragnarök*, a mythological battle for survival between the peoples of Earth. That endgame, however, has little to do with a clash of civilizations as Samuel Huntington foresaw, but rather with a clash of populations, a banal ecological struggle for living space as ecologist Paul Colinvaux understood in his book *The Fates of Nations*.

Because the Arab world cannot possibly supply its subjects with a future, Muslims will have to find the required wealth to feed their families elsewhere. They can do so by begging the West for food and luxury—in exchange for oil—or they can wait for the aging Europeans to die off and then take Europe's capitals without even shedding a drop of blood. In case of a lack of patience, our invaders may quicken our dispossession by cutting Europe's senile throats. It's obvious why Islamic leaders are advocating armed holy war, the *Jihad*.

Europeans have a choice: stand by, idly, while invaders murder their sons and gangrape their daughters, or stand up, fight back, and take back control over Europe's future. Our enemies know that wealth, luxury and hedonism have weakened the European fighting spirit to the level of that of an old snail. Within only a decade's time, Rome and Athens may fall to Islam.

Will Europeans find renewed strength to fight for their survival?

Globalism: Europe's Final Battle

May 9ᵗʰ, 2017
Young Macron has won the French elections. The old French voted themselves into the hands of a globalist Rothschild banker posing as a communist. Mainstream media gobbled it up, painting Macron's opponents as cowards. The other guys supposedly voted for right-wing contender Marine Le Pen out of an irrational fear of Islam.

But doesn't the accusation of fear fit the Left better? Didn't Macron's victory stem from a collective fear of terrorist attacks? France has revived the politics of appeasement, which is exactly what the terrorists wanted. An aging cohort of indigenous French over-40-year-olds voted to open their nation's borders to millions of immigrants, whose labor, they hope, will help fund their white pension plans.

That's not an act of progressive bravery. That's a cowardly act of egotism. The greatest danger to Western civilization isn't Islam, but a bunch of old farts voting to preserve their self-interests at the expense of the younger generations. That is the face of European globalism: a doctrine designed to protect the status quo, barring much needed indigenous rejuvenation.

Over in Germany, Chancellor Merkel has announced new partnerships between German and Saudi companies. Saudi Arabia is booming. Hundreds of billions of oil dollars, saved up over the past half-century, need to find a purpose. Saudi leaders have decided to invest in modernity and modern armies. By comparison, Saudi Arabia's high-tech cities make Europe look like the Third World. Most Saudi are Wahhabi fundamentalists. They hate non-Muslims.

Yet mainstream media continue to condemn those who oppose Arab neofascism as "Nazis", while the real new Nazis receive free housing and passports wherever they like to go in Europe. Money rules. Unlike conservatives, who are willing to pay for their principles, progressives trade their values faster than financial traders can short the stock market.

Besides, by the year 2070, nobody will be remembering the Holocaust anymore. There won't be enough indigenous Germans left to care.[2]

Globalists have global plans for Europe. A member of the European Commission, Sweden's Federica Mogherini, recently declared it time for Europe to assume the role of global leader. She wants to demote the United States to second place.

Sure, Europeans will welcome the revival of European might and the demotion of U.S. hegemony—as do I—but they should know that the likes of Mogherini and her globalist co-conspirators have been plotting to submit all of humanity to collectivist rule for at least a century.

In the European Union, globalists see the beginning of a world government that must eventually come to represent all humanity. They think long-term, very long term. For now, Russia remains an obstacle to the EU's eastward expansion but wars in Syria and Iran already serve to separate a failing Russian economy from its revenue streams, forcing it into a likely bankruptcy and then into the European Union, just like Ukraine after the Maidan Revolution.

Political scientist Zbigniew Brzezinski alluded to Europe's hostile takeover of the world in his book *The Grand Chessboard* almost 20 years ago.[3] Indeed, the European Union was never founded to serve and protect Europeans. Similar to the United Nations, the European Union functions as yet another vehicle to attempt to put a small clique of superrich in charge of the whole world.

Like the old Soviet Union, the new global European Union will be of a collectivist nature. The *world state* will be "animated by a common will",[4] directed by a "far-sighted, purposeful elite"[5] and inhabited by a mixed "future Eurasian-Negroid race [that] will replace the diversity of peoples ..."[6]. If it means European women have to be gang-raped to achieve this dystopian nightmare, there's always Wolfgang Schäuble to approve it, the German technocrat who fancies Arabs and Africans will save Germans from inbreeding.[7]

Arguably, 'globalism' is not even an ideology. Globalism has been around in the form of despotism since the beginnings of civilization in ancient Mesopotamia, well over 5,000 years ago. Globalism is just the modern equivalent of an ancient crime, namely to submit a people to collectivist rule under a despotic ruler. Early examples include Gilgamesh of Uruk and King Hammurabi of Babylon.

Today's despots have invented a new vocabulary to fool the people into submission. They call it a 'global open society', a society no one can escape from short of flying to the moon. 'Equality' denies your freedom to be unequal. 'Progress' means your progressive slavery. When globalists speak of 'diversity', they mean the complete homogenization of mankind.

Who are the globalists, really, and what do they believe in? "They" are not some sinister conspiracy. Their work is public and they do not hide their intentions. Pro-globalist intellectuals have been around for a while. Having published a large volume of books detailing their worldview, we can learn from them through their own thoughts.

In the early 1920s, when the city of Paris was booming because of industrialism and cheap labor, philosopher Henri Bergson wrote an influential work titled *The Two Sources of Morality*. In the book, he was the first to coin the phrase *open society*. He envisioned such a society as being represented by a universal open morality. He introduced the false, but powerful dichotomy of open-versus-closed and based his entire worldview on the following false assumption:

> "Who can help *seeing* that social cohesion is largely due to the necessity for a community to protect itself against others and that it is primarily as against all other men that we love men with whom we live."[8]

Bergson was wrong to assume people can only protect themselves "against all others". In reality, all people struggle side by side against the harshness of nature. It is in that mutual struggle that man also incurs casualties of war. However, the solution to the problem of war cannot be found in universalism. It was pluralism that helped mankind survive.

In a pluralist world, man can cooperate with all others against nature, but at the same time, *man does not have to be like all others*. True diversity trumps universalism. By contrast, in a universalist world, bureaucrats rule all and will send those who defy the Truth to the Gulag. Bergson's totalitarian philosophy undoubtedly inspired a great number of 20th-century thinkers and despots.

One thing globalists have in common is their perverse desire to melt all human difference into one. Globalists want to efface, not preserve, all differences between people. In their line of thinking, they follow the principle of 'from many to one' or *E Pluribus Unum*, the slogan so beloved by Americans. It is a globalist's creed, anti-diversity and anti-human.

Philosopher Karl Popper and financial terrorist George Soros expanded on Henri Bergson's ideal for the open society. In Popper's own words, he was "bent on destroying what is in [his] opinion most mischievous in [Plato's] philosophy."[9] Popper made it clear that he wished to destroy the entire Western philosophical tradition since Plato, whom he held responsible for fascism, Nazism, communism, and the Holocaust.

The modern progressive belief that Christianity is bad, that whites are privileged, that Western men are evil patriarchs, or that the world would be better off without people of European descent, found its legitimization with Karl Popper. For lack of a better word, I'd say Popper was a racist.

According to George Soros, the billionaire speculator, the European Union "embodies the principle of open society, which could serve as a force for a global open society."[10] It's a principle Soros helped design himself as a former student of Popper's. Globalist billionaires like Soros are abandoning the United States, which they see a failed experiment because "the most successful open society in the world, the US, does not properly understand the first principles of an open society."[11]

Rule 1. Never question the universal truth of globalism.

Rule 2. Never question rule number 1.

Political scientist Hans Morgenthau wrote the classic *Politics among Nations*, popular among students of geopolitics. In it, Morgenthau advocates the establishment of a world state. This world state, he believes, can be achieved in the same way that the United States of America once succeeded in uniting its many southern and northern states. By using war, deception, and propaganda!

To create a world state, Morgenthau suggests the peoples of Earth must be submitted to a single world public opinion, "The community of the American people antedated the American state, as a world community must antedate a world state."[12] But since America has failed to live up to the 'promise' of an open society, globalists have turned their attention to Europe like flies attracted to a decomposing body.

The list of globalist intellectuals, entrepreneurs, and politicians goes on and on. Even Catholic Pope Francis appears to have turned to the dark side. The Pope wants to fuse Islam with Christianity in order to create a single world religion. Endorsing mass migration to Europe, the Pope apparently supports Schäuble's plan to crossbreed Europeans with Arabs and Africans.

Cologne's NYE rapes were no accident. They were intentional policy and a taste of what's to come.

Facing this powerful enemy, we, Europeans, have no choice but to resist the rape of our continent. We must aggressively put a stop to globalism. We must stand up and fight for a free humanity, free from collectivism and despotism.

It is not too late. Confronted with an insurmountable setback, we can still change our attitudes towards it. This coming half century, Europeans will have an opportunity to transform their traumatic history into a triumph of humanity. We will fight the good fight, the fight for autonomy and identity.

Let us start a global resistance movement. Alongside millions of freedom-loving men and women, we shall face the enemy and meet the challenge. We shall march with a faith in our hearts, a plan in our heads, and if all else fails, with a gun in our hands. We shall defy the globalist enemy as we have defied all enemies before him: with fearless determination.

After the Roman Empire had expanded northward along the Rhine, a small but militarily powerful Germanic tribe from the south of The Netherlands revolted against it. Around 69 AD, the Batavi tribe's one-eyed leader, known by his Roman name Julius Civilis, called for a rebellion,

> "For [the Romans] no longer regard us as allies, as we once were, but as slaves. ... We are handed over to prefects and centurions ... We are threatened with a levy which separates children from parents and brothers from brothers, as if in death. ... Simply lift your eyes and do not fear the empty name of legions. But on our side are our strong infantry and cavalry, our kinsmen the Germans, the Gallic provinces that cherish the same desires as ourselves. Not even the Romans will regard this war with disfavor ..."[13]

Civilis' words still hold true today. The globalists no longer regard us as free citizens, as we once were, but as slaves. Simply lift your eyes and do not fear the empty name of globalism. On our side are our freedom-loving kinsmen, the Americans, the Canadians, the Australians, the New Zealanders, the South Africans, alongside a freedom-loving majority of humanity. They all cherish the same desires as ourselves.

Our battle against globalism is the mythical fight between good and evil. Let us harden our souls to win the fight we cannot afford to lose. In the name of self-determination, let us root out the filthy tentacles of globalism wherever we find them.

The Defense of Europe: If Not Now, When?

February 22ⁿᵈ, 2016

Arabs, guardians of Islam and its one and a half billion support-ers, know that one day their oil will run out. Then their only source of income will disappear because Arab nations don't produce anything else the world needs. But in order to secure Islamic power on the world stage, Arab leaders must go looking for a new source of income.

Europe is willingly offering them that source: an aging, eco-nomically weakened continent that has fallen asleep, inhabited by naive suckers. If now isn't the time to conquer Europe, when is?

The whole world has watched how Europe literally failed to defend the confines of its civilization against the stream of refugees pouring in. It's expected that over tens of millions of migrants are preparing to claim a better life as well. That will be the decline of Europe, the death of its civilization.

Opposite to Europe's naive leadership is the Islamic Trojan Horse: an army of unmarried Arab men of fighting age. They came to Europe posing as refugees, but of the nearly one million that have reached Germany, three quarters disappeared into an-onymity. They are plainclothes enemy soldiers. Still, Europe's corrupt media keep calling all newcomers "refugees".

Among the refugees, there are more than five thousand ISIS terrorists, only waiting for a sign from above to set fire to Eu-rope. Meanwhile, the first Muslim colonists have established their own 'jungle' caliphate in Calais, France. Thousands of ca-liphates will follow, others proclaim. But while European asy-lum centers are flooding with testosterone bombs, police knock down every sane citizen's protest.

The biggest danger, however, is Europe's political leaders. All at once, these 'old thinkers' exclaim that NATO will surely protect Europe. For who would be so crazy to attack a nuclear power? That's a nice idea, but thanks to open borders the enemy has already arrived. Moreover, nuclear arms cannot effectively protect against a guerrilla war in one's own cities, unless one is aiming for kamikaze.

And when Arabs proceed to attack, so the Russians will follow, dreaming of a return to the old Soviet Union, and the Turks, wishing to reinstate the Ottoman Empire. The Turks won't have to march to Europe because thanks to mass migration they're already there. All they have to do is put on their uniforms.

Never before in history have all Europeans fought for their collective survival. But they can draw inspiration from the richest, most heroic history. The Spartans stopped the Persians at the battle of Thermopylae. Arminius united the Northern Europeans against the advancing Roman army.

Godfrey of Bouillon reconquered Jerusalem. Europeans fought the Eastern hordes of Genghis Khan. Vlad the Impaler scared the living daylights out of the Turks. Jan Sobieski defeated them at Vienna. And let's take an example of the Bulgarians. They had to live under the yoke of Islam for five hundred years, but never relinquished their resistance.

Europeans must leave the failed multicultural utopia behind them and found a new Holy Europe. The time of self-hatred and self-loathing is over. Europeans will reconquer their future. Deo volente—God willing.

6

Economics of Decline

"Are capitalism and communism not both in the process of converging into a neo-feudalism, led and manipulated by big, powerful bureaucracies in which the individual loses his humanity?"

—Erich Fromm

When at sea, the naked eye cannot observe what great oceanic undercurrents move at great depths underneath. At surface level, we perceive a freedom to sail in any direction the winds take us, but the undercurrents we see cannot influence the direction of the wind.

Similarly, the human society operates on many levels, of which the naked eye can only observe most trivial matters. Why has the West embraced the emancipation of women? At first glance, merely touching the surface of the matter, we awaken to the progressive insight that women are equal and that their equality, therefore, warrants their emancipation. As far as the West is concerned, in hardly half a century, the women's movement successfully promoted their education, and less successfully their employment, but we will come to that.

Digging slightly deeper, we discover that the aging demographics of the West embraced women's employment for economic reasons of growth, global competition, and home-market expansion, but this truth is not even remotely interesting in comparison to the deepest and widest of undercurrents, the one most neglected by public conscience.

Ultimately, at the core of the matter, while the Western peoples—from America to Europe, South Africa, and Australia—find themselves in a state of collective denial and self-delusion, the educated Western women inevitably will take command of the societies they gave birth to. Not out of wanting or desire, not out of a demand to repay their oppressed history, but to free the men to go to war.

Yes, war. While some failing civilizations go out with a whimper, the West's historic aggression demands it go out with a bang. With women keeping the machinery at home running, sooner than later, Western men who have nothing left to live for will learn their destiny. Political correctness may obscure and deny this inevitable fate, perhaps because we unconsciously know that deluding ourselves is the best way to trick the enemy, but at the heart of the Western family, like everyone else, we will demand our survival—and we own the wealth to claim it.

Global Kleptocracy: The 'Progress' Globalists Speak about Means the One That Fills Their Pockets

March 19ᵗʰ, 2018

Thieving kleptocrats backing globalist and nationalist regimes both aim to exploit the common people. Globalists are just better at it. We must topple these criminal regimes, especially those in the West. Not to establish a global open society, but to return peoples of European descent to traditional values of God, family, and kin.

One can hardly read a Western European newspaper nowadays—Spain's *El Pais*, France's *Le Monde*, Germany's *Süddeut-*

sche Zeitung, and so on—without feeling disenfranchised by its journalists' incessant spouting of anti-Eastern propaganda. Russia and its (former) satellite states have refused to embrace the suicidal doctrines of multiculturalism, open borders, and mass immigration, even those embedded within the European Union, such as Hungary and Poland. For this failure, these nations and their innocent peoples must be berated, bullied nonstop, pressured and punished if not outright invaded by millions of African and Arab migrants.

The Western "regime media", as I called them, have united in their globalist attack on the nationalist East. Supposedly, gangs of thieves are running Eastern Nations. They are kleptocracies such as Macedonia, Hungary, and Russia. Indeed, perhaps they are. But are Western nations truly any better? No! The Netherlands, for example, my homeland and a self-proclaimed beacon of progressive politics, has long fallen to globalist kleptocrats who rob the people blind. Backed by EU bureaucrats, the owners of *The Netherlands Inc.* have reduced the Dutch people to "cash cows" in the parlance of a product lifecycle.

Multinational corporations such as Unilever, Shell, and Philips are effectively running The Netherlands, having planted one of their own—Mark Rutte, a brainless, soulless former Unilever bureaucrat—as the nation's Prime Minister. At best, Rutte is a serf of international capital. This man has a greater concern for Coca Cola's stock price than for the survival of the Dutch people. Nations and their peoples, apparently, have become expendable assets.

Even the socialist leaders of The Netherlands play foul. Either they come from a multinational background, such as the former leader of the Worker's Party, Wouter Bos, a former Shell manager. When they leave politics, they traditionally join the Boards of Commissioners, for example for KLM/Air France, Shell, the Dutch Central Bank or some other prestigious institute. Only a fool would believe social democrats give a damn about human beings.

The Netherlands is not and never has been a true democracy. Modern democracy, the kind exported to Europe and the rest of the world by the United States of America, appears to have been the greatest scam in the history of humankind. This brand of democracy served U.S. kleptocrats well. It let them plant their own candidates in foreign regimes, just as Unilever planted its candidate in The Hague. If you ever wondered why so many Russian opposition candidates have been assassinated in recent decades, it's because the Russians damn well knew these candidates were on the globalist cabal's payroll.

Western peoples exist to be milked and taxed until a new, more profitable people comes along to replace them. The true purpose of multiculturalism was always to erase native families and replace them with higher-grossing immigrants, who still need to buy all the wealth Westerners have grown tired of. Call it genocide, if you will, but I don't think that word is big enough to cover the extent of the crime being committed before our eyes. Deprecated, written off, the globalist cabal will happily dispose of all those who fail to hit their targets.

More recently, though, the tide has started to turn. China's Xi Jinping declared himself "president for life". Western media can't be too harsh on China because they know how much Western economies have to rely on Chinese labor (and Arab oil). I would have said "China has a new emperor," but I'm just a lone voice crying in the wilderness. Nevertheless, Xi's move proves the world has had enough of American dictates. The prestige that U.S. democracy once exerted, the kind U.S. kleptocrats used to hide behind, has worn off.

Increasingly, the ugly faces pulling the strings have emerged from behind the smoke screens. That's Donald Trump's legacy. A media showman, he gamed the system and checkmated the cabal. Swiss research group proved much of Western media is controlled by a very small group of hardly 5,000 members, namely the Council on Foreign Relations (CFR), who make up a large share of the owners and directors of the U.S. media empire. Before Trump, members or family members of the CFR had been elected U.S. President for twenty years. Democratic rotation loses its meaning when every new President is loyal to the same doctrine.

This means U.S. Empire as a whole is losing its grip on the world. That also means its owner will respond in increasingly panicked ways. When former Russian double agent Skripal and his daughter were allegedly poisoned, Western media united in their condemnation of Russia. More likely, the British poisoned him themselves, or staged the entire event, in order to have something to fight Russia with. Russia has no incentive to cause further conflict with the West because it knows it will either lose a Third World War or suffer extreme consequences, such as the extermination of half its people and its subjugation to U.S. kleptocracy like Western Europe after the Second World War.

That doesn't mean Europe should kiss Russia's ass, either. Come to think of it, if Russia and Germany would team up, and I'm not saying they should, together they could cleanse all of Europe of its ethnic immigrant populations and establish an empire so vast and powerful it would rule the world for many thousands of years. At the same time, that would leave the Anglo, the Atlantic world divided up by the United Kingdom and the United States, destitute. If the balance of power were to shift away from the Washington-London axis towards a Berlin-Moscow axis, North America would soon belong to the Third World.

All nationalist regimes are kleptocratic, but all globalist regimes are kleptocratic, too. Progressive liberalism is not the answer, it is part of the problem. To truly free ourselves from the thieves that govern us, we must return to the traditional values of a personal God (not the Church), a self-sustaining, autonomous family and the love for our kin. Only autarkic, autonomous societies can provide an answer to the evils of global capitalism disguised as "progress".

Globalized Brain Drain: By Centralizing Human Capital in the Hands of Globalists, Mass Migration Contributes to Worldwide Inequality

December 22nd, 2016

We all worry about our financial inequality relative to our peers, but do we understand its causes? Since the Second World War, modern mass migration has relocated millions of skilled individuals. But migration does not necessarily distribute skilled people evenly across the globe. In fact, it achieves the opposite. By centralizing both the world's most educable minds and its lowest cost laborers into the hands of Western globalists, multinational corporations have greatly benefited from globalism. At the same time, globalism has eroded the world's middle classes, directly contributing to worldwide inequality. To reverse it, middle classes have to step up and reclaim their economic freedoms.

Not only has globalism centralized ever more financial capital in the hands of ever fewer people, it has also drained the non-Western world of its most talented people. For decades, talented students, skilled workers and those looking for a 'better life' have often migrated from the Third World to the West, mostly to America and Western Europe. As a result, the division of global talent has become more unequal than ever before. The Third World that had always been an economic backwater has lost any and all means to do something about it. Globalism has condemned a large part of the world to eternal dependence on Western aid—colonialism by proxy.

Europe and America, on the other hand, have been able to pick and choose, selectively exploiting the global supply of brain and muscle. In exchange for the promise of a mythical better life, workers and students have sold themselves and their home nation's future into serfdom. Chinese elites study at Harvard, not Beijing. Indian technologists work for Silicon Valley, not Mumbai. Top scientists work in Germany and France, not Africa. The global brain drain has divided the world into a small but prosperous West, and a large but poor East. Mass migration has thus caused a practically irreversible state of global inequality.

Since financial capital crosses borders more easily than people can in order to escape a home nation's tax regime, national citizens increasingly carry the burden of corporate tax evasion. Globalism has disconnected multinational firms from the economic restrictions imposed on them by nation states. If nations wish to attract businesses and keep jobs within their borders, national governments must appease corporate money men. If nations would hit multinational corporations with tough tax laws, most corporations would simply move its local branch elsewhere. Multinationals have the economic power to settle for the least 'oppressive' tax regime available to them.

Struggling to tax international capital, national governments have had to cut back on investments in national infrastructure, social security or healthcare. Because of this, national governments have increasingly come to rely on a growing class of immigrants to do the jobs its middle classes can no longer afford to do. It may be called privatization, but it's really a race to the bottom. It isn't a problem of lazy white people either, but rather a problem of jobs that no longer earn enough pay to afford middle-class citizens a mortgage and their children's advanced education. It has become too expensive to be middle class. Large numbers of Western citizens increasingly struggle and fail to compete with immigrants, fueling the rise of populism.

Continuing along globalism's path, eroding the world's middle classes both in the West (by undercutting it) and elsewhere (by migrating it away), the world is headed for globalized communism. That's what politicians really mean when they speak of a New World Order. The new order divides people roughly into three social castes: a globalist owner caste, an educated managerial caste, and a bottom-feeding caste consisting of migrants and serfs. Members of the owner caste fully control the global economy and can establish birth-right dynasties to separate themselves from the peasants. Since a healthy middle class would be its biggest threat to its power, the globalist caste has an incentive in destroying it further, leaving nothing but a planetary lower class.

Dreams of democracy may soon be all that remains of the middle class's ideals. Instead, the declining nation states will be forced to dissolve into a borderless gray mass, giving way to a world government ruled by a handful of extremely powerful families. Modern mass migration has directly contributed to the creation of this steep economic hierarchy. Mass migration from sources to sinks of human capital has moved skilled and intelligent people from East to West and from South to North. Rather than being a solution to inequality, mass migration has thus caused the very global inequality globalists say they aim to cure.

To avert this nightmare, and to reverse the global trend of economic centralization, the world's middle classes have few options left. Ultimately, they may have to revolt against the owner caste and claim their rightful dues. If successful, a revolt of the middle classes would shift the balance of power back into their hands. However, in absence of such a revolution, middle-class citizens may still be able to take back their lives one step at a time. By consciously spending less of their hard-earned cash on consumerist items they don't really need, they could convert their cold cash into more meaningful experiences and a revival of tradition.

In conclusion, wherever migration from sources of human capital to human sinks leads to inequality, mass migration leads to mass inequality. The globalism that drives mass migration pushes wealth up and people down. To solve this, middle classes must turn their backs on multinational corporations, by either refusing to work for them or by refusing to buy from them. The creative and productive output of our brains and muscles belongs to ourselves, not to our self-appointed globalist shepherds.

Open Borders for Capitalism: Why Multinational Corporations Aim to Deconstruct National Government

May 14ᵗʰ, 2016

For centuries, national governments, or nation-states, have pursued a business model of taxing their citizens' productivity in exchange for the oft false promise of old age and security. Traditionally, such rent-seeking schemes benefit an inner circle of ruling families and their wealthy lifestyles, the nobility, and royalty. But today, nation-states and their ruling elites find themselves in direct competition with multinational (and transnational) corporations. In order to increase profits, powerful multinationals not only seek to evade taxation from national governments but also aim to expand their 'market share' by taxing and governing citizens themselves.

Multinationals want to govern their own affairs. With over-reaching transnational 'partnerships' such as TPP and

TTIP in place, we are witnessing the advent of a global neo-feu-dalism that will trap the lives of the 99%.

Some multinationals already wield the necessary financial power to compete with smaller nations. For example, Samsung Electronics spent about $14 billion on advertising and marketing in 2013 — more than Iceland's gross domestic product (GDP). Yet to their frustration, national and international laws still bind global firms to local taxation. Thus, if a collective of powerful multinationals acted together in a successful push to deconstruct national government, and in the process create a so-called borderless world, such corporations could effectively replace the nation-state with a privately-owned corporate-state.

Note that while some political activists adopted the phrase "borderless world" to promote their idea of global citizenship, multinational firms merely embrace it as a first step towards submitting ordinary citizens to their rule. Multinationals aim to ensnare such citizens, robbed of their national identities, in commercial rent-seeking schemes provided by them. For example, your security, healthcare, pension plan and even your children's education might one day come at a monthly subscription from the Republic of Wal-Mart.

This dystopian view of the near future will take some time to accustom to. But the idea of a political state owned by a commercial enterprise isn't new. Founded in the year 1602, the Dutch East India Company quickly rose to power as the world's first multinational firm, and also the first to be publicly traded on the first stock exchange. According to Wikipedia, "The [East India Company] was a powerful company, possessing quasi-governmental powers, including the ability to wage war, imprison and execute convicts, negotiate treaties, strike its own coins, and establish colonies."

The East India Company was its own economy, while its private shareholders crowned themselves king. Today, we can observe a similar tug of war between ambitious multinationals and their traditional home-states. For example, in 2014, ING Bank co-authored a piece of Dutch legislation that awarded banks a fiscal benefit when issuing risky bonds. Samsung's 2012 revenue equaled 17% of South Korea's GDP, affording it a degree of 'involvement' in its home nation's politics. That year, Royal Dutch Shell raised over $555 billion in revenue, matching over 84% of Dutch GDP. And what about Super PACs taking money from billionaires to influence US presidential elections?

While one cannot compare national GDP with corporate revenue, it is evident that some of today's multinationals can afford to maintain real armies, directing them to invade and usurp lesser nations. Would it really surprise anyone if a coalition of US oil companies and weapons manufacturers had pushed for the war in Iraq? Let us forever be done with nationalist naivety: there is now a market for peoples and nations. And among their prospective buyers, we find such names as Shell, Samsung, BP, Glencore, Nestlé, Volkswagen, and others.

A key development driving the transition from public states to privately-owned corporate-states has been the historically recent rise of mega-cities. With over half of the world's populations living in cities —in Europe nearly three-quarters— national governments have largely driven their political responsibilities in the hands of commercial enterprise. The privatization of housing, sanitation, transportation and even prisons and pensions has shifted the center of political gravity away from political representation to multinational bureaucracy.

But what was the purpose of establishing democracies only to sell them off to the highest bidder? How can we reverse this neo-feudal trend? Can individual men and women escape modern slavery? The answer may lie in a simple insight formulated by late social philosopher Erich Fromm, who proposed a humanistic socialism that puts human needs before anything else.

In an essay bundle titled On Disobedience (1984), he reasons, "At this point in history the capacity to doubt, to criticize and to disobey may be all that stands between a future for mankind and the end of civilization."

Fromm concludes:

"A person can become free through acts of disobedience by learning to say no to power. ... In order to disobey, one must have the courage to be alone, to err and to sin. But courage is not enough. The capacity for courage depends on a person's state of development. Only if a person has emerged from mother's lap and father's commands, only if he has emerged as a fully developed individual and thus has acquired the capacity to think and feel for himself, only then can he have the courage to say "no" to power, and disobey."

The greatest threat to a collective is a single individual demanding freedom. Just say "no".

The Imploding G7: If the European Union Was a Business, Its Investors Would Put It up for Sale

April 12th, 2017

Comparing each state's relative share of the global economy, or its 'market share' as measured by its gross domestic product (GDP), I noticed four of the G7 states have been steadily losing their share since at least 1900. They are the four largest European economies of Germany, France, Italy and the United Kingdom. Much unlike the US, Canada, and Japan.

How will Europe's decline affect the world?

Graph 1. German share of the global economy (1900-2008), including both East and West Germany. (Notice that volatility flat-lined since 1950—evidence of a communist plan economy?)

Since 1900, Germany has lost around two-thirds of its share of the global economy, down from nearly 12% at its peak to below 4% today.

Hitler's Third Reich briefly restored German power, but only because of its expansionist economy that robbed neighboring countries. In the subsequent decade, Germans would pay for their hubris with economic demise. Despite having rebuilt their economy during the 1950s, the German economy is no more powerful today than it was immediately after Hitler's defeat in 1945.

German economic influence in the world isn't just waning, it's dying. One doesn't need to wonder why Germany decided to open its borders to millions of cheap labor immigrants. Not just to prove how progressive they have become, but because native German workers so accustomed to richer lifestyles cannot compete with Chinese and Indian wages.

Third World immigrants to the West can easily underbid their hosts. Not, as Indian supremacist, Fareed Zakaria, would like us to believe[1] because Indian immigrants supposedly are more productive, but because immigrants can undercut Western salaries by accepting poorer lifestyles. Although immigrants are *less productive* than native Westerners, they are willing to do the same work for far less money.

Globally, the threat of a Chinese-Indian miracle forces further mass immigration to the West: the only people still able to underbid Asian and Indian wages are Africans (from Africa). Unsurprisingly, Italian President of the European Parliament, Antonio Tajani, recently told German newspaper *Die Welt* that Europe will have to absorb 30 million black Africans over the next decade. They will supply factories and assembly lines with fresh workers.

Note that progressive ideology has played no role whatsoever in the decision to open Europe's borders. Economics comes before political fantasy, although the multicultural worldview conveniently serves to keep native Europeans in a passive state of denial, as their lives are gradually being supplanted by foreign populations.

Children of rich white parents will never be able to compete with Third World immigrants.

Graph 2. French share of the economy (1900-2008).

Like Germany, France has also lost over half of its global economic influence since 1900. The Second World War briefly hurt the French economy from 1939 to 1945 during its Nazi occupation, but unlike Germans, the French were then able to rebuild their economy rather quickly.

France, too, has joined the race to the bottom and opened its borders to mass immigration. In need of low-wage labor in order to remain economically competitive, France already houses Europe's largest North African, Central African and Muslim populations. Immigrants are the only people willing to work below livable French wages.

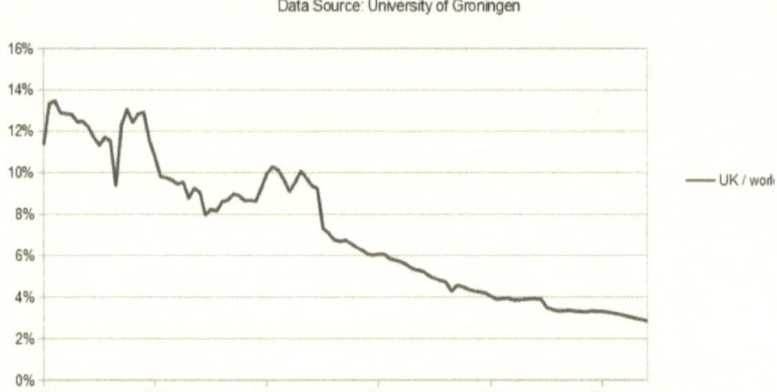

Graph 3. The British share of the global economy (1900-2008).

In 1900, the British economy was as powerful as that of Germany (12% of the global economy), despite having had a smaller population at the time. British citizens were more productive, perhaps thanks to resources it could obtain from its colonial empire.

Not having been occupied by Nazi forces, the British economy appears to have benefited from war efforts. Nonetheless, the British economy as a whole has kept on sliding into forgetfulness since. Today, the British economy represents a measly 3% of the global economy, even less than that of Germany (4%). Perhaps #Brexit will help Britain regain some of its lost pride.

Having lost nearly 75% of its global power since 1900, British economic power is clearly dying.

Graph 4. Italian share of the global economy (1900-2008).

Unlike Germany, the formerly fascist state of Italy hardly suffered from its military defeat after World War II. Italy recovered within several years and was even able to maintain a relatively stable share of the global economy since until decline finally set in around 1980.

Why are European G7-economies failing to maintain their global relevance? Aging demographics and a subsequent shortage of native laborers explain why politicians must invite Third World immigrants to come and apply for jobs, but it doesn't explain why Europe's economies had already begun to decline *before* the advent of mass immigration and even *before* the Second World War.

We must conclude that immigrants haven't caused Europe's economic decline. Immigrants have likely postponed Europe's impending collapse, but that doesn't mean they've prevented it indefinitely. If the process of mass immigration continues, Europe's economies eventually won't be run by Europeans, but by Arabs, Asians, and Africans. In the very long term, Europeans are facing both their economic and biological extinction.

What, then, should European peoples do differently in order to turn the tide and defend a future for native progeny? If Europeans continue to cling to their wealth, preferring luxury cars over children, they will never be able to underbid Chinese and Indian wages. Western addiction to wealth has certainly condemned Europeans. (Evolution obviously does not favor the rich.)

If, on the other hand, Europeans were to forgo luxury goods and divert their wealth to raising family sizes, aside from rendering itself less attractive to immigrants, their slightly rising numbers would still not be enough to compete with four to six billion Asians, nor with a projected two to four billion Africans before the end of this century. Europeans, it seems, stand to lose no matter what they do.

There is, of course, one unspoken approach to this European dilemma that may yield a solution. According to ecologist Paul Colinvaux, author of *The Fates of Nations*, richer nations always resort to war against poorer nations whose continuously rising populations pose an economic threat.

He writes, "Aggressive war is caused by the continued growth of population in a relatively rich society." In our time, that rich society is the globalized world, and the growing Third World populations certainly threaten to crush the richer West. If Colinvaux's historical analysis proves correct, we're in for a show.

World War's Winners and Losers: Participants' Economic Gains and Losses in Terms of Gross Domestic Product

April 13th, 2017
Who won the First and the Second World Wars? History says German lost both, and the United States of America won both.

Economic data supports the historical record. Comparing participants by their share of global GDP, or gross domestic product, I've identified which countries benefited most from either world war.

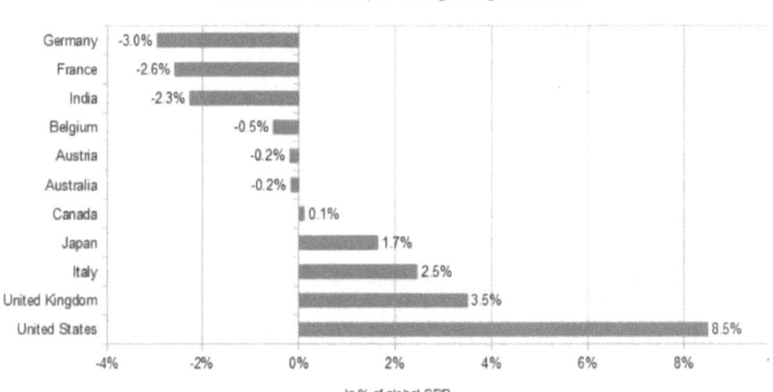

Graph 1. Gains and Losses in Global GDP Share for World War I (1914-1918).

How to read the graph: the graph shows the *absolute* gain/loss in global GDP share, which is itself a %. For example, Germany lost 3% of its absolute global GDP share, namely down from 11% to 8%. Relatively speaking, that would have meant a loss of 28% (3%/11%) of its gross domestic power relative to the world.

Germany (-3%), France (-2.6%) and India (-2.3%) appear to have been the biggest economic losers of the First World War, although India's GDP had already been in decline naturally and did not seem to have been impacted by the war.

The economic winners of the First World War were Japan (+1.7%), Italy (+2.5%), United Kingdom (+3.5%) and the United States (+8.5%). At the time of the war, they were Entente Powers that opposed Germany. France lost despite being an ally.

See here for a list of World War I participants. In the graph above, I only included those with significant gains and losses.

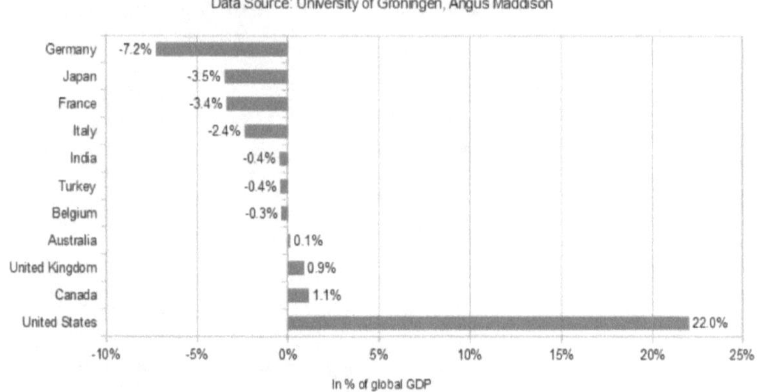

Graph 2. Gains and Losses in Global GDP Share for World War II (1939-1945).

After World War II, the United States (+22%) emerged as the sole victor. Its main ally, the United Kingdom (+0.9%) under Winston Churchill, only gained a small piece of the global economy. The war's losers count Fascist Italy (-2.4%), Imperial Japan (-3.5%) and Third Reich Germany (-7.2%). As during the First World War, allied France incurred a loss, of -3.4%.

It is important to note that the aforementioned gains and losses quickly disappeared again after the war was over when the global economic balances reverted back to their respective trend lines. France recovered shortly after the war, as did Germany during the 1950s.

War can be profitable, but only if you win by remaining relatively unharmed. The United Kingdom was heavily bombed during WWII, but America was not. Countries occupied by

Axis powers, such as France, generally lose economically, since the aggressor plunders their economies.

Both world wars funded the rise of the U.S. Military-Industrial-Complex that would police the world for decades to come. The incredible economic benefits to be gained from winning world wars *make it a very attractive proposition* to try and challenge world order.

On a disturbing note, I don't think the potential of nuclear war will deter challengers. It's expensive to feed billions of people. Military strategists will likely be willing to sacrifice the urban lower classes in order to divert resources to military victories. The belief in lasting peace is grounded in denialism.

Capital, Labor, and Reproduction:
Why Socialist Technocrats Must Ignore the Real World

May 21ˢᵗ, 2018

I finally got around reading Thomas Piketty's 2013 *Capital in the Twenty-First Century,* in the original French edition, a 700-page tome. With just three remarks I can dismiss the entire work as a useless exercise in ignorance.

First of all, Piketty centers his work on (financial) inequality but fails to provide a definition of what inequality is, why it matters, and why (and to whom) it would be beneficial to make the world more equal. He assumes this rationale as a given, i.e. as religious doctrine. He never explores the possibility that, depending on circumstances, an unequal system sometimes yields greater benefits than an equal one. For example, during the Second World War, the majority of casualties were young men. As a result, both post-war Russia and post-war Germany suffered a population surplus of millions of women. This allowed both nations to replenish their populations, following the principle that 100 women and 10 men can produce 100 pregnancies, whereas 100 men and 10 women can only produce 10 pregnancies. In times of war, therefore, leaders ought to prefer male soldiers over (fertile) female ones if they wish to preserve their people after a defeat. It doesn't even matter whether women are equally or more competent soldiers. What matters is that surviving men can't give birth to children. (Present-day 'progressive' regimes seem to prefer their people's extinction by sending more females to war.)

Secondly, Piketty defines capital as that which excludes human capital. He argues that human capital can't be traded on a market, can't be valued properly etc. But isn't it convenient to discount human capital *ex-ante*? By ignoring human capital in his equations, the professor can ignore the real-world source of inequality: innate and learned inequalities between individual capabilities. By ignoring this human factor, socialist economists can conveniently ignore insights offered by biology and ecology. The sheer fact that human beings are not equal provides such a nightmarish scenario to the technocrats that they must uphold a self-imposed mind-blindness to ignore reality.

Thirdly, Piketty explores the Marxist theme of capital and labor, while, once again, ignoring an important biological component. No study of capital and labor can provide a complete picture of reality without factoring in female reproductive rates. Studies should not focus on the capital-labor dichotomy but on the capital-labor-reproduction trichotomy. For example, women in Central Africa may be very poor today but they produce, on average, five to six children per woman *before* age thirty. European women produce hardly two children *after* age thirty. The wealth of Western families may thus be explained by concentrating a larger share of inheritances among a smaller number of offspring. This is the wealth-first strategy. African women pursue an offspring-first strategy. As a result, potential inheritances are rapidly diluted within just several generations' time.

In conclusion, by solely focusing on the strictly rationalistic and measurable part of the world of economics and finance, further ignoring truths and insights provided by biology and ecology, Piketty's book becomes a useless exercise in ignorance. His book is one written by a technocrat written for a technocrat audience. It serves no purpose to people looking for a greater understanding of the world.

Piketty never asks *cui bono*—who benefits from equality? So, let me answer it with an analogy. In Finland, decades ago, the forestry department decided to plant new forests. Unlike in a wild forest, where stronger trees outcompete weaker trees, the foresters planted new trees in equal measures from one another to give each tree equal access to soil and sunlight. As a result, the thickness of each tree was indeed more equal but the wood from these trees was also considerably weaker than the wood from wild forests, where only strong trees could win the competition for resources. Still, the experiment was a success: the local sawmills greatly profited from sawing the more equally-shaped trees into planks!

In other words, if your government is trying to make you more equal to your neighbor, it's because it will make it easier for governments to control you both.

The Changing Face of the U.S. Economy: This Graph Shows What Open Borders Are Doing to America

April 5ᵗʰ, 2017

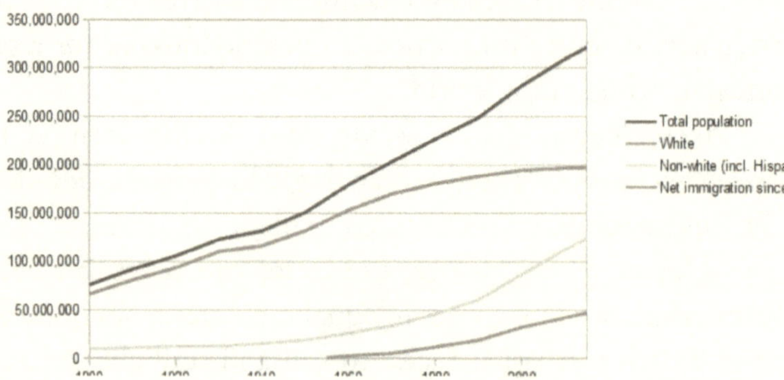

Graph 1. U.S. Population: Whites vs. Non.Whites (1900-2015)

The blue line in the graph above shows how the total U.S. population has developed since 1900. The red line represents white people's share of the population (not counting Hispanics). The graph shows that America been a white Christian nation for a long time, at least up until 1960, when U.S. demographics suddenly began to change.

Since 1980, the aging white demographic has been stagnating, while its non-white population, represented by the yellow line, has grown exponentially. As the green line shows, though, much of non-white growth didn't come from non-white births, but from open borders. In only half a century's time, nearly 50 million immigrants entered the country.

It's true that the United States has always been an "immigrant nation", but up until the Second World War, those immigrants had been mostly white, Christian and European. For centuries, no more than 10% of the U.S. population had been non-white. Today, non-whites make up almost 40% of the total population: they come from Latin America, Asia, India and the Arab World.

So what happened? What happened was the passage of Ted Kennedy's *Immigration and Nationality Act* of 1965. As Breitbart explains:

"The passage of the act marked a fundamental change in America's immigration policy: Rather than serving the interests of Americans and national unity by setting limits on immigration, the act *put* 'family unification' as the top priority, serving the interests of foreigners first."

Rather than investing in the white middle class, corporate lobbyists realized they could pay non-white immigrants far lower wages. Hijacked by corporations, the U.S. government began putting private profits before making long-term investments in its own people.

U.S. Share of World GDP (1900-2008)

Data Source: University of Groningen

Graph 2. U.S. Share of World GDP (1900-2008)

But did open borders affect the economy as a whole? The graph above shows America's share of the global economy as measured by its *gross domestic product*. Rising from 20% to 30% during the roaring 1920s, the Great Depression hit the U.S. hard before rewarding the U.S. economy for its liberation of Europe from the Nazis.

In 1945, American economic activity briefly represented 45% of the world's economy—American exceptionalism at work.

The American economy has since steadily lost a third of its share of the global economy. By 2015, the U.S. share had dropped from 30% back down to 20%, the same level as in 1900. Here's an important lesson to be learned: *opening the borders to low-wage, non-white immigrants failed to strengthen the economy*.

It would be inaccurate to put the blame for America's relative economic decline on immigrants. In fact, the decline came from within:

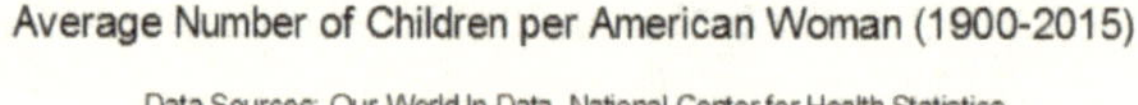

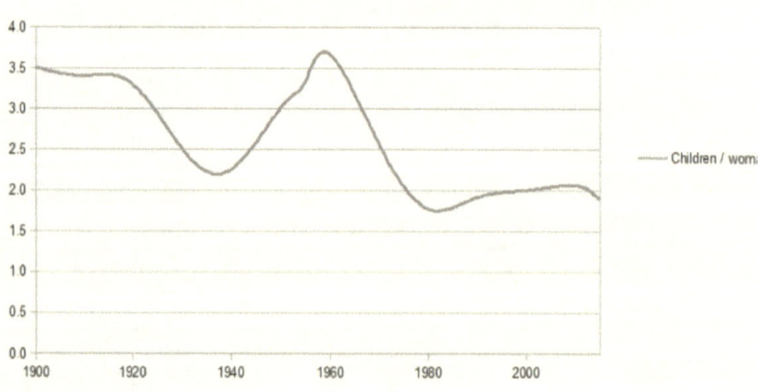

Graph 3. Average Number of Children per American Woman (1900-2015)

This graph shows the development of American fertility over time for both white and non-white women combined. From 1800 to 1900, the American family size had already dropped from 7 to 3.5 children per woman. During the 20th century, U.S. fertility further dropped to below two children per woman.

American fertility briefly boomed during the 1960s, the reward for having emerged victoriously from the Second World War. This was the *baby-boom generation.* Demographically speaking, baby boomers are the great white whale that helped elect Donald Trump into office.

Nonetheless, if white fertility does not increase, and borders remain open to non-white immigrants, then perhaps Americans ought to listen to this century-old warning:

> "Thus, white men, of whatever country and however far removed from personal contact with colored competitors, must realize that the question of colored immigration vitally concerns every white man, woman, and child; because nowhere, absolutely nowhere, can white labor compete on equal terms with colored immigrant labor. The grim truth is that there are enough hard-working colored men to swamp the whole white world."[2]

If Americans of European descent don't treat the U.S. economy as their sole responsibility, the United States may already be headed towards becoming a gigantic new South Africa, an economic junkyard condemning whites to a fringe minority in the country their ancestors built.

If that's what Americans want, they might want to google what *necklacing* means.

The West versus the Rest:
Diminishing Western Power as an Incentive for War?

March 21ˢᵗ, 2017

How do civilizations compare economically? Dividing up the world into roughly nine civilizations,[3] we can sum their member nations' *gross domestic product* (GDP). This allows us to track a civilization's share of the global economy over time.

Economists have long questioned the use of GDP as a financial measure, but in this study, I only look at relative differences. I define economic power as a relative advantage that one party holds over others.

The nine civilizations used for this study include: *Western* (Western Europe, Northern America and Australia), *Sinic* (China and its satellites), *Orthodox* (Russia, former Soviet states and Greece), *Latin American*, *Japanese*, *Islamic* (including the Arab World, Turkey, Northern Africa, the islands of Oceania and Iran), *Hindu* (India), *Buddhist* (southeast Asia and Mongolia) and *African* (below the Sahara).

Figure 1. Germany's GDP between 1900 and 2000.

Before clashing into civilizations, have a look at the above graph. It shows the development of Germany's share of global GDP during the 20th century. German economic power, relative to the world, has been in decline for at least a century, dropping from around 12% of global GDP in 1900 to 4% in 2000. As we will see later, this decline also applies to the West as a whole.

The diminishing share of global GDP did not mean Germany was becoming poorer. The global economy was still growing and German wealth per capita increased throughout the 20th century. But Germany's share of the global economy kept sliding down, eventually losing almost 75% of its economic power in only a single century's time.

The graph also tells us that from the day Hitler became Chancellor, in January 1933, the Nazi economy immediately began seizing a larger share of global GDP, fueled in large part by aggressively occupying and colonizing neighboring lands (Austria, Poland, etc.). German expansionism came to a halt by 1939 when allied forces started to fight back.

In the final year of the Second World War, the German economy collapsed, losing 75% of its share of global GDP in a single year. But during the 1950s, Germans managed to rebuild their economy. In a single decade's time, the *Wirtschaftswunder*, or the German miracle, successfully healed the damage done by the collapse of the Third Reich.

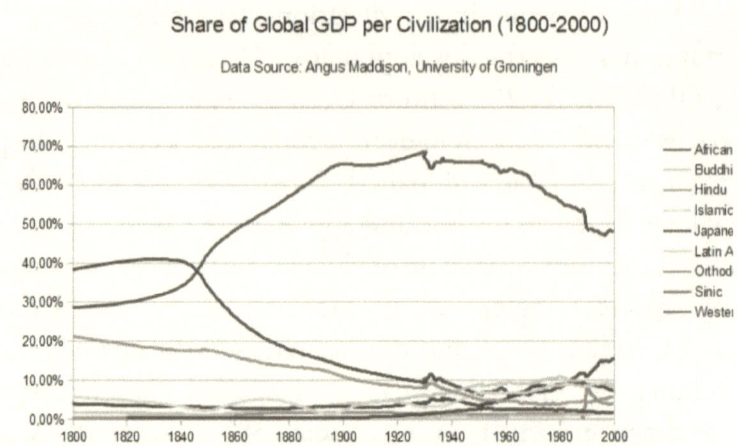

Figure 2. The share of GDP per Civilization (1800-2000).

Professor Angus Maddison has gathered historic GDP values for the University of Groningen.[4] In the graph above, I have plotted these values for each of Samuel Huntington's nine civilizations for the time frame 1800-2000.

The purpose of this graph is to show the sudden rise and fall of Western economic supremacy. For the first time in history, the industrial revolutions that began in Great Britain put the West firmly in charge of the global economy. Before that, the Silk Road civilizations of East Asia (China and India) had dominated human economic activity for thousands of years.

By disrupting the old order, the West condemned the rest of the world to an economic backwater, but the age of Western supremacy arguably lasted only about 150 years, from 1850 to 2000. Immediately after the Second World War, the West began losing its comparative advantage again. That's because technology and knowledge transfer from the West to the Rest democratized industrial wealth.

As a result, the West's relative share of global GDP dropped from around 70% in 1950 to about 50% by 2000. Western civilization lost almost a third of its economic power relative to the world, in only half a century's time.

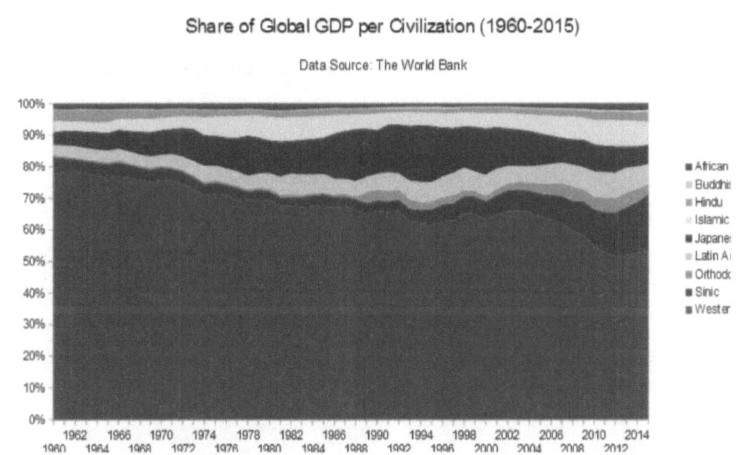

Figure 3. The share of Global GDP per Civilization from 1960 to 2015.

Using a different data set provided by the World Bank, the earlier results can be reproduced. The graph above shows a stacked comparison of each civilization's relative share of the global economy (in GDP). According to the World Bank, the West controlled over 75% of the global economy by 1960.

Again, the following five decades paint the economic decline of the West, its relative GDP share dropping to 50%, a loss of a third of its relative economic power.

The graph shows that East Asia began to threaten Western dominance. For a short period of time, from 1960 to 2010, Japan managed to conquer a significant share of the global economy. Around 1995, Japan alone controlled nearly 20% of the global economy. But by the 2000s, Japan would hand its momentum over to China.

When the West decided to outsource its factories to China, rather than invest in new births, the West appears to have committed cultural suicide, handing China a ticket to global dominance. Western support for globalism should, therefore, be understood in this manner: globalism is a hastily formulated answer to try and compensate for failing Western economies.

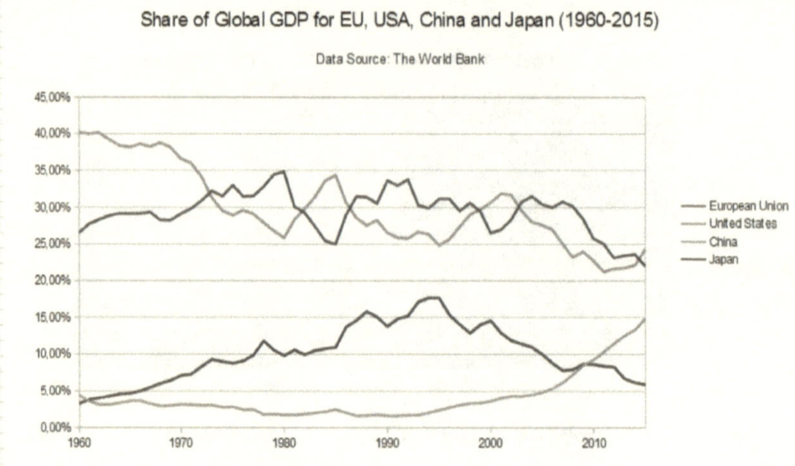

Figure 4. The share of global GDP for major players.

The global economic power shift from West to East will have social, political and cultural implications.

The *Pax Americana*, the world order provided by American economic dominance, has come to an end. Between 1960 and 2010, Americans lost nearly half of their GDP share relative to the world, down from about 40% to about 20%, as shown in the above graph. But with only 20% of the economy in American hands, the United States has ceased to be an economic superpower.

In turn, China alone now controls 15% of the world economy; the combined Sinic civilization nearly 20%—on par with the United States. With China's population nearing 2 billion, the Chinese will undoubtedly attempt to do what the Japanese could not, namely overtake America and the West in the continuous struggle for global economic dominance.

Unsurprisingly, China has already ended its one-child policy in 2015. This move brings a Chinese baby-boom. The new Chinese births are set to guarantee a large influx of cheap labor into China's working class between 2030 and 2040.

Unlike Europe and America, China won't need immigrants to fuel its economy.

How will the West respond to its economic downfall? In his book *The Fates of Nations*, ecologist Paul Colinvaux pointed out that aggressive wars are always started by rich nations. When confronted with rising population numbers, rich nations respond with war and oppression in order to protect their wealth from angry masses.

As African and Chinese populations are set to grow explosively, the West may decide that war is in its best interest. The very real threat of being flooded, raped or genocided by hundreds of millions of angry Arab, African, Latin American and Asian immigrants will certainly drive (white) Europeans and Americans to despair—and into the hands of a 'savior'.

Colinvaux further noted that aggressive wars are not won by numbers, but by superior technology. And indeed, the Western world still holds a technological and military advantage over the Rest. Will the West, faced with decades if not centuries of economic humiliation, follow in German footsteps?

I hereby predict that, for economic reasons, Western Europeans and Northern Americans will eventually come to support a modern-day Hitler in order to wage nuclear war on the world's surplus masses.

7

The Progressive Fraud

"An authoritarian conspiracy that cannot think efficiently, cannot act to preserve itself against the opponents it induces."

—Julian Assange

Exposing WikiLeaks:
The Plot to Overthrow the U.S. Deep State

March 30ᵗʰ, 2018
In a 2011 interview with former Executive Chairman of Google, Eric Schmidt, Julian Assange of WikiLeaks said that "populations basically don't like wars and they have to be lied into it. That means we can be 'truthed' into peace. That is cause for great hope."[1] It is hopeful thinking, indeed, but false. First of all, it isn't true that people are *only* lied into wars. From time to time, we also embrace wars willingly. Secondly, the majority of people isn't interested in the truth as long as they're doing better than their neighbors.

But thirdly, and this is the crux, Assange's thinking has fallen for the power fallacy, the false belief that the world is strictly ruled by top-down hierarchies of power. It denies that power often results from bottom-up competencies that are, in fact, beneficial to the world. Psychologist Jordan Peterson correctly pointed out that if a society were solely based on power, instead of on "the competence necessary to get important and difficult things done, it [would] be prone to collapse."[2]

Sabotaging competency to fight power spells catastrophe.

So, what exactly does the Australian hacker want? As stated, Julian Assange believes the world is ruled by hierarchies of power and that, therefore, average citizens such as you and I are the oppressed victims of powerful people. It is a stereotypical belief perpetuated by classical Marxists. Among them, we find thinkers such as Karl Popper, Noam Chomsky, Jacques Derrida, Michel Foucault, and Herbert Marcuse. They are anarchists with a self-declared mission to destroy Western civilization.

But we don't have to speculate. In November and December 2006, Assange wrote two fairly identical papers and published them on his website, "iq.org". The first paper is titled *State and Terrorist Conspiracies*,[3] the second *Conspiracy as Governance*.[4] In the papers, Assange distills lessons learned from studying terrorist conspiracies. He then applies these lessons to combatting authoritarian governments.

Assange seems to suggest that national governments, too, are authoritarian conspiracies. He wants to sabotage all such governing regimes by cutting the communication links between their conspirators. In a blog post dated December 31st, 2006, (following a post titled *The pending total annihilation of the U.S. regime in Somalia*) he explains,

> "The more secretive or unjust an organization is, the more leaks induce fear and paranoia in its leadership and planning coterie. ... Hence in a world where leaking is easy, secretive or unjust systems are nonlinearly hit relative to open, just systems."[5]

This summarizes the WikiLeaks mission statement. With WikiLeaks, Julian Assange hopes to collapse the despised hierarchies of power that rely on secret communication to operate. By making secrecy costlier, he believes a world where leaking is easy makes it harder for one group of people to conspire against another. (That's not really true. More likely, leaking would escalate a cold war of technology and repression to outsmart the leakers; think "Seth Rich".)

Assange's motives are noble, in theory, but what exactly are these "open, just systems" he spoke of? This phrase echoes a belief in the Open Society. The global open society was first envisioned by the French mystic Henri Bergson, weaponized by the philosopher Karl Popper, and its development now funded by U.S. billionaire George Soros. WikiLeaks and its ideological co-conspirators believe that somehow, magically, better forms of government will emerge from the initial anarchy after all authoritarian regimes have been toppled.

I have serious doubts whether that is possible and whether Assange, like so many other gifted people, has submitted himself to intellectual tunnel vision. By sabotaging hierarchies of power, WikiLeaks also ends up sabotaging *legitimate* hierarchies of competence. That's because power and competence so often happen to be linked qualities. Rather than establish a utopian global society free from authority, the radical Marxists may leave behind an ungovernable world.

Not unlike the over-socialized leftists described in Ted Kaczynski's *Unabomber Manifesto*,[6] Assange solely preoccupies himself with the fight against authoritarianism. In his worldview, all authority is malign. His focus is on destroying authority, not on building a better world per se. On February 26th, 2007, he writes (with 'X' obviously referring to himself),

"X is an 'average shy intellectual' and in that is *a sounding* for characters of his type. This type is often of a noble heart, wilted by fear of conflict with authority. The power of their intellect and noble instincts may lead them to a courageous position, where they see the need to take up arms, but their instinctive fear of authority then motivates them to find rationalizations to avoid conflict."[7]

Does he fancy himself a Messiah? Nonetheless, Julian's courageous yet conflict-avoiding, Christ-like behavior has landed him in London's Ecuadorian embassy without contact with the outside world. Let there be no doubt, though, that Julian Assange is a classical Marxist from the activist end of the spectrum.

My earlier warning that we must preserve hierarchies of competence by accepting some degree of authority should not be understood as an attempt to whitewash criminal conspiracies. Secret governments really do exist and they do lie to coax a people into war. We remember George W. Bush and the alleged Iraqi weapons of mass destruction. The weapons were claimed to be so powerful that Saddam Hussein could bomb U.S. soil,[8] just as Hitler had once pounded London's neighborhoods with V2 missiles.

But it never happened. The fantastical weapons were never found. Then what was the purpose of such lies? A late 19th-century French thinker who wrote the classic on crowd psychology, *La psychologie des foules* by Gustave le Bon, gave the world the insight that "a hundred petty crimes or accidents will not strike the imagination of crowds in the least, whereas a single great crime or accident will profoundly impress them."[9]

Ruling families around the world took heed. With this observation, Le Bon laid the basis for a century of deception. His lessons are still being applied to control the masses today.

German citizens of the early 1930s, for example, were nothing like the bloodthirsty savages depicted by postwar fiction. Thomas Sowell cites that Hitler had trouble pushing the Germans to war. The Führer had to "stage border incidents, using Germans in Polish uniforms to fire weapons and leaving concentration camp inmates dying as 'casualties' of the purported Polish attacks."[10] Just one month after Hitler had been sworn in as Chancellor, the Nazi conspiracy staged the famous 1933 Reichstag fire. The Nazis pinned it on a lone-wolf Dutch terrorist, 24-year-old Marinus van der Lubbe, but they handily exploited the event as an excuse to consolidate power.

The 'Reichstag fire'-method proved to be so effective in manipulating public opinion that conspiracies around the world would copy it. In 1946, members of the Zionist Irgun organization bombed the King David Hotel—the British headquarter in Palestine. Disguised as Arabs, they killed 91. As Le Bon had predicted, this great crime shifted the British public opinion. Britain had been fighting Jewish paramilitaries, successfully, but the media aftermath convinced Britons their government had gone too far, to the point of inflaming the Arabs instead.

The most famous of all Reichstag fires is still officially denied. Although fewer than half of respondents in the latest 2008 World Poll believed in the official story that Al Qaida had done it, one in five respondents thought the U.S. government and its Israeli ally are guilty of bringing down the Twin Towers on September 11th, 2001. On the attack's ten-year anniversary, a group of scientists convened at Ryerson University in Toronto, Canada. They proved that the Twin Towers had to have been pulled down by controlled explosives from within the building, contradicting the official government report.[11]

The conspirators behind the 9/11 attacks succeeded in altering the U.S. public perception of prolonged war in the Middle East, namely in Afghanistan, Iraq, Libya, and Syria. (Coincidentally, these countries were the avowed enemies of two important U.S. allies, Saudi Arabia and Israel. Logic dictates that Iran is next.)

No one with a brain still believes a bunch of camel-riding desert nomads could stage a successful attack on New York City and the Pentagon without being detected and intercepted by the world's most advanced army. Besides, if Bin Laden could attack the United States so easily, then why didn't Russia and China, upon smelling the fear and weakness of a crippled animal, immediately gang up on the USA to finish the job? Well, they didn't even try, because the United States was perfectly prepared to intercept them.

Under President Trump, Reichstag fires kept burning. Just several months after having taken his oath, the new President approved a U.S. airstrike on Syria in response to alleged chemical and gas attacks by the Assad regime.[12]

It would be foolish to think that a showman President had anything to do with staging a false-flag attack. It merely offered Trump an opportunity to deliver on his election promise, namely to "bomb the hell of out ISIS".[13] The real U.S. conspirators are the same group of people who have been in charge of North American society since 1921, namely the several thousand members of the Council on Foreign Relations (CFR).

For twenty years between 1996 and 2016, every single POTUS had either been a member of the CFR or a family member of a member.[14] The CFR and its global media tentacles are indeed the U.S. 'Deep State'. Assange is right to expose them.

Reichstag fires can burn in virtual dumpsters, too. During and after the Trump win, a frenzied, CFR-controlled media accused Putin and the Russians of hacking the U.S. elections. It turns out that the Democratic National Committee's servers haven't exactly been hacked at all,[15] but were more likely infiltrated by a disgruntled employee with direct access. Not the

Russians, but a British company called Cambridge Analytica used stolen Facebook data to sway the 2016 election in Trump's favor. Russians trolls had nothing to do with it.

And what to think of the downing of Malaysia Airlines flight 17 that crashed over Ukraine in 2014, close to the Russian border? It was another Reichstag fire, meant to coax Europeans into war against Russia. It failed for a reason few U.S. pundits understand. Ever since the black Obama took to the White House, especially rural and Eastern Europeans began seeing Putin as the leader of the West. Not everyone is prepared to swallow multiculturalism as hard as Americans do.

Ultimately, the Anglo-American attacks serve to sever Europe, especially Germany, from Russia. That's because a Euro-Russian alliance could easily dethrone the United States as the world's singular superpower for thousands of years to come. Luckily, Western European elites are so heavily invested in American capitalism that they will happily sell out their own peoples for profit.

I can understand what Julian Assange is trying to do. But I question whether you can establish lasting global peace by sabotaging social hierarchies, even if only targeting the most powerful ones. Another reason why you can't 'truth' people into peace is that you don't really need a secret conspiracy to wage war. Religious fundamentalists, for example, don't need to use secret communications to get their message across. They wage their war on the non-believers in plain sight. (That's probably the reason why radical Marxists want to outlaw religion.)

More problematically, Assange's thinking hinges on the false assumption that people *never* want war. That's just not true. People will go to war for various reasons other than being coaxed into them by conspiracies. Natural catastrophes may naturally push people to war for their survival. Perceived historical humiliations may erupt in unpredictable conflict. Complex group dynamics may produce wars without a cause.

There are many reasons for war, but Assange has only tackled one of them. I believe lasting global peace simply isn't a goal worth pursuing. It's not realistic. It's naïve. One can't lock the world into an eternal state of pacifism without exposing mankind to the wolves and the bears. At some point, even the most over-socialized leftists must burst out of their safe spaces and experience real life.

War, like death, is an inevitable part of life, but to say wars are inevitable does not mean we must surrender to them. From a complex systems' perspective, we should rather aim to minimize the number of war casualties, precisely by accommodating small-scale, regional conflict. Allowing regions to let off steam in contained wars may prevent a global catastrophe, assuming that's a goal worth fighting for.

The End of Progress and the Last Struggle: The Decline of the West Heralds Its Rebirth

February 4th, 2016
After the European colonial era, globalization opened the world markets to Western consumption and technology. But because Western populations are aging, stagnating or even shrinking in the 21st century, modern means of communication and transportation are helping the world's poor to move to the West, tens of millions at a time. The economies of their homelands in Africa, Asia, Latin America and the Middle East have proven unable to provide their explosively growing populations with a meaningful future.

Conversely, Westerners flee into politically correct naivety, alcohol, drugs or consumer hedonism while both the Left and the Right privately condemn mass immigration. As long as Westerners can still afford to do so, they will keep fooling themselves that everything will be okay again. Despite Western self-delusion, the Syrian refugee crisis that began in 2015 heralded the beginning of the decline of Europe. Perhaps that of America, too.

In the interest of our collective self-preservation, the time has come for the rebirth of the West.

Globalization has driven urban man to his highest productivity yet with the smallest specialization. To facilitate billions of individuals living on Earth, we've narrowed our lives down to that of gears in a machine. To cope, we've fled in mind-altering drugs and virtual computer worlds that simulate long-lost worlds of freedom. The success of mass man has no equal. Never have so many people lived so close to each other as, for example, in Paris, Seoul or Mumbai, cities housing over fifteen thousand people per square mile.

Cities have become human cowsheds, self-regulated prison equipped for the tax industry. The pressure of mankind's explosively growing numbers has reduced man to an obedient executioner in an incomprehensible system. Although modern 'progress' changed feudal serfs into modern employees with more prosperity than medieval kings, it did so at the expense of their humanity. The majority of people alive today live out their lives as sardines, stuffed together in residential towers like termite colonies.

The modernity that promised people infinite opportunities brought them boundless self-deception. The technological revolution that Europe has cranked up since the 17th century, accelerated by the invention of the combustion engine and later atomic energy, had only led to worldwide overproduction and overpopulation. While the rest of the world, out of fear of losing the struggle for existence, is blindly running after the drunken Western example, the fate of mankind is rooted in the tragic question,

"What are we willing to sacrifice for our survival?"

The billions of people on Earth live in relative harmony, thanks to a historically tried and tested system of hierarchy and order.

This human hierarchy is like a steep mountain made of loose sand. The more effort a subordinate makes in order to climb to the top, the further he will drop back down again. This discourages many to even try. You have to be born at the top. There's no path to the top but when everyone takes the hierarchy by storm, the sands will disperse in all directions, eventually dropping the elites to the bottom.

Because a people always possess this latent power to humiliate its elites and because the elites can only defend their power by oppressing the people, both parties must treat each other with the friendliest contempt. What we generally call 'peacetime' is a ceasefire between the people and its elites, between ordinary folks and special snowflakes, between the quantitative mass man and the self-proclaimed man of quality.

Human organization is based on a holy trinity.[16] At the top of the hierarchy, a governing power elite rules with the help of its slavish civil servantry. Below it, the relatively autonomous but loyal security forces operate, including a police force and an army. Down at the bottom live the people. The security forces have the exclusive right to use violence against civilians. In exchange for their loyalty, the security forces share in the elite's prestige. As a consequence, people experience relative peace of the sort shepherd dogs maintain by barking at a herd of sheep.

The people are being oppressed. Society is not free because people are required to obey the social order. I call this the *basic order*. To maintain the basic order, great civilizations invented principles of wide-scale social oppression. Governing elites rule the people by means of social taboos, traditions, religious doctrine, one-sided news coverage, and arbitrary legislation.[17] In East Asia, for example, Confucius formulated the values of obedience, pacifism, and what we would nowadays call mindfulness. In the West, Catholic clergy spread the teachings of Jesus Christ, the slave who submitted to his suffering.

Those social precepts are not set in stone but continuously adapt to changing circumstances. Social taboos serve to control the reproductive rate of the people as well as its economic output.[18] Because the tameness of the people benefits larger numbers, which helps increase the military might of its controlling elites, spiritual leaders submitted the masses to their leadership by means of most deceitful manipulation, for example, by the promise of an afterlife, reincarnation or, nowadays, capitalist riches, like a pot of gold at the end of the rainbow.[19]

Although the role of tradition and religion appears to have decreased in the increasingly irreligious West, popular television hosts now formulate the political correct taboos that media elites impose a gullible people by threat of social exclusion. Political correctness is the religion of modernity.

In the basic order, the people are serfs. They accept their fate because, in the long term, the social order brings them social security. That social stability is the strongest argument for democracy. Through consensus-driven decision making, a democracy moves considerably slower than other forms of organization. This has the advantage that governments must avoid reckless behavior and side-track autocratic rulers who think the State exists to afford them their adventures.

What is the benefit of democracy? By slowing down decision making, democracy makes the future more predictable for its citizens. Democratic citizens can invest more in the longer term which benefits the creation of great public works such as infrastructure, health, and education. A well-governed democracy guarantees its citizens a certain peace of mind.

However, democracy also saddles citizens with annoying drawbacks. Democracy brings along a cumbersome civil servantry, as well as an inefficient if not pointless hierarchy. Democracy can often adequately respond to internal crises, but not always and even less so in case of unpredictable anarchy coming from the outside world.

In addition, democracy erodes administrative responsibility because even in case of big mistakes by her governing officials, the people foot the bill for their vote. Democratic officials hold less power than autocratic rulers, but as a consequence, they also feel much less responsible for the result. They can always pass that responsibility on to the people. The people, acting like a herd, fears individual responsibility and preferably wants to give it back to politicians.[20] Thus, people flee into politically correct conformism—e.g. into bipartisan uniformity.

It's a misconception to think democracy leads to prosperity naturally. It's also untrue that building high-quality governing institutions lead to the foundation of a democracy. In reality, precisely the opposite is true: democracy presupposes prosperity[21] and without democracy, high-quality institutions have no use.[22] Only prosperous peoples can afford the governing inefficiency of a democracy. Poor peoples have no use for impractically expensive institutions.

To ensure the survival of sometimes up to hundreds of millions of people, governing elites encourage their citizens to keep the economy 'running' from their cradle to their grave. This is to say: each day anew, the masses must commit their physical and mental productivity for the benefit of the collective survival of the people.

We call this system capitalism. Despite the fact that every human being on Earth owes his existence to this never-ending struggle against nature, capitalism harvests little appreciation due to its unfair distribution of the outcome. That doesn't mean people have any other choice.[23] Capitalism arises from the need to feed billions of people. The desire to treat people equally does not affect it. The system that feeds so many people may, under no condition fail. Capitalism protects itself, counter-intuitively, with a buffer of inefficiency that leads to inequality. Besides, capitalism isn't an 'ism'. There is no ideology. Capitalism is a de-centralized system of people going to work each day.[24]

When Marxists criticize capitalism, they mean the centralization of capital. Their only criticism is that the men who are in charge of it are not the intellectuals.

The basic order discussed earlier has transformed its citizens into land-based (or urban-based) slaves. Because humankind's survival depends on the collective productivity of collaborating individuals, the economy has driven man to reduce cost by all means necessary. We house people in unnatural, square boxes we call city apartments. Like capital, we centralize the workers in working-class neighborhoods. The economy forces most citizens to perform their productive duties at fixed times and locations.

Modern citizens are not much better off than medieval serfs. They just have more luxury and more money to buy drugs. We live longer and healthier lives but the healthy years won rather serve our continued exploitation than our personal freedom. Few manage to escape this mechanical existence—a rich minority—but the masses never can. The ordinary man is born and raised in the System, conditioned to accept his artificial reality as real. The promise of old age and security motivate him like the carrot before the donkey.

Because the *System* may not fail, freedom of opinion makes way for intellectual conformism. Bureaucracy tempers entrepreneurial freedom. Politically correct taboos have replaced an individual outlook on life. Parents impose the System's ideals onto their children because they too don't know any better. Even judges and psychiatrists, who have internalized the System's ideals, make sure to calm down rebellious citizens. A 'good' child learns to sit still, waiting for the teacher's, priest's or king's lessons. A strong-willed child that wants to be an independent individual has 'issues', is 'maladjusted', needs 'discipline' or suffers from a 'disorder'.

The law of diminishing returns controls the economy like a law of physics, so, increasingly, people have to work harder for increasingly less life. Men and women go through the motions of life but without really living. They have become machines. They work as gears in factories, as tools in construction, or at the office as computer extensions. Citizens have become the living furniture in the households of their elites.

The System puts a lot of pressure on people, on men to become achievers and on women, too. Many Western women did not stay childless because they wanted to study but decided to study because they could not have children.

Modern life is in stark contrast to the life in, for example, Europe around the year 1000. Almost all inhabitants of Norway were still free farmers that didn't owe anyone a dime in taxes. The Viking-age Norway was an egalitarian society—socialists' wet dream—until King Harald introduced taxes for the first time to fund his wars against England.[25]

Times change. To keep the economy running and the people in check, socialism plays a particularly mean double-play. In theory, socialism means to strive for the emancipation of the working classes. Socialism wants to make it possible for workers to provide themselves with their daily needs without having to submit to artificial consumption, according to the definition of socialism as understood by Noam Chomsky,[26] similar to what Karl Marx pursued.[27]

At least, that's the philosophy. In practice, socialism rather plays the role of an *urban religion* that seeks to reduce the people to servile sheep, or "turn tigers into cats."[28]

Socialism serves as the lubricant between the gears in densely populated human machinery. More conservative values can only survive in the countryside. Once people had mastered modern city planning that allowed for millions of people to live together in small spaces, city dwellers were forced to become more tolerant of deviating behavior by their neighbors in order to maintain social harmony. This has consequences for the psyche. The modern family, locked between four walls, is the source of violence in the lives of many young children.[29]

In our time, globalization has led to the emergence of a sort of hyper-socialism that tries to assimilate people from all corners of the world, of all cultures, beliefs, and traditions. This hyper-socialism cannot succeed without a high dose of self-deceit. The so-called multicultural societies push the boundaries of tolerance so far, they can only succeed in their intent by distorting every child's psyche through far-reaching propaganda. Nowadays, the lies we have to take for truths have become as indispensable to world peace as the air we breathe.

That makes multicultural societies unstable—at any given moment, the whole thing threatens to fall apart. The basic order remains standing with great effort. We have reached the limit of the humanly possible.

The state of the present world order is tragic: predatory capitalism, which feeds man but plunders nature, and predatory socialism, which brings a man peace but plunders his freedom, have pushed both man and nature towards the edge of the abyss. Already condemned to a life of labor and maximal productivity, social precepts imposed from above further restrict man's life. The slavery of his mind is complete.

The rigidity of the basic order clashes with the human need for freedom and self-determination. In world history, this conflict shows itself in periodic waves of war and peace. Near the end of a long peace period, the masses, who now experience their slavish existence as degrading to their humanity, reach a boiling point. The people demand new leaders, a new future, and a revolution. Under pressure from a forlorn lower class, the middle classes rise up and seize the opportunity to steal back their rightful dues from the egocentric elites.[30]

Both revolutionary radicals, as well as reactionaries, then pursue the same goal: to overthrow the current order in favor of an idealized future.[31] In most cases, revolutions strand because the security forces remain loyal to the elites. Only in extraordinary cases do the security forces side with the people. That happens, for example, when governing officials have endangered the survival of their people through corrupt governance.

Economies behave irrationally. They are driven by positive feedback loops. For example, families see that their neighbors are getting a loan for a second car, so they also decide to do so themselves out of fear of falling behind financially. Both unjustly assume that the economy will always continue to grow.

History shows that economies do collapse. The Viennese stock market crash of 1873 signaled the end of half a century of economic growth. During this so-called *Gründerzeit* or Founder's Era, German and Austrian entrepreneurs became rich overnight. Thanks to the construction of an elaborate network of railroads, people from the countryside migrated to the city *en masse* to meet economic demand. After the crash, the German industry came to a standstill for almost twenty years, called the *Gründerkrise* or Founder's Crisis. The new middle class again threatened to drop back into a starving lower class.

Professor Didier Sornette (ETH Zurich) researched if perhaps the world economy is also a bubble in crisis. He sketched three scenarios for the future:

1. we may unexpectedly invent new means of transportation that will enable us to colonize other worlds so that we can relieve the exhausted Earth;
2. people satisfy their economic appetite and voluntarily reduce their family size;
3. we hit a world market crash after which only the super-rich and their private armies manage to survive among clans of barbarians—the scorched Earth scenario.[32]

But before it even comes to a global economic collapse, the current situation in the West already strongly resembles that of the German *Gründerzeit*. Just like then, we have experienced half a century of economic prosperity. Like then, millions of people from the countryside, this time from Middle-Eastern, East-Asian, Latin-American and North-African areas, migrated to European and American cities. Like then, our economy characterizes itself by unfounded expectations; we think it's normal that virtual companies that produce nothing can be valued at over a hundred billion dollars.

Westerners are living in the repetition of the *Gründerzeit*, on the eve of their economic destruction. But what will Westerners do in case of a total crisis—fight or flight?

An economic crash of this proportion means that the money and the means to sustain multicultural appeasement politics will dry up. We will no longer be able to afford our progressive values. In times of crisis, we shall witness a return to conservative values.

Will the West choose collective suicide or will it embrace a combative people that won't hesitate to reconquer its world?

Rules for Alt-Radicals:
How to Destroy the Left Using Their Tactics against Them

February 15th, 2017

In his 1971 book *Rules for Radicals*, left-wing activist Saul Alinsky wrote, "Organization for action will now and in the decade ahead center upon America's white middle class. That is where the power is."[33] This line came from the same man who defined the American radical as "that unique person who ... genuinely and completely believes in mankind".[34] I'm sure Salinsky meant his narcissistic self.

For some reason, left-wingers, Salinsky included, believe white people were born "powerful" and, therefore, deserve to be persecuted by the powerless. It is the ideology of the incompetent who in the face of drive and talent respond with jealousy rather than magnanimity.

Can you guess who was a young admirer of Alinsky and his subversive work? *Hillary Diane Clinton*. In her 1969 Bachelor's thesis for Wellesley College, she presented an analysis of Alinsky's methods, but she did not disapprove of her ideological mentor's anti-white rhetoric.

Instead, in her thesis, Clinton struck a combative tone, quoting T.S. Eliot[35] that "there is only the fight to recover what has been lost and found and lost again and again",[36] inspiring her to title the thesis "*There Is Only the Fight*". She, too, meant the fight against white people. The Clintons are no friends of the West.

Don't be fooled by appearances. The mere fact that Alinsky's followers, such as Hillary Clinton, cite the occasional anti-Semite (Eliot), openly criticize Israel, or publicly act the part of devout Christian Methodist[37] does not acquit them of dabbling in revenge fantasies that aim to destroy Western civilization from within.

Whatever their personal motives, Clinton, Alinsky and many others, including the most wretched thinkers Karl Popper,[38] Noam Chomsky, financial terrorist George Soros,[39] and former Secretary of State Henry Kissinger have come to believe that not just Nazi Germany, but all of Western civilization carries responsibility for the Holocaust.

All white people are born guilty; the Christian original sin only applies to the "powerful".

Leftists believe that the West let the Holocaust happen by not doing enough to stop it, a belief perfectly oblivious to the millions of (white) Americans, Europeans, and Russians who sacrificed their lives to *fight* Hitler, including my own grandparents. Sadly, such convictions drive the progressive movement: an entrenched hatred of white people.

Leftist radicals preach the end of "white privilege" through affirmative action; the deconstruction of 'whiteness' through diversity; the collapse of white nations through open borders and mass immigration; the genocide of white people through their displacement and dispossession. None of these things are coincidental. They are policy. Progressive politicians dream of the complete eradication of European civilization and its peoples.

Now you know why Hillary Clinton thinks half of white Americans belong in a *basket of deplorables*. Why won't these "racist, sexist, homophobic, xenophobic, Islamophobic"[40] taxpayers vote themselves into poverty? The radicals of the seventies have become today's status quo. They have become the powerful people they sought to destroy, but the irony eludes them. They are globalists, they manipulate the media, and they police academia.[41]

If we want to dispose of them, we will have to take Clinton's own advice at heart:

"Those possessing power want to retain it and often extend the bounds of it. Those desiring a change in the power balance generally lack the established criteria of money or status and so must mobilize numbers."[42]

Indeed, if alt-right radicals (*alt-radicals*) could master the art of mobilizing the people, I believe they could crush the progressive left before the end of the next decade. In support of the coming insurgency, I've partly rewritten Alinksy's thirteen rules for radicals[43] below. In fact, to mess with people's heads, I've cut them down to ten:

1. *Make the enemy think you have more power than you really have.*
2. *Build future action based on past experiences.*
   People can only understand new things in terms of old things. The same is true for political action. If you venture too far from your people's past experiences, you will confuse them and the mission will fail.
3. *When in doubt, confuse the enemy.*
   By doing things the enemy has never experienced before, you will confuse him.
4. *Tirelessly ridicule the enemy and point out his flaws.*
   Conservatives all too often try to sway their opponents with sound arguments, but the leftist enemy couldn't care less about facts. Leftists know the truth does not persuade anyone.
5. *Keep reinventing yourself and your tactics.*
   When Hitler threatened to invade France, the French built their defenses on the same spot they had fought the First World War. Hitler responded by ordering his troops to take a detour and surprise the French from behind.

6. *When you can back it up with force, threaten the enemy.* The threat is usually more terrifying than the thing itself.

7. *The truth is malleable. Bend anything the enemy says to your advantage.*
   When leftists accuse you of racism for wanting to close the border, point out that U.S. tax dollars can buy far more food and shelter abroad than at home. The border is just there for national security.

8. *Provoke the enemy to act by applying constant pressure.*

9. *When you attack the enemy's plans, make sure you have first prepared viable alternatives.*

10. *Blame visible targets for complex problems.*
    It's Hillary Clinton's fault refugees are coming to America, because she bombed the Middle East and funded ISIS. It doesn't even matter if it's true or not. Just keep repeating the accusation until people believe it.

On the Purpose of Socialism: Self-Determination or Managed Freedom?

April 20ᵗʰ, 2017
In *On Anarchism*, famed intellectual Noam Chomsky writes,

"And that's one of the main purposes of socialism, I think: to reach a point where people have the opportunity to decide freely for themselves what their needs are, and not have the 'choices' forced on them by some arbitrary system of power."[44]

Most of us will agree with this statement, but Chomsky being a linguist, one has to wonder why he thinks 'people deciding freely' deserves the label socialism. Similarly, one author pointed out that Karl Marx himself intended his socialist doctrines to stand for nothing other than freedom.[45] Still, why call freedom socialism? I previously suspected this Orwellian belief—freedom=socialism—-to serve a wholly different purpose, in my book *Return to Freedom*:

> "If Marx's philosophy was really about freedom, then why call it socialism? Socialist freedom is managed freedom, 'for your own good'. Socialism does not, cannot and will not elevate the working classes, because doing so makes socialism superfluous. To stay in power, socialists, therefore, reduce the people to lemmings that no longer have a say in the direction of their own lives."[46]

Both Chomsky and Marx represent a class of power-hungry intellectuals. While they may claim to represent the interests of the people, their personal interests do not align at all with the working classes. Most intellectuals wake up every day to the reality that the capitalist owner classes, despite being far less educated, nonetheless succeeded in accumulating masses of wealth, influence and power. The intellectual's own investments in the life of the mind often hardly paid off. The poor intellectual, in other words, is jealous. How come the intellectual elites are not in power?

Socialism, it seems, is not really about freeing the workers from corporate slavery, but about jealous leftist intellectuals scheming to install themselves as the new power elite. Merely out of convenience have socialist thinkers appropriated the struggles of the worker, inventing class warfare as a weapon against those currently in power. But that would make socialist leadership no different from its supposed enemy. As I already concluded in my book (Ch. 7),

> "Politics is about powerful families competing for the right to exploit the masses. The 'leftists' wish to tell the people how to live, the 'rightists' wish to tell the people what to consume. Neither regime gives a damn about you."

The purpose of socialism is not to free the working classes, but to deceive the masses into worshiping new masters. This managed freedom, 'for the good of the people', is not freedom at all, but outright manipulation. While capitalism at least to some extent offers working men and women the means to live and feed their families, socialism offers them nothing substantial other than the loss of their global competitive strength.

The Socio-Capitalist Complex: The Survivors of the 22ⁿᵈ Century Will Be the Most Aggressive Oppressors of the 21ˢᵗ

November 12ᵗʰ, 2015

The problem with socialism is that it is inherently a lie. Capitalism and socialism are not opposing but complementary forces. Working together, this socialist-capitalist Chimera maximizes an economy's population size. Through 'equality' socialism effaces the masses in preparation for mass consumption, allowing for capitalist economies of scale. Capitalism serves these effaced masses efficiently, and in doing so increases the economy's capacity for carrying bigger populations. Bigger populations afford more socialism. Therefore, capitalism is socialism's precondition: only wealthy nations can afford the cost of 'progress'.[47]

We have a resource problem. If every Chinese citizen wants to own a car like Americans and Europeans do, we'll need four

Earths just to produce enough cars. Unless we find new Earths to exploit, the Chinese will not be able to drive cars. Herein lies the invention of social oppression, but it is a mistake to believe that capitalism is the cause of it. Instead, all social oppression is the consequence of continued population growth.[48]

Consequently, the 21st century will see the emergence of highly oppressive ideologies to prevent the have-nots from becoming have-alls. Wealthier peoples will exert social oppression by using their weapon of choice, e.g. discrimination by economic class, birth caste, tribe, nationality, religion, race or otherwise. All but one thing is clear: the richest, most technologically advanced peoples will be the ones oppressing the 'others'. What remains open for debate is whether that still means the West, or whether East-Asia will take the world by surprise.

The underlying message is: humanity has entered the final stage of a global-scale Tragedy of the Commons, but neither socialism nor capitalism can solve it. New, socially oppressive ideologies can because the only real solution to a Tragedy of the Commons is to reduce the number of consumers. Reducing the population can be done either voluntarily through birth control—which requires social oppression—or involuntarily through famine, war and, ultimately, deliberate extermination and genocide (e.g. as ISIS already practices).

Unless we find new worlds to colonize and alien peoples to submit to our greedy system, the current system will inevitably collapse. The survivors of the 22nd century will be the most aggressive oppressors of the 21st.

The Collectivization of North America: Why European Culture that Founded American Civilization is Rapidly Losing Ground to Collectivism

February 17ᵗʰ, 2018

Canada's *Maclean's* magazine recently increased its prices for men. Men ought to pay 26% more for the same magazine. It's supposed to be a clever social commentary, but what exactly is the commentary? Must men die in all wars and pay for everything, too?

Something else is going on here. After the Second World War, feminism was supposed to make women financially independent, liberating women from their evil, patriarchal husbands (who forced young women into marrying them, obviously), but it turns out most women can't compete in a fair economic competition against men.

That's the sort of problem social engineers love to solve. To keep themselves employed, they recommend the State to step in and enforce equality of outcomes. Next, the U.S. government may begin redistributing men's incomes to women — *enslaving both.*

How did we go from "husbands should take their wives out to dinner" in the 1950s to "independent women can pay for their own meals" in the 1990s to "it's sexist if a man doesn't pay 26% more for the same dish to compensate for women's lower earnings"?

Well, that was always the plan! Feminism never meant to make women financially independent, but rather meant to *deconstruct traditional marriage* by pitting women against men, by breeding resentment between the sexes.

By comparison, back in those dreaded, single-income 1950s, married women spent over three-quarters of their husband's income. Women were in charge of household expenses. They were more powerful than today's liberated, unmarried women, who are struggling to make enough money to feed the child their Tinder date left behind.

No wonder, then, that women welcome Father State to take on the role of husband. Woman's psychology hasn't changed, her society has. Fewer women marry than ever before, but as a consequence, more women prostitute themselves than ever before, and more women work in porn than ever before.

The purpose is to create a global society in which women sleep with everyone but are married only to the State.

The strong marriage tie long formed a bulwark against collectivism, but thanks to crypto-communist feminist ideology, American women are on the verge of submitting both themselves and their reproductive function to government planning. That is what progressives call "progress", namely the gradual transformation of an individualist society into a communist one.

After the deconstruction of marriage came the deconstruction of race, culture, 'whiteness', the nation, sex and gender, "euro-centric" science and Western civilization itself.

There's a very simple explanation for the speed at which European culture began to disintegrate in North America. The Kennedy Immigration Act that brought over 60 million non-Europeans and their offspring to the United States since the 1960s simultaneously brought in an equal number of state-dependent citizens.

It just turns out societies are the product of a people's dreams and desires, and the immigrant *Dreamers* are dreaming of socialism. If Americans of European descent want to defend their civilization, they will have to convince millennial women to embrace traditional marriage again.

Ending the Gender Holocaust:
The Attack on Birth Sex is a Crime Against Humanity

April 2nd, 2018

May disappointed parents play 'Hitler' and brainwash children to adopt a different gender?

The Western world has chosen to normalize gender dysphoria. A previously rare condition now springs up in nearly every kindergarten. No one asks why. Government-appointed activists posing as therapists claim they can tell when a 2-year-old boy wants to be a girl. Risking ostracization for being too conservative, parents try to raise their children gender 'neutrally'. Western societies are breeding a neutered generation that will no longer reproduce.

The gender movement—led by the usual rabble of progressive liberals, social democrats, Marxist-feminists, and whatnots—wants to legitimize the right of parents to change their child's sex. It robs children of their particular identity. The particularism of a birth sex threatens the worldview of a class of universalists so much that they're willing to justify a war on children.

The universalist standpoint is particularly racial. The madwomen want to deconstruct especially white boys and prevent them from having families in adulthood. When a society allows parents to brainwash their children into taking sex-blocking chemicals, we are speaking of chemical oppression. Men are facing a hybrid war fueled by non-stop media attacks.

The death of the West is the real goal. In the face of economic and demographic changes, it has become evident that the West has chosen the path of collective suicide. But the suicide is not voluntary! The anti-white movement's infiltration of Western media and politics has made it so.

Like the mother who suffocates her child, Western leaders work to suffocate a generation of boys and prevent the next from being born. If we want to undo this progressive sickness, Western peoples must rise up against their manipulators down in Washington and Brussels. We must end the gender Holocaust.

> "For as photographs from this period reveal, [David], for all her attempts to drag a smile onto her face, had the wounded eyes of *a shamed* and hunted animal."[49]

David Reimer and his twin brother were born in Canada on August 22nd, 1965. When David was a seven-month-old baby, a medical doctor burnt off his penis during a failed circumcision. Dr. John Money, a progress-liberal psychologist, seized the 'opportunity' to experiment on the twins, David and his brother Brian.

The doctor pressured the parents to raise David as a girl instead. Astonishingly, both parents complied. They would raise David as a girl, calling her Brenda. Even more astonishingly, David/Brenda's parents kept this secret from him for fourteen years. They dressed David up as a girl and forced him to play with girl's toys.

The abuse didn't end there. Dr. Money wanted to prove that one's gender is learned, not innate. Two months before David's second birthday, the doctor convinced David/Brenda's parents to have his testicles surgically removed. Surgeons gave him a provisory vagina—a hole between his legs that looked nothing like the real thing.

Making sure David/Brenda would be conditioned into being a girl, Dr. Money had David and his twin brother spend sessions in his office. There, the doctor ordered the underage kids to perform sexual acts on each other. Brian would play the male and David/Brenda the female. They were ordered to practice missionary and doggy-style positions. Sometimes, a handful of colleagues attended.

The sexual roleplay was supposed to brainwash David/Brenda into believing he really was a girl. As a teenager, doctors injected David with the female estrogen hormone. He developed breasts. Still, he never became a woman. Despite a life of psychological abuse, David/Brenda would later testify that he had never felt like a woman.

One cannot imagine a greater crime committed against a child. Everything goes in the name of 'progress'.

It had been David's parents who had sent him to Dr. Money. They would insist that David obey the doctor's every command. At age 13, the doctor proposed David/Brenda have another surgery, one to widen the hole between his legs so he could have intercourse. This is when David threatened his parents to commit suicide. He still didn't know that he had been born as a boy.

One year later, at age 14, his father finally admitted to the conspiracy he and his wife had kept from their son. During the next seven years, David demanded reconstructive surgery. He wanted to be what he had always been—a man.

Things didn't work out. In 2002, David's twin brother Brian killed himself with an overdose of antidepressants. Two years after his death, David ended his own life, at age 38, by blasting shotgun hail through his head.

The story of David/Brenda is the true face of today's gender movement. Rather than learn from the mistake, the gender movement became more aggressive. Rather than accept that gender is determined at birth, the movement began waging war on the truth.

For fourteen years, the sort of people who run Western societies today attempted to program David into being a girl. For thirty years, well after David's suicide, the psychological industry kept referring to his case as a "success". This deliberate denial has led thousands more boys and girls down the path to the gender-Auschwitz.

When a journalist of *Rolling Stone* interviewed David Reimer before his death, he stated that,

> "What they did to you in the body is sometimes not near as bad as what they did to you in the mind – with the psychological warfare in your head."[50]

Society condoned what was done to David but his parents were equally guilty. His mother admitted she thought she could train her boy into being a girl,

> "It was a pretty, lacy little dress," Linda recalls. "[David] was ripping at it, trying to tear it off. I remember thinking, 'Oh, my God, she knows she's a boy and she doesn't want girls' clothing. She doesn't want to be a girl.' But then I thought, 'Well, maybe I can teach her to want to be a girl. Maybe I can train her so that she wants to be a girl.'"[51]

Apparently, you cannot teach children to be something other than they really are. Not without inflicting serious psychological damage, that is. David later testified how hard it was to fight his parents,

> "I remember saying, 'Oh, can I shave, too?'" [He] says of this incident, which forms his earliest childhood memory. "My dad said, 'No, no. You go with your mother.' I started crying, 'Why can't I shave, too?'" [Brian] says that the incident was typical of the way their parents tried to *steer* them into opposite sexes – and how such efforts were, inevitably, doomed to failure."[52]

Of course, society took notice. On the first day of kinder-garten, not even the teacher accepted that David was a girl.

So, what sort of decent, good-thinking person would dare deny that the psychological warfare waged on David and his brother Brian is what drove them to suicide? Who would dare maintain that children can be born gay, trans, neutral, or Tin-kerbell?

The truth is that sex is determined at birth. In fact, sex is de-termined at conception when the male sperm that carries either an X or Y chromosome melts with the female egg that hosts an X. Not birth sex, but rather homosexuality, transgenderism, and other disorders are *learned behaviors*,

"A very important determining influence in the development of homosexuality is the child's awareness that his sex was a disappointment to his parent, especially if their disappoint-ment leads them to treat the child as if he were of the oppo-site sex."[53]

Parents disappointed with their child's sex *cause* the child to suffer feelings of psychological invisibility. Knowing that its sex was the 'wrong' one to make mommy or daddy happy, the child will do whatever it takes to win its parents' love. Under pressure from disappointed parents, the child will behave as though it was the opposite sex.

According to psychiatrist Paul McHugh, such gender-con-fused children suffer a personality disorder. They were not born with a disorder. The disorder is the child's response to a society that disapproves of its sex. In some cases, such as in David/Bren-da's case, parents even help brainwash their children into having a sex change operation.

The progressive attack on children doesn't stop there. In the states of Carolina, New Jersey, and Massachusetts, lawmakers have enacted laws that forbid psychiatrists to treat gender-confused children. Instead, they must refer them to gender surgery. Under these laws, even parents who are trying to help their children risk being sued by the state.

There's no reason to offer a child gender therapy. Research shows that 80% of children who are left alone heal their confusion before age 10.[54] Among people who did receive sex-change operations, none have become happier. The Swedish Karolinska Institute discovered that patients who had surgery had a twenty times higher chance of committing suicide.[55]

No wonder! You didn't really expect you could amputate your genitals and become 'better', did you? Besides, a sex change doesn't change your sex, it just mutilates your body.

I come to the conclusion that the progressive attack on a child's birth sex is a crime against humanity.

Who Interfered in Manning's Gender? Certain Assumptions Are So Painful Society Chooses to Hide Them

November 28ᵗʰ, 2016

When a journalist for *The Intercept*, Glenn Greenwald, referred to Charles Manning as a 'she' on Twitter, I commented that Manning is technically still a 'he'. It provoked Greenwald to classify myself as a sort of *Untermensch*, a being undeserving of participating in public debate,

> "It takes a very warped sickness to want to interfere in and dictate other people's gender identity. You should focus on that."

Was he talking about his mother? Whatever Greenwald was projecting, there is an enormous dose of latent irony in that statement. Of course, it wasn't I who had interfered in Manning's gender nor had I dictated what it ought to be. However, I did refuse to call people by whatever made-up gender they've come to identify themselves with, other than their birth sex, either male or female.

Why won't I go along with other people's fiction of themselves like a proper liberal would? It's partly because I refuse to go along with other people's psychological problems. More importantly, I am convinced that people who invent their own gender are suffering from a psychological and not from a physical problem.

In terms of Manning's imprisonment, I believe 'Chelsea' should be pardoned and released from prison as soon as possible. But unlike Greenwald, I don't believe people are born with a transgender psyche. In fact, I believe it was our society that first interfered with Manning's gender by disapproving of his birth sex, i.e. by making him aware that he was unwanted as a boy and that he would be loved more if he had been a girl. Perhaps a traumatic life experience triggered Manning to hide his original male identity in favor of a female one.

Where Greenwald and I hold a difference of opinion thus comes down to us having made different assumptions about the world. But these assumptions remain unchallenged on both sides. We should, therefore, be able to discuss those assumptions openly.

I find it a "warped sickness" that our society has trapped many so-called transgenders in a gender that was never *really* of their own choosing. For example, a disappointed parent may feel entitled to play God and choose his child's gender. I don't consider that progress, but rather a crime against children if not against humanity.

In Greenwald's world, such a child cannot escape its conditioning. Condemned to a life of psychological suffering, the

Mannings of our world must hide their true selves behind the mask of desirable behavior. I believe men like Manning should receive recognition for their suffering. Society should protect transgenders not only against their original abusers but also against themselves.

By offering transgenders a way out of their artificially induced gender trap, I believe my assumptions about them are more progressive than Greenwald's.

8

Philosophical Ponderings

"The 'apparent' world is the only one: the 'real world' has only been lyingly added..."

—Friedrich Nietzsche

Millennials' Search for Meaning

December 31ˢᵗ, 2016

A civilization's main export product is its constituents' behavior, especially abroad. The West, judging by the millennial generation's monomaniac party drive, scouring the world's pristine island beaches and trashing them in raves of binge drinking and electronic music, suffers more than a PR problem, but an existential crisis.

While their grandfathers, and great-grandfathers, unflinchingly stormed the beaches of Normandy in defense of freedom, this wealthiest, most privileged generation to have ever lived in human history remorselessly spoils that freedom on beach festivals and full moon parties, turning tropical coasts into dumping grounds of plastic cups, glass bottles, and wasted potential.

Nothing says "I can afford not to care about you" like the economic colonialism of the West's roving youths whose flyover lifestyles trample on starving Third World populations, only to spend long vacations losing themselves to their favorite deejays' dance tunes and in mind-altering drugs.

What went wrong? What happened to the idea of leaving behind a better world for future generations? When did we decide to make hedonism foreign policy?

Twenty-somethings call it "life before work". The phrase's negative connotation not only exposes a deep lack of purpose among young Westerners, but also a wholesale rejection of Western society. The pride earlier generations once took in carrying the responsibilities to keep their economies afloat simply no longer balances out the social cost of a sixty-hour-or-more workweek.

Had the millennial generation possessed their grandparents' economic opportunities, perhaps these party armies could have ended many of the world's humanitarian crises. They could apply their wealth to preventing the refugee crisis from having happened in the first place. Why can't droves of party-goers make a stop in Aleppo to do the right thing and end human suffering?

The purposelessness the youngest Western generations experience poses a problem the world cannot afford to ignore. A lack of meaning in one's personal life may cause a depression, but a broad sense of meaninglessness afflicting an entire generation of wealthy people spells catastrophe.

Catastrophe has hit the West before. Writing in 1936, three years before the outbreak of the Second World War, psychoanalyst Carl Jung recognized this problem among Germany's youths:

"Armed with rucksack and lute, [blond youths] were to be seen as restless wanderers on every road from the North Cape to Sicily, faithful votaries of the *roving* god. [Later], the wandering role was taken over by thousands of unemployed, who were to be met with everywhere on their aimless journeys. By 1933 they wandered no longer, but marched in their hundreds of thousands."

Jung understood that war happens when the young grow frustrated and collective reject their parents' society.

Surely, many in the West preoccupy themselves each day with providing aid to the Third World, working hard to solve wars and crises all over the globe. But they do so while dangerously ignoring a rapidly growing problem within their own ranks. If the West fails to provide its youths with a meaningful future, their survival instincts will send them looking for one elsewhere — one way or another.

If Western civilization wants to survive, its leaders will have to change their attitude towards the world. The West is at a crossroads. Like the cathedral builders of medieval Europe, this generation of Westerners holds a potential to become the architects of new civilization.

And if we can do all that, perhaps then, too, we can stop trashing the world's most beautiful beaches.

Solving the Riddle of Happiness

January 1ˢᵗ, 2017

No one should have to earn the right to be happy. No one ought to go to Kafkaesque lengths to achieve happiness either. Despite the unalienable right to life, liberty and the pursuit of happiness granted by the U.S. Declaration of Independence, happiness probably isn't something you'll need to pursue at all as if the pursuit itself were a substitute for some mythical, yet unattainable ideal.

In fact, I believe happiness is available to everyone. Finding it requires no superhuman achievement, nor someone else's permission. Rather, I believe true happiness comes from establishing a secure and supportive relationship with just one other human being. No matter how unhappy you feel right now, your salvation may lie one meaningful connection away.

People have been looking for happiness since the beginning of history, but that does not mean they have been looking in the right places.

Writing over 2,300 years ago, in his book Ethics, the Greek philosopher Aristotle presumed the chief determinant of happiness — or, as he called it, *eudaimonia* — lay in one's virtuous character. He dismissed happiness to mean a life of pleasure, wealth or honor. Instead, he defined happiness as "an activity of the soul in accordance with virtue".

But living a virtuous life may sound like an awful lot of work, especially since Aristotle believed happiness took one's whole life to achieve it. Another Greek philosopher, Epicurus, didn't think living virtuously was necessary to become happy. He thought happiness could be attained by simply maximizing pleasure and minimizing pain. In his view, it is the absence of suffering that makes people happy.

Eight centuries later, Christian philosopher Boethius echoed Aristotle's views of happiness but connected it to a relationship with God. Writing his book The Consolation of Philosophy while imprisoned to be executed, Boethius agreed that the road to happiness lay not in money, status, power, glory or pleasure, but within ourselves. Boethius concluded true happiness is God and that people can achieve happiness through prayer and love.

Many others have proposed different definitions of happiness, but it wasn't until modern times that psychologist John Bowlby discovered a crucial component of what really makes people happy:

"For not only young children, it is now clear, but human be-ings of all ages are found to be at their happiest and to be able to deploy their talents to best advantage when they are confident that, standing behind them, there are one or more trusted persons who will come to their aid should difficulties arise."

Like Aristotle, Bowbly stresses that people may find happi-ness in the life of virtue, but that in order to be securely happy they will need the support of people they trust and respect. So, there we have the solution to the riddle of happiness: since it's impossible to be happy on our own, what we need to be happy lies one meaningful connection with a supportive human being away from us.

Now that we know what happiness is, the question is: How do we get it? To be happy, we will need to find trusted others who can provide us with a secure base from which we operate, Bowbly suggests. We may find it tempting to acquire or enforce such a base quickly using money, status or power, but in order to cement real happiness, we will have to invest in others.

Bowlby warns, though, that the more people take a secure relationship for granted, the more they risk overlooking its im-portance. The first step in getting happiness, therefore, means to avoid losing it in the first place. Happiness demands us to make small but daily investments in our existing social relationships.

Conversely, relationships that do not offer us the support we need may be the reason we feel unhappy. That's why we need to expand our social networks to spread the risk. The more se-cure connections we've established, the more stable our base from which we operate, the happier we become.

We can expand our relationships in two ways. One, we can build a mutual relationship with someone who reciprocates the support we offer them. Two, we can start a chain and pass on the support we've received ourselves to others who need it too, like a mother caring for her baby who is securely supported by her husband.

Getting What We Want from Life

November 13ᵗʰ, 2015
As newborn babies, we rely on our parents' ability and willingness to provide for us. We're at their mercy. All children come into this world equipped with the social skills needed to secure the shelter and safety they need for their survival. A baby's silky skin communicates it needs gentle touches. Babies' cries signal hurt, danger, hunger or loneliness. Children have real needs and parents must find ways to meet them. In turn, children quickly learn to psychologically reward their parents by mimicking their facial expressions, and by offering smiles and giggles. Bluntly speaking, we manipulate them, though for the sake of humanity's continued existence we have no other choice. We do as adults. In adulthood, we can either choose to manipulate others for our personal gain or learn to get what we want from life through self-directed action.

Our individual ability to get what we really want from life can serve as one way to measure what we call freedom. This definition hints that the freedom of one may come at the expense of another. We live in a dog-eat-dog world where life preys on other life. Human beings generally don't eat each other, but the financial success of one 'gifted' stockbroker often comes at great losses to less fortunate speculators. Like stock markets, civilized societies codified and institutionalized the competition for better lives.

Children are innocent and deserve to be loved unconditionally, but more than through self-directed action, we picked up from early childhood experiences that it is easier to get what we want from life when we manipulate others. This manipulation no longer merely serves our basic needs, but the exploitation of those around us for personal gain and self-aggrandizement, for narcissistic attention and hedonistic pleasure. "We can never have enough of what we do not really need," wrote American longshoreman and philosopher Eric Hoffer.

As children, most men learn to manipulate others from manipulating their mothers. The experience leaves a permanent psychological impression. Perhaps it explains why adult men can feel entitled to women's subservience, a psychological remnant from their nursing mothers that attended to their childhood needs. For women, it is more complicated. Girls more frequently wave their fathers goodbye when they have to go to work in the morning, even in feminist societies. Whatever the case may be, absent fathers leave their daughters with no one to manipulate other than the very person they psychologically identify with — their mothers. Girls have a harder time getting what they want from their less available fathers than boys do from their more reliable mothers.

Both men and women never forget their childhood lessons. We can easily observe manipulation whenever two or more people meet. The sly salesman sells goods and services people don't really need, to customers he despises, yet his financial successes leaving him frustrated why nobody will give him the genuine recognition he really seeks. The office manager deceives herself into thinking that she found her passion, while she spends her days plotting new ways to 'motivate' her subordinates to donate more of their productivity to corporate profits.

Learning to manipulate our parents came at a cost because our parents, in turn, convinced us that we had to be 'good boys' and 'pretty girls' to deserve their attention. We paid for our survival by giving up our right to unconditional love. In our earliest attempts to get what we want from life, we had to adopt a false self-image. We play smart to impress our intellectual parents. We take up sports we don't really like to play out of fear of disappointing athletic mothers and fathers. In adulthood, this socially desirable image frustrates even our best attempts at living a fulfilling life, because we can never get enough recognition for who we are not.

As long as we keep deceiving ourselves, the pursuit of happiness can only bring more unhappiness. The slavery of a false self-image leads to self-destruction. What we really need is unconditional positive regard for our true selves. This we can only achieve when we stop being who we are not. Then we cease to manipulate others for artificial satisfaction. We return to our true selves and find that the freedom we look for lies within, in confident, self-directed action.

Becoming Your True Self: Reflection on the Suicide of a Former High School Classmate

November 10th, 2015
Recently, one of my former high school classmates committed suicide by leaping off his apartment balcony. The eerie thing about the internet is that his LinkedIn and Facebook profiles lived on. I had not been in touch for nearly fifteen years, but I was tempted to have a look.

The thing that worried me was his show of pride for supposedly having graduated high school — because I knew he had not. He had flunked the final year, had not been allowed to redo it and was forced to get a job. To keep up appearances he had spent a lifetime fooling himself, his friends and family into believing something that was not so. Could the weight of this lie have been the real cause of his depression?

It is self-evident that most of what drives society can be attributed to people's need for chasing substitutes, such as money, status or diploma's. Using those substitutes, we try to make up for the lack of love and appreciation we really crave. We go to work for the promise of a promotion we may never get. We put in unpaid overtime hoping that someday we'll get a raise. We give up on our social lives to study straight A's in hopes of appreciation.

But "we can never have enough of the things we don't really need," wrote longshoreman philosopher Eric Hoffer. What drove my former classmate's depression was that he did not feel valued for who he was, but for having to live up to some impossible condition. Why do we allow others to so destructively communicate to us their sense of our worth?

We carry with us this learned attitude, submitting our inner needs to external validation, our whole lives. We elect political leaders that promise a "better future" or a "return to prosperous times" — the straight A's of the people — but their ideals often come at our expense. We've imprisoned ourselves beneath layers of ideological dirt to hide from the view that all of us flunked the school of humanity.

The root of the problem is that we've been trying to 'fix' with technology that which was never broken: our capacity to love, respect, recognize and appreciate others, and in doing so, ourselves. What we need is a society built on unconditional positive regard, as psychologist Carl Rogers called it. If we learn to let go of substitutes and embrace our real needs, then we cease to live the lives of others and finally become our true selves.

Why We Need 'Fake' News: Alternative Media Help Restore the Balance of Power between People and Politics

May 24ᵗʰ, 2017

Researcher David Lazer and others state that "shifts in the media ecosystem raise new concerns about the vulnerability of democratic societies to fake news and the public's limited ability to contain it."[1]

The public's ability to vet the mainstream media is equally limited, but why has that never been considered a threat to democratic societies? Modern democracies seem to have elevated official media to the position of government soothsayers whose truths may not be questioned.

And that is why democratic societies need 'fake' news, or alternative news, in order to democratize the official narratives. The fake news phenomenon, although indeed moving between inaccurate, subjective and provably false, provides a necessary check on the balance of power between a people and its government.

Governments no longer dictate the truth. When democratic governments think they ought to engineer the truth, or that they have a mandate to nudge an 'ignorant' citizenry into obedience, are they still democratic? By democratizing the truth, alternative news media may prevent democratic societies from slipping into totalitarian states.

Of course, powerful special interest groups operating behind the curtains of democratic elections have reason to fear fake news, since an "abundance of information sources online leads individuals to rely heavily on heuristics and social cues in order to ... shape their beliefs, which are in turn extremely difficult to correct or change."[2]

Lazer and his colleagues thus admit that the real problem societies face is not fake news, but the increasing difficulty government educators face in engineering their people's beliefs. In other words, the abundance of alternative news has drowned out the official narrative.

The internet has created a market for alternative news. This development seems inevitable and irreversible, a consequence of the democratization of news brought about by social media. But the social engineers who think they ought to design our societies to match their own best interests feel they are losing their grip on a stubborn people.

The methods Lazer et al promote to combat fake news amount to nothing short of communist censorship. Even more hilariously, Lazer recommends "involving more conservatives in the discussion of misinformation in politics".[3] Fake news isn't just fake, it's conservative. Lazer sees no problem stating that "misinformation is currently predominantly a pathology of the right".[4]

The word "pathology" means *diseased*—anyone who does not support the progressive narrative is written off as mentally ill, a maneuver to disable political opponents once applied on an apocalyptic scale by Joseph Stalin.

Of course, a lot of what progressives call news is perceived as fake by others, and not just by conservatives. The political spectrum isn't as bipolar as mainstream media want us to believe. The only difference is that progressive activists have long seized control of mainstream media to spread their own fake news.

That's why the public needs a healthy dose of alternative news in order to correct the one-sided progressive worldview that confuses opinion with universal truth. The belief that the world is somehow moving towards Elysium may very well turn out to be progressive self-delusion.

The False Promise of Future Gains: The Cynical Truth about What Really Drives Human Behavior

April 29th, 2016

When I was an intern at a major car manufacturer in southeastern Germany, I asked another intern colleague why he had decided to apply. The colleague held hopes the internship would land him a full-time job because it came with a new company car once every two years. He had reasoned that, if he would not get a company car, he would end up spending most of his future savings to afford them anyway. He worked relentlessly to prove himself and even extended his unpaid internship by six months. He got the job. But to his shock, it came with a contractual provision that excluded the sought-after company car. He would ultimately spend several extra car-less years before finally earning that promotion.

My colleague fell for what I call the false promise of future gains. Once you fall for it, you keep on falling, because you invested too much to quit. It's a most deceitful trap, promising people a false certainty that they will get ahead in life, and be "successful", if only they show enough loyalty to someone else's cause, put in their overtime, and without complaining, patiently wait for rewards to come—someday. More often than not, the reward never comes.

Creative freelancers know what I'm talking about. A customer may ask you to work on "their idea" for free, but they'll promise you more paid work in the future if you do the job well. They'll promise to send more customers your way by dropping your name. In reality, that scheme hardly ever pays off.

Consider the following example. In high school, during math class, I sat next to a girl who knew early on she wanted to become an econometrician, someone who applies math and statistics to economic data. She had learned that recent university graduates in econometrics could land entry-level jobs handling "half a million" dollars of clients' money. Obviously, the dollar signs in her own eyes had lured her into the industry. She loyally finished her studies and slaved away at crunching numbers for many years to come, but without ever getting close to earning such wealth herself. She, too, fell for the false promise of future gains.

Generation after generation, people fall for this false-promise scheme, because society teaches children from a young age to think that way. In fact, ruling elites have long understood the scheme and made it their preferred tool of public governance. Falsely promising people "they can be rich too if they work hard and put their minds to it" works in the same manner as the carrot-and-stick approach does to motivate donkeys, but with one minor difference: donkeys rest when they're tired.

Such learned behavior governs most of modern civilization. Besides ruining unfulfilled lives, the false-promise scheme has disastrous global implications, captured best by Michael Lewis, author of The Big Short, who explained in two sentences why the 2008 housing crash had happened:

> "A thought crossed his mind: How do you make poor people feel wealthy when wages are stagnant? You give them cheap loans."

Promising people cheap loans for homes they could never have afforded otherwise is a false promise. Most people still don't understand they don't actually own their mortgaged homes until they've paid them off in full. Until that time, the bank that supplied them a loan owns their home. Mortgages were designed for this purpose. The false promise of future gains isn't just some quirky tool to rob a handful people, it's the global financial system's business model.

Here's how the false-promise scheme works to enslave entire nations of people:

Apart from food and shelter, human beings have several innate needs or real needs. These include the need to be with friends and family; to move and travel freely; and to spend time reflecting on their personal lives.

Rather than fulfilling said real needs directly, public education enforces social taboos and accepted behaviors that fool people into thinking they need to get something else first.

This belief then pervades every aspect of life. Men supposedly need a luxury car to "get the girl". Women need to show up at church every Sunday to be accepted by their community. Children need to do their chores before they can have time to themselves. And we all need to be law-abiding taxpayers in order to earn our right to "live free".

Financial, clerical and governing elites and the likes thus sell their subordinated peoples a false promise of future gains, one that continuously benefits them at everyone else's expense. They may call it "World Order", but it really means your feudal slavery.

My intern colleague didn't really need a new luxury car once every two years. He needed friends who respected him for he was. The girl from my high school math class didn't really need to prove herself competently handling other people's money. She needed the freedom to move and travel as she pleased. People don't need cheap loans to buy material wealth they can't afford. They need free time to ponder the meaning of their lives.

Increasingly, modern civilization has gotten in the way of fulfilling our real needs. While I believe an overwhelming majority of people will continue to fall for the false promise of future gains, informed individuals like yourself can learn to recognize it. By becoming more aware of our real needs, and the tricks governing elites play on us to deceive us, we can begin to appreciate more meaningful lives as independent, responsible people who don't need to be told what to do.

Science Does Not Think: Science Has yet to Become Scientific

April 18th, 2017
Philosophy questions itself, wrote German philosopher Martin Heidegger (1889-1976) at a young age, "In contrast to researchers in other fields of science, it appears to be a particular quality of the philosopher that he always first and foremost questions his science. What is philosophy?"[5] The natural sciences, on the other hand, capitulate by virtue of famous physicist Stephen Hawking, who says, "There is no picture- or theory-independent concept of reality."[6] Science does not know what reality is and must invent its own models for it. Hawking has based his theories of the origin of our universe on what he calls "model-independent realism", but if by definition the natural sciences cannot know *what* the reality she claims to be researching is, then what is science?

Science appears to be practicing religion. She believes in an unproven or perhaps even unprovable reality that she assumes to be true and that she, ceteris paribus, might as well call God: *There is no picture- or theory-independent concept of God.* Now, what is the difference between God and reality? If science wants to be scientific, she must first subject herself to questioning. And that is something only philosophy can do. A philosopher can ask *why* science does not know a model-independent reality. All of science stands or falls on a single unscientific assumption about what reality is. What does it actually say about the nature of reality that it does not expose itself to scientific methods?

Supposedly, our reality would be physical and tangible, ruled by time and space. This prevailing yet unproven model of reality determines and influences the science that moves within its contours. Would we choose a different model of reality based on mathematical self-similarity, then reality would lure science into an infinite, self-repeating trap from which science cannot escape without annulling itself. In mathematics, an object's self-similarity means "that this object is precisely or approximately similar to a part of itself"[7] and infinitely so. Take time, for example. A second resembles a minute; a microsecond resembles a second; and so on. As scientific instruments are able to measure time with ever greater granularity, those instruments will infinitely be able to measure ever shorter periods of time, but they will never discover an elementary particle "time".

The same would hold true for spacial reality. We start with bodily organs and enzymes and arrive at quantum particles via molecules and atoms, and beyond. Just as in the example of time, it applies in this model that we, as we refine scientific equipment, will continue to discover ever smaller particles. Yet, we will never arrive at an elementary particle 'matter'. In this model, reality keeps repeating itself indefinitely. The deeper we dig, the more we find, but by no means do we find anything that has something to do with a real reality. This infinitely repeating reality possesses an elastic attribute that science can infinitely stretch out without ever discovering anything about the nature of that reality because it is grounded in an eternal return of the same.

Thus, one cannot say that science is not influenced by the model we choose for reality. A science that does not know the nature of reality remains subject to cosmic ignorance. For example, were science to reach a definitive consensus following a certain model of reality, then the eternal doubt remains whether the chosen model was the right one and if we, in case humanity would be able to redo the past 2,500 years of history, would really have arrived at the same consensus. Is science the outcome of real reality or of some arbitrary set of historical choices? In an alternative model, in which science never arrives at a definitive consensus, the question remains whether man influences the nature of his own reality. Does the scientist excite his own results?[8] And in another model, in which we assume the nature of reality to be variable, science makes a fool of itself, because in that case, she doesn't have any predictive value left.

But science, using her methods, cannot determine which model of reality is the right one. Nor can she say anything meaningful about her own nature; science does not think. During his only television interview, Martin Heidegger responded to the question on science:

"Science does not move in the dimension of philosophy. She is, however, without her knowing, dependent on this dimension. For example, physics moves in the field of space and time and movement. What movement, what space, what time is, science as science cannot decide. Therefore, science does not think. That means, she cannot even think, in this *sense*, with her methods. I cannot, for example, say physically or with physical methods what physics is, but what physics is I can only say when thinking, philosophizing. The sentence science does not think is not a reproach, but only an observation of science's inner structure, which belongs to her nature that she, on the one hand, depends on that which philosophy thinks, but forgets and ignores this herself."[9]

With the statement that science does not think, Heidegger does not say that scientists do not think about their formulas, but that they do not first question the unproven assumptions upon which they base those formulas. What would later happen to libraries full of physics research if it were to come to light that movement does not exist? Can the human senses, including measurement instruments developed by and for human senses, ever observe a real reality? People with akinetopsia disorder, for example, do not register movement. Instead of seeing smooth transitions, these patients perceive the world as consecutive photographic images that suddenly skip ahead. But there is nothing wrong with their eyes. Experts are looking for the cause in a brain disorder that makes the brain forget to process movement, but the reverse is also possible: what if movement *does not really exist* and our brains *simulate* movement as an evolutionary response to an reality otherwise incomprehensible to us?[10]

In case movement would not be an attribute of reality's hardware, but only a simulation of our own brain's software, then the science that measures said movement would not be scientific, but psychological. In that case, science does not measure a real distance that an object traverses between points A and B, but only the psychological illusion of a distance that the human brain projects. Scientific instruments we use to measure such illusory movement would not be the product of independent technology, but of psychological projection in the world. The science that wanted to remove human observers from her equations in order to measure reality directly, without human interference, would not really exist.

The crisis of science is that she can neither prove nor disprove the above observations using her methods. She cannot determine whether movement would be a property of a real reality or an attribute of man's psychological projection. Science only knows a model-dependent reality. That's why we must conclude the following about science: *Not only does science not think, science is not what she claims to be. Science is not scientific.*

Philosopher and physicist professor Carl Friedrich von Weizsäcker (1912-2007) argued as follows against Heidegger's reproach regarding thoughtlessness:

"I think a direct influence of the Heideggerian thinking on present-day natural sciences hardly exists. I think that people shouldn't be so surprised about that either, because to me the relation between natural sciences and philosophy appears to be somewhat as follows: Heidegger has sometimes said—and he has annoyed scientists with it, but he has said something very important with it—that science does not think. That means: science, in contrast to philosophy, does not doubt her own assumptions, does not question them. That is what he meant here. Now, a science that does not question her own assumptions, of course, will not be influenced by a philosophy that does precisely this. In reality, however, I think that the process is so that modern natural sciences, and all sciences at that, precisely do think there, *where* they make really big steps, and do so in the Heideggerian sense, namely: her big jumps mean exactly that they *question* their assumptions. And that has happened in our century in the theories of relativity, in the quantum theories. But that happened without Heidegger's influence, however not without the *influence* of philosophy."[11]

Weizsäcker claims science does question her own assumptions and is able to make big jumps because of that, as happened with Einstein's theory of relativity. But Einstein did not answer the questions what time, what space and what movement is. Unsurprisingly, in the above quote, Weizsäcker sheepishly introduced a refined sophism by applying to the phrase "own assumptions" his own meaning. It is correct in the Weizsäckerian sense that Newton's geometry replaced that of Euclid by questioning Euclid's assumptions. It is true that Einstein's theory of relativity questioned Newton's assumptions, but that questioning was limited to the assumptions posed *within science*.

Neither Euclid, nor Newton, nor Einstein questioned science herself by asking: what is science? They did not doubt space, but *Euclidian* space. They did not doubt movement, but *Newton's* concept of movement. Modern science does not question time, but *Einstein's* concept of time. By only limiting oneself to such "own assumptions", science remains forever trapped within itself. Real science does not begin by questioning merely a single assumption, but by questioning all assumptions. And that's exactly what science cannot do without concluding that she is not scientific yet.

Which purpose does a science serve that cannot and does not want to investigate real reality? Just like primitive technology in the hands of chimpanzees, rocks, and sticks, 'thinking' man's fundamental science primarily serves his survival in an endless reproductive struggle for resources with both other people and other life forms. Human science might as well be a reproductive strategy of mostly collaborating males who commit their subjective science in order to increase the reproductive chances of their own group members—this, then, is called progress. When they apply science to reduce competing groups' chances by means of intimidation, sabotage, slavery, oppression or destruction, then we call that war.

So what is science? Science is a weapon in service of human progress and war, intended to benefit one group or specific groups at the expense of others. The fact that there exists an international scientific community does not invalidate this statement. The exchange of scientific insights between two groups may offer a mutual advantage in comparison to yet another, third group. The existence of an international community in which all groups attain a mutual benefit does not mean that they all do so equally. There are still relative winners and losers.

Modern science has a Western, even American, bias. That not only means new scientific insights coincidentally mostly come from American institutes but also that Americans can defend their own insights with money and violence to their own benefit.

One cannot say that the West stands on the shoulders of classical scientists as if science has followed along a road of cumulative progress. Progress is a subjective Western idea. It was a modern Western decision to pick up science where classical antiquity had left off. Moreover, by modern standards, the ancient Greeks and Romans have hardly been right about anything. Almost all of their scientific ideas have been invalided since. Why couldn't same happen to modern science? Two thousand years from now, new civilizations would likely be able to disprove Einstein's truths, just as we have disproved those of Euclid, but this also won't indicate objective progress, but rather subjective change.

We also don't know, and will never be able to know, if it is possible that Euclid's laws were entirely or partially true *in his day* and that the reality we live in has since changed *so that* Einstein's laws became true? Is it possible that the laws of nature are not constant, but arbitrary? If so, a *Theory of Everything* could never remain true for long, since even the slightest change of the nature of reality would invalidate it. Science can neither confirm nor deny the existence of such a changing universe, because science remains subjected to her own assumptions at all times.

Claims that science would be scientific and that reality would be real are subject to subjective human interests. America and the West currently have an interest to sell their science to the world as being absolutely true. As long as they have the power to do so, Western nations will be able to suppress unwanted insights from others that might damage the West's position of power. According to the law of diminishing returns, new scientific insights will come to cost the West ever greater investments, but with ever smaller returns. In the long term, science always risks becoming too expensive to afford. The best scientists will then leave science to focus on other, more profitable fields.

Seen in this light, it is not even an established fact that the Earth is round. A new world civilization that amasses the means to shoot down all satellites, to destroy all Western knowledge and to rewrite all schoolbooks, can make the Earth 'flat' again. That's because all science is, and will always remain, subjective science, namely *science in service to something else:* human reproductive struggle.

He Who Thinks Greatly Must Err Greatly: What Did Martin Heidegger Mean by This Sentence?

January 9th, 2017
On May 1st, 1933, Martin Heidegger, the obscure German philosopher from Meßkirch, became a member of the Nazi Party. With his misstep, Heidegger tainted his philosophical legacy. Today, Heidegger's thinking doesn't wield much influence on academic German philosophy.[12] Not only the German but also the international community blamed him for never offering explicit apologies for his support to the Nazi regime, despite the fact that his membership legitimized Hitler's movement in the eyes of many young people. In one of his many writings, Heidegger, at first sight, appears to have pleaded his innocence when he wrote, "Wer groß denkt, muß groß irren."[13] He who thinks greatly must err greatly.

What does this sentence mean? According to one commentator, Heidegger's statement betrays his "overbearing hubris".[14] One interpretation might be that the great thinker has the right to err greatly. His greatness places him above others. That narrow mind that errs little must learn to overlook the great mistakes of his great master, "Indeed, Heidegger emphasizes that the philosopher who thinks greatly must necessarily also err greatly."[15]

Peter Trawny, philosopher, and editor of some of Heidegger's works went looking for the meaning of the sentence *Wer groß denkt...* in Heidegger's "ambivalent"[16] use of the concept of *greatness*, but as so many others, Trawny treats the line in isolation of its context. We find that context in Heidegger's publication *Aus der Erfahrung des Denkens*, in the 13th part of his collected works spanning over 100 works. In that work, the sentence *Wer groß denkt...* forms the closing line in a cursive text—a thought—that sprung up in Heidegger's mind when he made an observation in outdoor nature. The whole is part of a series of multiple poetic tryouts in each of which an observation provokes a thought in Heidegger.

The concerning observation goes as follows (in German),

"Wenn am Sommertag der Falter sich auf die Blume niederläßt und, die Flügel geschlossen, mit ihr im Wiesenwind schwingt..."

The translation reads as follows, "When on a summer day the butterfly settles down on the flower and, wings closed, swings along with it in the meadow wind..." Having observed this, Heidegger penned the following thought,

"Aller Mut des Gemüts ist der Widerklang auf die Anmutung des Seyns, die unser Denken in das Spiel der Welt versammelt.

Im Denken wird jeglich Ding einsam und langsam.

In der Langmut gedeiht Großmut.

Wer groß denkt, muß groß irren."

The translation: "All spirit of the mind is the resonance on the vague impression of Being that gathers our thinking in the world's play. In thinking, each think becomes lonely and slow. In long-suffering flourishes magnanimity. He who thinks greatly must err greatly."

As Trawny remarked, this passage does not contain a direct reference to Heidegger's support for national socialism.[17] There is no reason to suggest that Heidegger meant to distance himself from his mistake with this sentence. In the media's mangle of things, the oft-cited sentence *Wer groß denkt...* has begun to lead its own life. The sentence has given commentators a sound-bite to reject Heidegger's legacy along with his person with one strike. The man actively supported Nazism so no one ought to study his thinking, let alone take him seriously. But we still don't know what the line really means.

Let's analyze the fragment in its contextual entirety. For starters, the thought *Aller Mut...* and the previous observation *Wenn am Sommertag...* form an analogy together. Heidegger's first thought *Aller Mut...* echoes the earlier observation. The courageous butterfly, a puny creature, nests itself on the flower, *die Anumutung des Seyns.* The flower and the butterfly gather together in the game the wind plays with the meadow, *unser Denken im Spiel der Welt.* As the butterfly lands on the flower, our thinking requires courage to interact with the world. In only two sentences, Heidegger has shown us that the thinking man not only observes his reality, as if the world were to play before our senses like a film we uncritically acknowledge, but rather that such observations elicit a counter-reaction, a thought of our own. Our own thinking resonates on the vague impression of Being in the world.

In fact, having noticed Heidegger's poetic choice of words, we see this impression resonating through the sentences: *Mut... Gemüts... Anmutung, Denken... Denken... Ding, einsam... lang-*

*sam... Langmut, Langmut... Großmut, groß denkt... groß ir-
ren.* Heidegger often applies this chaining of similar sounding
words. It is the echo of his thinking. It offers an insight into his
manner of philosophizing. Heidegger does not jump around.
The philosopher follows along with his thinking in so-called
Holzwege, wood paths through a forest, the difficult to pass or
even impassable paths he either visits or which appear to him.
With each dead end, he returns to the last known point from
where he looks for another path. He traverses the paths in his
thinking in a careful manner, one by one, and meanders thus
way then that way through his wood of thoughts, looking for a
clearing where the light, *Die Lichtung*, presents him with new
insight. But by traversing each possible path, he must also fall
into all traps, even the biggest ones.

In the next line, *Im Denken wird jeglich Ding einsam und
langsam*, Heidegger elaborates on the meaning of our thinking
in the play of the world. The *Ding* is the butterfly that, wings
closed, now rests on the flower, lonely and slow. Together, they
swing in the wind but in thinking, each only knows his own
thoughts. We are always alone in our thinking and we progress slowly. Then Heidegger writes, *In der Langmut gedeiht
Großmut.* It is the long-suffering flower, the vague impression of
Being, that must bear the wind and the butterfly with patience
because it cannot escape them. The flower, Being, behaves itself
magnanimously and generously towards the butterfly, thinking.
Together, they gather Being and thinking in reality.

It is clear that the first 'groß' from the line *Wer groß denkt...*
must refer to *Großmut*, the last word from the previous line.
We, therefore, don't have to regard Heidegger's great thinking
as a sort of abstract notion of the concept of greatness, but rather as the magnanimity of the long-suffering thinker. A great
thinker is not someone who is great himself, but rather someone who offers the world his greatest thought, both his best and

his worst. He presents the world his whole, uncensored think-ing, because he, like the flower, does not choose the thoughts that land on him.

So, we arrive at the meaning of Heidegger's sentence. It is not the case that the philosopher who thinks greatly must nec-essarily err greatly, but rather the other way around: only the philosopher with the courage to err greatly can become a great thinker. The explorer who has given mankind his best discov-eries cannot discover new worlds without risking catastrophe. The magnanimous thinker who offers humankind his best work cannot acquire valuable insights without simultaneously open-ing himself up to the worthless and despicable. The way towards the clearing in the woods is found by getting lost because the way is not known to anyone yet. Great mistakes make for a great thinker. *Wer groß denkt, muß groß irren.*

The Will to Meaning:
Who, after All, Moves Whom First, Man or His Reality?

January 26th, 2016
"What is the meaning of life?" That question is wrong because life doesn't have meaning. Life is meaning. Moreover, a mean-ing in life isn't something you claim for yourself, but that which you grant others. Life grants the universe its meaning. We cre-ate meaning by making room for meaning. Meaning fights a counter force it must push away—a counter-meaning. Life is that pushing force.

The fact that life is meaningful suggests a free will shaping that meaning. After all, what kind of meaning can be discovered in a purely deterministic universe without a free will? In case the universe would indeed be deterministic, we must wonder where the idea of a free will comes from. How can something that wouldn't possess free will come up with the idea that there exists such a thing as a free will?

We agree that a concrete slab can't possess free will, but neither does a concrete slab suspect itself of having one. The only man suspects himself. The idea of free will came into being in us. What kind of thing suspects the universe of harboring a free will, unless it is will itself that thinks so? Man is the will that grants the universe its meaning.

Psychiatrist Viktor Frankl posed his idea of the will to meaning opposite to that of Nietzschean will to power.[18] However, according to philosopher Sam Harris, free will is an illusion. Mathematical and physical formulas supposedly control people's behaviors and feelings. We experience a free will that isn't really there, Harris thinks, because our brains believe in the illusion that we made the choices ourselves that our unconscious subconscious had already decided for us.

The large secondary brain, peeled around the primary brain, supposedly only comes up with the arguments as to why we executed the primary brain's 'will' in hindsight. Simpler put: the brain fools us. This illusion is called cognitive dissonance.

For his ideas, Harris seeks to join evolutionary biologist Richard Dawkins and physicist Lawrence Krauss.[19] Together, this trinity explains human actions away as a natural phenomenon in which man plays no role. According to them, man appears as a computer program on a cosmic display on which man executes his predictable routines. This so-called scientific worldview leaves no room for meaning.

These wise men may very well be right, but man can't survive without meaningfulness, even if that's an illusion. Should we really believe in the mechanical meaninglessness of our existence, then we would become depressed, we would sleep without dreaming and we would lose hope for progress. Isn't it peculiar that a thing of which one assumes it is a deterministic thing becomes ill from a lack of meaningfulness if that meaning were nothing more than an illusion?

Science wants to measure the world without scientists' interference, but it pays for its knowledge with the unprovable assumption that there exists such a thing called 'real' reality which comes into being outside of man. Scientists admit they cannot possibly prove what reality might be: "There is no image- or theory-independent concept of reality."[20] Science cannot know what reality is!

Is it possible that human observation provokes its own reality, thus that man creates his own reality by simultaneously taking part in it?[21]

Brain researchers couldn't uncover a free will in the human brain's nerve paths. However, that doesn't prove will doesn't exist. After all, geologists looking for Earth's gravity won't find it by digging in the earth. Yet there is gravity: the Earth doesn't possess gravity, but it is heaviness. Man doesn't harbor a willpower in his nerves, but he is will.

The phenomenon known as life is an appearance of the universe's will to meaning; man is the highest consciousness of that will. We can grant ourselves and others meaning by suspecting life of being meaningful. We find meaning where we want to find meaning. Will has meaning.

Who, after all, moves whom first, man or his reality?

Nature vs. Nurture Revisited

April 6ᵗʰ, 2018
A meta-study showed that IQ has a heritability between 40% to 80%. However, the thing inherited is not a specific IQ score. People aren't born with a genetic IQ of, say, 110. Your genes predispose you to a certain range of intelligence, for example

between 80 and 140. Your actual IQ score depends on this genetic range, your childhood history (both psychological and physical), and your social circumstances.

There's a problem. The nature vs. nurture debate presents us a false dichotomy. Your intelligence not only depends on genes and circumstances. This worldview reduces people to puppets. Perhaps it's easier to blame bad genes and discrimination for your lack of ability. But what if you actual intelligence depends as much on your past as on your own actions? I call this nature versus nurture *times effort*.

Your intelligence is not only determined by your genes. It's not only determined by your circumstances either. It's determined by what you do with those givens. The conservative worldview dictates you are a victim of your biology. Although your DNA doesn't change, the expression of specific genes does change over the course of your life. As a child, for example, different genes are active. In adulthood, other genes are dormant.

The socialist worldview dictates that you are a victim of the society you were born into. Both the socialist and the conservative worldview are false. Your biology and your society have provided you with a range of opportunities. It is still up to *you* what to do with that range. Your brain can rewire itself after prolonged exposure to a new situation. So, if you want to become smarter, you must expose yourself to new situations that require you to think smarter. Over time, your brain will adapt and the problems you face will become easier.

One way I've found people can become smarter is by *reading books* and by *learning languages*. Reading not only increases your knowledge, it also trains you to think. Reading exposes you to new situations you might never have encountered yourself. Books offer the opportunity to think through solutions for situations otherwise alien to you. Your brain will adapt.

Learning languages provides one with access to more reading material and even more diverse situations to encounter. The real strength in language learning lies in seeing the world in new ways. When you acquire a second language, you have learned to see the world from that language's perspective. Each problem you encounter now has at least two equally valid solutions.

People can also become less intelligent. Prolonged exposure to rote tasks that require little to no thinking will make you dumber. Menial tasks hurt your verbal skills, your problem-solving skills, and your intellect. It will blur your imagination, it will kill your social skills. It will diminish your ability to learn. It will lower your IQ.

So, my advice is: reject the notion that either your biology or your society has imposed limitations. Instead, embrace the platform provided to you. Start reading books and lots of them. Start learning new languages and lots of them. Start using that mind for thinking and think your way out of your circumstances. I promise you, with this mode of thinking you will achieve greater successes in life than by blaming your mom's bad genes or condemning an 'oppressive' society.

Notes

2: Identity and Diversity

1. Meadows, Donella, Jorgen Randers, and Dennis Meadows. *Limits to Growth: The 30-Year Update.* 1st ed. White River Junction: Chelsea Green Publishing Company, 2004.
2. Potter, David M. *People of Plenty: Economic Abundance and the American Character.* 1st ed. Essex: Phoenix Books, 1965.
3. Martin Bosma, *Minderheid in eigen land: Hoe progressieve strijd ontaardt in genocide en ANC-apartheid* (Bibliotheca Africana Formicae, 2015), sec. epiloog.
4. Paul Colinvaux, *The Fates of Nations: A Biological Theory of History* (Penguin Books, 1983), 48.
5. Ibid., 55.
6. Ibid., 60.

3: Reviving the West

1. Simon Busuttil, "Report on a Common Immigration Policy for Europe" (Brussels: Committee on Civil Liberties, Justice and Home Affairs, April 6, 2009), http://www.europarl.europa.eu/sides/getDoc.do?pubRef=-//EP//NONSGML+REPORT+A6-2009-0251+0+DOC+PDF+V0//EN.
2. Jan Van Herwaarden, "Erasmus En Zijn Vaderland: Variaties Op Een Rotterdams-Gouds Thema." *Tidinge van Die Goude*, 2006, 139–60.
3. Jan Papy, *Erasmus: Een Portret in Brieven*, trans. Marc Van der Poel and Dirk Sacré, 1st ed. (Utrecht: Boom, 2001), 37.

4. Ibid., 38.

5. Ibid., 30.

6. Ibid., 39.

7. Erika Rummel, ed., *The Erasmus Reader* (Toronto: University of Toronto Press, 2013), 325.

8. Ibid., 317.

9. Ibid., 316.

10. Ibid., 315–16.

11. Ibid., 318.

12. Erika Rummel, ed., *Erasmus on Women*, 1st ed. (Toronto: University of Toronto Press, 1996), 68.

13. Bastiaan T. Rutjens et al., "A March to a Better World? Religiosity and the Existential Function of Belief in Social-Moral Progress," *The International Journal for the Psychology of Religion* 26, no. 1 (January 2, 2016): 1, doi:10.1080/10508619.2014.990345.

14. Karl Marx, "Zur Kritik Der Hegelschen Rechtsphilosophie," in *Karl Marx/ Friedrich Engels - Werke*, Band 1 (Berlin: Dietz Verlag, 1976), 378.

15. Stéphane Courtois, *The Black Book of Communism: Crimes, Terror, Repression* (Harvard University Press, 1999), 2.

16. Ibid., 4.

17. Martin Heidegger, "Gelassenheit," in *Reden Und Andere Zeugnisse Eines Lebenswegens*, vol. 16, Gesamtausgabe (Frankfurt am Main: Klostermann, 2000), 517–29.

18. Population Reference Bureau, "Human Population: Population Growth," accessed February 14, 2017, http://www.prb.org/Publications/Lesson-Plans/HumanPopulation/PopulationGrowth.aspx.

19. Ami Gazin-Schwartz, "What the Islamic State's Destruction of Antiquities Means to Archaeologists," *New Republic*, March 18, 2015, https://newrepublic.com/article/121324/isis-destroys-precious-historical-artifacts-all-not-lost.

20. Morris Jastrow and Albert T. Clay, *An Old Babylonian Version of the Gilgamesh Epic: On the Basis of Recently Discovered Texts* (New Haven: Yale University Press, 1920), 44.

21. W.M. Flinders Petrie, *Egyptian Tales: Translated from the Papyri (First Series: IVth to XIIth Dynasty)*, 2nd ed. (London: Methuen & Co, 1899), 48–49, https://archive.org/details/egyptiantalestr00elligoog.

22. Ibid., 45.

23. Ibid., 45.

24. Jastrow and Clay, *An Old Babylonian Version of the Gilgamesh Epic: On the Basis of Recently Discovered Texts*, 44–45.

25. Genesis 1:28, King James Bible.

26. Diane Wolkstein and Samuel Noah Kramer, *Inanna, Queen of Heaven and Earth: Her Stories and Hymns from Sumer*, 1st ed. (New York: Harper & Row, 1983), 46, https://archive.org/details/input-compressed-2015mar28a29.

27. Petrie, *Egyptian Tales: Translated from the Papyri (First Series: IVth to XIIth Dynasty)*.

28. Hoffer, Eric. *The True Believer: Thoughts on the Nature of Mass Movements*. Kindle. Titusville: Hopewell Publications, 2011, p. 14.

4: Demography is Destiny

1. Tainter, Joseph A. The Collapse of Complex Societies. 1st ed. Cambridge: Cambridge University Press, 1988. (p. 13)

2. Ibid., p. 14.

3. D'Vera Cohn and Andrea Caumont, "10 Demographic Trends That Are Shaping the U.S. and the World," *Pew Research Center*, March 31, 2016, http://www.pewresearch.org/fact-tank/2016/03/31/10-demographic-trends-that-are-shaping-the-u-s-and-the-world/.

4. D'Vera Cohn, "It's Official: Minority Babies Are the Majority among the Nation's Infants, but Only Just," *Pew Research Center*, June 23, 2016, http://www.pewresearch.org/fact-tank/2016/06/23/its-official-minority-babies-are-the-majority-among-the-nations-infants-but-only-just/.

5. Cohn and Caumont, "10 Demographic Trends That Are Shaping the U.S. and the World."

6. Josiah Brownell, *The Collapse of Rhodesia: Population Demographics and the Politics of Race* (London: I.B. Tauris & Co, 2011).

7. W. K. Hancock, *Smuts: The Sanguine Years 1870-1919*, 1st ed., vol. 1 (Cambridge: University Press, 1962), 219.

8. S.H. Steinberg, ed., *The Statesman's Year-Book, 1967–1968*, vol. 104 (London: Macmillan, 1967), 1405–24.

9. "South African National Census of 2011," *Wikipedia*, January 19, 2017, https://en.wikipedia.org/w/index.php?title=South_African_National_Census_of_2011&oldid=760854616.

10. BusinessTech, "South Africa's White Population Is Shrinking," accessed February 5, 2017, https://businesstech.co.za/news/business/128732/south-africas-white-population-is-shrinking/.

11. Jan Sariman and Henk Chin A Sen, eds., *De Decembermoorden in Suriname: Verslag van Een Ooggetuige* (Bussum, 1983).

12. Anadolu Agency, "More than 1,000 White Farmers Killed in South Africa since 1990," *DailySabah*, accessed February 5, 2017, http://www.dailysabah.com/africa/2016/04/27/more-than-1000-white-farmers-killed-in-south-africa-since-1990.

13. David Masci, "Europe Projected to Retain Its Christian Majority, but Religious Minorities Will Grow," *Pew Research Center*, April 15, 2015, http://www.pewresearch.org/fact-tank/2015/04/15/europe-projected-to-retain-its-christian-majority-but-religious-minorities-will-grow/.

14. Commission Staff, "Demography Report 2008: Meeting Social Needs in an Ageing Society" (Brussels: Commission of the European Communities, 2008), 52, http://www.igfse.pt/upload/docs/gab-doc/2008/11-Nov/Demography2008_Full_reports_annexes.pdf.

15. Russell Shorto, "No Babies? - Declining Population in Europe," *The New York Times*, June 29, 2008, http://www.nytimes.com/2008/06/29/magazine/29Birth-t.html.

16. Ben Freeth, Desmond Tutu, and John Sentamu, *Mugabe and the White African*, 1st edition (Oxford : Chicago, IL: Lion Hudson, 2011).

17. Al Jazeera and agencies, "Zimbabwe Pleads for Cash to Stop Mass Starvation," accessed February 4, 2017, http://www.aljazeera.com/news/2016/02/zimbabwe-pleads-cash-stop-mass-starvation-160209181824106.html.

18. Manitra Rakotoarisoa, Massimo Iafrate, and Marianna Paschali, *Why Has South Africa Become a Net Food Importer? Explaining African Agricultural and Food Trade Deficits* (Rome: FAO of the United Nations, 2011), http://www.fao.org/docrep/015/i2497e/i2497e00.pdf.

19. Garrett Hardin, "The Tragedy of the Commons," *Science* 162, no. 3859 (December 13, 1968): 1243–48, doi:10.1126/science.162.3859.1243.

20. Ibid.

21. Ibid., 1244.

22. Ibid.
23. Ibid., 1248.
24. CLAUDIA PAP MANGEL, "Licensing Parents: How Feasible?," *Family Law Quarterly* 22, no. 1 (1988): 17–39.

5: *The United States and Europe*

1. Daniele Ganser, *NATO-Geheimarmeen in Europa: Inszenierter Terror und verdeckte Kriegsführung* (Zürich: Orell Füssli Verlag, 2008), chap. 4.
2. David Engels, *Le Déclin: La crise de l'Union européenne et la chute de la République romaine* (Paris: Editions du Toucan, 2013), chap. 2.2: "Le respect de la vie humaine: famille et déclin de la population."
3. Zbigniew Brzezinski, *The Grand Chessboard: American Primacy And Its Geostrategic Imperatives*, 1St Edition edition (New York, NY: Basic Books, 1998), chap. 2: The Eurasian Chessboard.
4. Henri Bergson, *The Two Sources of Morality and Religion*, trans. Ashley R. Audra and Brereton Cloudesley, 1st ed. (London: Macmillan and Co., 1935), chap. 1: "Moral Obligation."
5. George Soros, "Europe's Global Mission," *Project Syndicate*, November 17, 2006, https://www.project-syndicate.org/commentary/europe-s-global-mission.
6. Richard N. Coudenhove-Kalergi, *Praktischer Idealismus: Adel—Technik—Pazifismus* (Wien-Leipzig: Paneuropa Verlag, 1925), 23.
7. Moritz Schuller, "Auf Dem Terrain von Erdogan Und Sarrazin," accessed May 9, 2017, http://www.tagesspiegel.de/politik/schaeuble-ueber-die-degeneration-der-deutschen-auf-dem-terrain-von-erdogan-und-sarrazin/13713574.html.
8. Bergson, *The Two Sources of Morality and Religion*, chap. 1.
9. Karl Popper, *The Open Society and Its Enemies: The Spell of Plato*, Reprint (London: George Routledge & Sons, 1947), chap. 3: Plato's Theory of Ideas.
10. Soros, "Europe's Global Mission."
11. George Soros, "The New Bush Doctrine," *Project Syndicate*, January 25, 2005, https://www.project-syndicate.org/commentary/the-new-bush-doctrine.

12. Hans Morgenthau, *Politics among Nations: The Struggle for Power and Peace*, 1st ed. (New York: Alfred Knopff, 1948), 406.

13. Tacitus, *Tacitus: Histories, Books IV-V, Annals Books I-III*, trans. Clifford H. Moore and John Jackson (Harvard University Press, 1931), bk. IV, §14.

6: *Economics of Decline*

1. Fareed Zakaria, *The Post-American World: Release 2.0* (New York: W. W. Norton & Company, 2012), chap. 1.

2. T. Lothrop Stoddard, *The Rising Tide of Color Against White World-Supremacy* (New York: Charles Scribner's Sons, 1921), 270–71.

3. Samuel P. Huntington, *The Clash of Civilizations and the Remaking of World Order*, E-book (Simon & Schuster, 2011).

4. Angus Maddison, "Statistics on World Population, GDP and Per Capita GDP, 1-2008 AD" (University of Groningen, March 2010), http://www.ggdc.net/maddison/Historical_Statistics/horizontal-file_02-2010.xls.

7: *The Progressive Fraud*

1. Julian Assange, When Google Met WikiLeaks (OR Books, 2014), chap. "Ellingham Hall, June 23, 2011: Censorship is always cause for celebration."

2. Jordan B. Peterson, 12 Rules for Life: An Antidote to Chaos (Random House Canada, 2018), chap. "Rule 5: Do Not Let Your Children Do Anything That Makes You Dislike Them."

3. Julian Assange, "State and Terrorist Conspiracies" (November 10, 2006), https://web.archive.org/web/20061114014042/http://iq.org/conspiracies.pdf.

4. Julian Assange, "Conspiracy as Governance" (December 3, 2006).

5. Julian Assange, "The Non Linear Effects of Leaks on Unjust Systems of Governance," iq.org, January 10, 2007, https://web.archive.org/web/20070110200827/http://iq.org:80/#Thenonlineareffectsofleaksonunjustsystemsofgovernance.

6. Theodore Kaczynski, The Unabomber Manifesto: Industrial Society and Its Future (New York: Unabomber, 1996), paras. 9–37.

7. Julian Assange, "Average Shy Intellectuals," iq.org, August 24, 2007, https://web.archive.org/web/20070824010259/http://iq.org:80/.

8. TheMiddleBlitz, Earth to Liberals: Robert Mueller Lied Us into the Iraq War!!, 2017, https://www.youtube.com/watch?v=mNeqrTb-kZmM.3,31]]}}}],"schema":"https://github.com/citation-style-language/schema/raw/master/csl-citation.json"}

9. Gustave Le Bon, Psychologie des foules, 1895, chap. 3.

10. Thomas Sowell, Black Rednecks and White Liberals, 1st ed. (San Francisco: Encounter Books, 2005), 188.

11. 9/11: Decade of Deception, Documentary, 2015, http://www.imdb.com/title/tt6061892/.

12. Michael D. Shear and Michael R. Gordon, "63 Hours: From Chemical Attack to Trump's Strike in Syria," The New York Times, April 7, 2017, sec. Politics, https://www.nytimes.com/2017/04/07/us/politics/syria-strike-trump-timeline.html.

13. Jenna Johnson, "Donald Trump Promises to 'Bomb the Hell out of ISIS' in New Radio Ad," Washington Post, November 18, 2015, sec. Post Politics, https://www.washingtonpost.com/news/post-politics/wp/2015/11/18/donald-trump-promises-to-bomb-the-hell-out-of-isis-in-new-radio-ad/.

14. Swiss Propaganda Research, "The American Empire and Its Media," Swprs.Org (blog), August 16, 2017, https://swprs.org/the-american-empire-and-its-media/.

15. George Parry, "Mr. Mueller: Was the DNC Server Actually Hacked by the Russians?," The American Spectator, March 29, 2018, https://spectator.org/mr-mueller-was-the-dnc-server-actually-hacked-by-the-russians/.

16. Yuval N. Harari, *Eine Kurze Geschichte Der Menschheit*, trans. Jürgen Neubauer (München: Deutsche Verlags-Anstalt, 2013), 112.

17. Paul Colinvaux, *The Fates of Nations: A Biological Theory of History* (Penguin Books, 1983), 55–67.

18. Ibid., 55.

19. Ibid., 67.

20. Amaury De Riencourt, *The Coming Caesars* (Coward-McCann, 1957), 328–42, http://babel.hathitrust.org/cgi/pt?id=mdp.39015039745933.

21. David M. Potter, *People of Plenty: Economic Abundance and the American Character*, 1st ed. (Essex: Phoenix Books, 1965), 111–12.

22. Dambisa Moyo, *Dead Aid: Why Aid Is Not Working and How There Is a Better Way for Africa*, trans. Ronald Kuil, 1st ed. (Amsterdam: Olympus, 2012).

23. Richard N. Coudenhove-Kalergi, *Praktischer Idealismus: Adel—Technik—Pazifismus* (Wien-Leipzig: Paneuropa Verlag, 1925), 100.

24. Thomas Sowell, *The Vision of the Anointed: Self-Congratulation as a Basis for Social Policy* (New York: BasicBooks, 1995), chap. 10: The Legacy of Marx—The Marxism of Marx: Price-Allocation and Crises.

25. Leifur Eiricksson, ed., *Egil's Saga*, 1st ed. (Penguin Books, 2004).

26. Noam Chomsky, *On Anarchism*, 1st ed. (New York: Penguin Books, 2014), 35–36.

27. Erich Fromm, *Marx's Concept of Man* (New York: Open Road, 2003), chap. 6: Marx's Concept of Socialism.

28. Coudenhove-Kalergi, *Praktischer Idealismus: Adel—Technik—Pazifismus*, 24.

29. Murray A. Straus and Denise A. Donnelly, *Beating the Devil out of Them: Corporal Punishment in American Families and Its Effects on Children* (New Brunswick, New Jersey: Transaction Publishers, 2001), 25.

30. Colinvaux, *The Fates of Nations: A Biological Theory of History*.

31. Eric Hoffer, *The True Believer: Thoughts on the Nature of Mass Movements* (New York: First Perennial Classic, 2010), 52.

32. Didier Sornette, *Why Stock Markets Crash: Critical Events in Complex Financial Systems* (Princeton: Princeton University Press, 2003), chap. 10.

33. Saul D. Alinsky, *Rules for Radicals: A Practical Primer for Realistic Radicals* (New York: Vintage, 1989), 184.

34. Hillary Diane Clinton, "'There Is Only The Fight': An Analysis of the Alinsky Model" (Bachelor's Thesis, Wellesley College, 1969), 4, http://www.hillaryclintonquarterly.com/documents/HillaryClinton-Thesis.pdf.

35. Louis Menand, "Eliot and the Jews," *The New York Review of Books*, June 6, 1996, http://www.nybooks.com/articles/1996/06/06/eliot-and-the-jews/.

36. Clinton, "'There Is Only The Fight': An Analysis of the Alinsky Model."

37. CBS News Staff, "Hillary Has Jewish Roots," *CBS News*, August 6, 1999, http://www.cbsnews.com/news/hillary-has-jewish-roots/.

38. Karl Popper, *The Open Society and Its Enemies: The Spell of Plato*, Reprint (London: George Routledge & Sons, 1947).

39. Qiao Liang and Wang Xiangsui, *Unrestricted Warfare: China's Master Plan to Destroy America*, Reprint ed. edition (Echo Point Books & Media, 2015), chap. 5.

40. Charles M. Blow, "About the 'Basket of Deplorables,'" *The New York Times*, September 12, 2016, https://www.nytimes.com/2016/09/12/opinion/about-the-basket-of-deplorables.html.

41. John J. Mearsheimer and Stephen M. Walt, "The Israel Lobby and U.S. Foreign Policy," *Middle East Policy* XIII, no. 3 (Fall 2006): 45–48.

42. Clinton, "'There Is Only The Fight': An Analysis of the Alinsky Model," 8.

43. Alinsky, *Rules for Radicals*, 127–30.

44. Noam Chomsky, *On Anarchism*, 1st ed. (New York: Penguin Books, 2014), 35–36.

45. Erich Fromm, *Marx's Concept of Man* (New York: Open Road, 2003), 315.

46. Mathijs Koenraadt, *Return to Freedom: A Traveler's Thoughts on Life, Love and the Fate of the World*, 1st ed. (Amsterdam: Morningtime, 2015), chap. 7: The Illusion of Progress.

47. David M. Potter, *People of Plenty: Economic Abundance and the American Character*, 1st ed. (Essex: Phoenix Books, 1965).

48. Paul Colinvaux, *The Fates of Nations: A Biological Theory of History* (Penguin Books, 1983).

49. John Colapinto, "The True Story of John/Joan", *The Rolling Stone*, 11 december 1997, 54–97.

50. Ibid.

51. Ibid.

52. Ibid.

53. Ibid.

54. Paul McHugh, "Transgender Surgery Isn't the Solution", *Wall Street Journal*, 13 mei 2016, sec. Opinion, http://www.wsj.com/articles/paul-mchugh-transgender-surgery-isnt-the-solution-1402615120.

55. Cecilia Dhejne e.a., "Long-Term Follow-Up of Transsexual Persons Undergoing Sex Reassignment Surgery: Cohort Study in Sweden", *PLOS ONE* 6, nr. 2 (22 februari 2011): e16885, doi:10.1371/journal. pone.0016885.

8: *Philosophical Ponderings*

1. in Journalistic Practice et al., "Combating Fake News: An Agenda for Research and Action," *Shorenstein Center*, May 2, 2017, https:// shorensteincenter.org/combating-fake-news-agenda-for-research/.
2. Ibid.
3. Ibid.
4. Ibid.
5. Martin Heidegger, *Frühe Schriften*, vol. 1, Gesamtausgabe (Frankfurt am Main: Klostermann, 1978), 69.
6. Stephen Hawking and Leonard Mlodinow, *The Grand Design* (New York: Bantam Books, 2010), chap. 3: What is reality?
7. "Zelfgelijkvormigheid," *Wikipedia*, March 10, 2016, https://nl.wikipedia.org/w/index.php?title=Zelfgelijkvormigheid&oldid=46271722.
8. Richard Conn Henry, "The Mental Universe," *Nature* 436 (July 7, 2005): 29.
9. Martin Heidegger, *Von der Sache des Denkens: Vorträge, Reden und Gespräche aus den Jahren 1952 - 1969* (München: der Hörverlag, 2009).
10. Justin T. Mark, Brian B. Marion, and Donald D. Hoffman, "Natural Selection and Veridical Perception," *Journal of Theoretical Biology* 266, no. 4 (October 21, 2010): 504–15, doi:10.1016/j.jtbi.2010.07.020.
11. Ulrich Boehm and Rüdiger Safranski, *Philosophie Heute: Martin Heidegger - Der Zauberer von Meßkirch* (Junius Verlag GmbH, 1989).
12. Peter Trawny, *Freedom to Fail: Heidegger's Anarchy*, vertaald door Ian Moore en Christopher Turner (Cambridge: Polity Press, 2015), 14.
13. Martin Heidegger, *Aus der Erfahrung des Denkens: 1910-1976*, vol. 13, Gesamtausgabe (Frankfurt am Main: Klostermann, 1983), 81.
14. Ulrich Greiner, "Darf groß irren, wer groß dichtet?", *Zeit Online*, 2006, 24 editie, http://www.zeit.de/2006/24/Handke_Grn__xml.
15. Trawny, *Freedom to Fail: Heidegger's Anarchy*, 12.
16. Ibid., 10.
17. Ibid.

18. Viktor Frankl, *Der Wille Zum Sinn: Ausgewählte Vorträge Über Logo-therapie* (Bern-Stuttgart-Wien: Hans Huber, 2005).
19. Sam Harris, *Free Will* (New York: Simon and Schuster, 2012), 5.
20. Stephen Hawking and Leonard Mlodinow, *The Grand Design* (New York: Bantam Books, 2010).
21. Richard Conn Henry, "The Mental Universe," *Nature* 436 (July 7, 2005): 29.

Other Books by Mathijs Koenraadt

Revival of the West: Securing a Future for European People (2017)

The Ignorant God: Thoughts about Time and Eternity (2017)

Return to Freedom: A Traveler's Thoughts on Life, Love and the Fate of the World (2015)

A Teenage Philosophy of Awareness and Existence: Analysis of the Columine Shooters' Worldview (2014)